Jacqueline

edited by Lu

'A
pro
co
— *l*

Over
over
child
varie
cism
she r

This
ture 1
of W
and t
relati
of te
an in
challe
writi

Lucy
Chilc

This l
specia
texts
appro
and c

Series Editor: Martin Coyle

This book is due for return on or before the last date shown below

New Casebooks
Collections of all new critical essays

CHILDREN'S LITERATURE

MELVIN BURGESS
Edited by Alison Waller

ROBERT CORMIER
Edited by Adrienne E. Gavin

ROALD DAHL
Edited by Ann Alston & Catherine Butler

C. S. LEWIS: *THE CHRONICLES OF NARNIA*
Edited by Michelle Ann Abate & Lance Weldy

PHILIP PULLMAN: *HIS DARK MATERIALS*
Edited by Catherine Butler & Tommy Halsdorf

J. K. ROWLING: *HARRY POTTER*
Edited by Cynthia J. Hallett & Peggy J. Huey

J. R. R. TOLKIEN: *THE HOBBIT & THE LORD OF THE RINGS*
Edited by Peter Hunt

DAVID ALMOND
Edited by Rosemary Ross Johnston

NOVELS AND PROSE

JOHN FOWLES
Edited by James Acheson

JACQUELINE WILSON
Edited by Lucy Pearson

POETRY

TED HUGHES
Edited by Terry Gifford

Further titles are in preparation
MEDIEVAL ENGLISH LITERATURE
Edited by Beatrice Fannon

For a full list of published titles in the past format of the New Casebooks series, visit the series page at www.palgrave.com

New Casebooks Series
Series Standing Order ISBN 978–0–333–71702–8 hardcover
Series Standing Order ISBN 978–0–333–69345–2 paperback
(*outside North America only*)

You can receive future titles in this series as they are published by placing a standing order. Please contact your bookseller or, in the case of difficulty, write to us at the address below with your name and address, the title of the series and the ISBN quoted above.

Customer Services Department, Macmillan Distribution Ltd, Houndmills, Basingstoke, Hampshire, RG21 6XS, UK

Jacqueline Wilson

Edited by

LUCY PEARSON

 palgrave

Contents

Series Editor's Preface   vii
Notes on Contributors   viii
Acknowledgements   xi

Introduction   1
Lucy Pearson

1   A Publishing Phenomenon: The Marketing and Branding
    of Jacqueline Wilson   16
    Julia Eccleshare

2   From Realism to Romance: The Early Novels   34
    Ika Willis

3   'This Started Like a Fairy Story': Fantasy, Realism and
    Bibliotherapy in Jacqueline Wilson   55
    Lucy Pearson

4   Feisty Girls and Fearful Boys? A Consideration of Gender
    Roles and Expectations in the Work of Jacqueline Wilson   78
    Kay Waddilove

5   The Illuminated Mums: Child/Primary Carer
    Relationships in the Fiction of Jacqueline Wilson   102
    Helen Limon

6   The Irrepressible, Unreliable, Lying Tracy Beaker: From
    Page to Screen   119
    Helen Day

7   'I'm Not Used to Writing about Me. It's Always Us':
    'Double Acts' in Jacqueline Wilson's Metafictional Novels   141
    Clémentine Beauvais

Contents

8 Coming of Age in Jacqueline Wilson's Victorian Fiction   160
   Sheena Wilkinson

9 Jacqueline Wilson and the Problem Novel in
   Comparative Context   176
   Rebecca Morris

10 A Writing Life: Interview with Jacqueline Wilson   198
   Lucy Pearson and Jacqueline Wilson

Further Reading   212

Index   221

Series Editor's Preface

Welcome to the latest series of New Casebooks.

Each volume now presents brand-new essays specially written for university and other students. Like the original series, the new-look New Casebooks embrace a range of recent critical approaches to the debates and issues that characterise the current discussion of literature.

Each editor has been asked to commission a sequence of original essays which will introduce the reader to the innovative critical approaches to the text or texts being discussed in the collection. The intention is to illuminate the rich interchange between critical theory and critical practice that today underpins so much writing about literature.

Editors have also been asked to supply an introduction to each volume that sets the scene for the essays that follow, together with a list of further reading which will enable readers to follow up issues raised by the essays in the collection.

The purpose of this new-look series, then, is to provide students with fresh thinking about key texts and writers while encouraging them to extend their own ideas and responses to the texts they are studying.

Martin Coyle

Notes on Contributors

Clémentine Beauvais is Junior Research Fellow at Homerton College, University of Cambridge (UK). She is the author of *The Mighty Child: Time and Power in Children's Literature* (John Benjamins, 2015), which explores adult–child power dynamics within children's literature, with an emphasis on politically committed contemporary picture books. Her current work focuses on the construct of child precocity and giftedness in the twentieth century. Her main interests are theory, metacriticism and the links between philosophy and children's literature.

Helen Day is Senior Lecturer in Children's Literature at the University of Central Lancashire and Course Leader of the MA Writing for Children. Her teaching interests include crossover fiction, histories of children's literature and the fairy tale. Her most recent publication is 'Simulacra, Sacrifice and Survival in *The Hunger Games*, *Battle Royale*, and *The Running Man*' in *Of Bread, Blood and The Hunger Games* (MacFarland Press). She is currently working on lying and unreliable narrators in young adult fiction, exploring the difference between unreliable narrators and those who admit to the reader that they are liars. This involves bringing together work on lying from linguistics, psychology and sociology as well as blending cognitive stylistics and literary theory.

Julia Eccleshare is children's books editor of the *Guardian* and a writer, broadcaster and lecturer. She is chair of the Guardian Children's Book Prize and founder/chair of the Branford Boase first novel prize. She has judged numerous other prizes including the Booktrust Teenage Prize and the Whitbread Children's Book Prize. She won the Eleanor Farjeon Award 2000 in recognition of her outstanding contribution to children's books and in 2014 was appointed MBE for services to children's literature and awarded an honorary DLitt for her contribution to children's literature by the University of Worcester. In addition to numerous anthologies her books include *Treasure Islands: The Woman's Hour Guide to Children's Reading* (BBC Books, 1987), *A Guide to the Harry Potter Novels* (Continuum, 2002), *Beatrix Potter to Harry Potter: Portraits of Children's Writers* (National Portrait Gallery,

2002), *The Rough Guide to Picture Books* (Rough Guides, 2007) and, with Nicholas Tucker, *The Rough Guide to Teenage Books* (Rough Guides, October 2002). She is the editor of *1001 Children's Books to Read Before you Grow up* (Cassells, 2009). She is a founder member of the steering committee for the Children's Laureate, and a trustee of Reading is Fundamental, Listening Books and the Poetry Book Society.

Helen Limon is a Teaching Associate in Creative Writing at Newcastle University, and is currently Writer in Residence at Seven Stories: the National Centre for Children's Books. Helen completed her PhD in Creative Writing at Newcastle in 2012, and is the author of *Om Shanti Babe*, which won the Frances Lincoln Diverse Voices Award in 2011.

Rebecca Morris is a PhD candidate in Texas A&M University's Department of English where her dissertation work focuses on holidays in American children's literature from the nineteenth century to the present. She is co-editor of *Representing Children in Chinese and American Children's Literature* (Ashgate, 2014).

Lucy Pearson is Lecturer in Children's Literature at Newcastle University. She is the author of *The Making of Modern Children's Literature: Publishing, Criticism and the Children's Literature Scene in the 1960s and 1970s* (Ashgate, 2013) and, with Peter Hunt, *Children's Literature* (Longman, 2011). She works closely with Seven Stories: the National Centre for Children's Books and is currently working on the history of children's publishing in the twentieth century.

Kay Waddilove is a librarian and teacher who works with national and international programmes to promote reading for teenagers. Her interests include twentieth-century post-war children's literature, in particular domestic novels and historical writing. Previous research work has focused on gender issues in children's texts, especially as these relate to representations of family life and the position of women in society. She has published on a range of topics, including children's book awards, 1950s series for girls, fathers in picture books, Noel Streatfeild, Penelope Lively and Sophie MacKenzie. She is currently researching at Roehampton University for a PhD in children's literature, looking at the construction of motherhood in twentieth-century children's fiction.

Sheena Wilkinson's first book *Friends in the Fourth* (Bettany Press, 2007), based on her doctoral research, was unusual in discussing children's fiction (the girls' school story) alongside adult fiction. Since then, she has concentrated mostly on writing fiction. Her first young adult novel *Taking Flight* (2010) won a number of awards in Ireland and internationally, while the follow-up *Grounded* (2012) was the overall Children's Books Ireland Book of the Year 2013. Her latest novel is *Still Falling* (2015). Historical fiction includes the story 'Each Slow Dusk' in *The Great War: An Anthology of Stories Inspired by Objects from the First World War* (2014), and the forthcoming novel *Name Upon Name*. Sheena was Writer in Residence at the Church of Ireland College of Education in Dublin in 2013/2014.

Ika Willis is Senior Lecturer in English Literature at the University of Wollongong. She specialises in reception theory – the relationship between texts, contexts and readers – and has published on a wide range of topics, including Harry Potter fan fiction. She is currently working on a book called *What We Talk About When We Talk About Books*.

With thanks to Jacqueline for her generosity and time.

Introduction

Lucy Pearson

Jacqueline Wilson has formed an important part of the British children's literature landscape in the last 20 years. She has published well over 100 titles, ranging from picture books for very young readers (*Ricky's Birthday* 1973; *Lizzie Zipmouth*, 2000) to challenging young adult fiction (*The Dream Palace*, 1991; *Love Lessons*, 2005). Although best known as a writer of social realism (most notably *The Story of Tracy Beaker*, 1991 and its sequels), she has also written fantasy (*Glubbslyme*, 1987; *Four Children and It*, 2012) and historical fiction (*Hetty Feather*, 2011; *Queenie*, 2013). Since 1997, Wilson has occupied a place among the top 20 children's authors borrowed from public libraries, and in 2002 she ousted Catherine Cookson from the top spot of most-borrowed author across both adults' and children's books.[1] Wilson's books regularly top the bestseller lists – she had the fourth highest UK sales in the first decade of the millennium – and a 2005 survey of children's reading habits identified Wilson as one of the top three favourite authors (alongside J. K. Rowling and Roald Dahl).[2] This is reflected in Wilson's regular appearance on the shortlists of awards chosen by child readers themselves: her awards include the Red House Children's Book Award (1996), the Smarties Prize (1995, 2000) and the Blue Peter People's Choice Award (2002). Her popularity with child readers has given her superstar status: in 2004 she was nominated for a Guinness world record after a mammoth eight-hour book signing which attracted more than 8,000 fans.[3] Several adaptations have further raised her profile: the BBC adaptation of *The Story of Tracy Beaker* ran for five seasons (2002–2006), and it was followed by two 'spin-off' series, *Tracy Beaker Returns* (2010–2012) and *The Dumping Ground* (2013–). *Hetty Feather* has also been adapted for the BBC (2015), and is the most high profile of several stage adaptations of Wilson's books: the spectacular production by Novel Theatre debuted at the Rose Theatre, London, in 2014 before going on to the West End later that year. Wilson's significance as a children's writer has also received more formal recognition: she was made Children's Laureate in 2005, awarded an OBE in 2002 and in 2008 was made Dame Jacqueline Wilson. In 2011, her work was recognised

1

in 'Daydreams and Diaries', a major exhibition at Seven Stories, the National Centre for Children's Books. The exhibition attracted over 65,000 visitors at the Centre's home in Newcastle and was visited by a further 364,837 people when it toured the rest of the country, making it Seven Stories' most-visited exhibition to date.

To the casual observer, Wilson might appear an almost overnight success, springing onto the children's literature scene in 1991 with *The Story of Tracy Beaker*. Certainly her rise following *Tracy*'s debut was meteoric: within five years Wilson's name was a familiar sight on award lists as well as on the public libraries lists of most-borrowed books.[4] *Double Act* (1995) won both the Nestlé Smarties Book Prize (ages 9–11 years and overall) and the Red House Children's Book Award, and was highly commended for the Carnegie Medal. In fact, this success was a long time in the making: Wilson's first book for children appeared in 1973, almost 20 years prior to *Tracy Beaker*, and her career as a professional writer predates this by almost a decade. Her writing career thus spans a period of significant change in British children's literature, beginning in the midst of the so-called second golden age of children's literature in the 1960s, spanning the 'difficult' years of the late 1970s and 1980s (when recession and changing market conditions posed new challenges for children's publishing) and coming to fruition at the dawn of a new period of vibrancy in British children's literature. A critical evaluation of Wilson's work therefore offers the opportunity to understand not only her individual contribution to the world of children's literature – which is significant – but also the development of children's books in Britain as a whole. Curiously, however, children's literature scholarship has lagged behind in recognising Wilson's significance: with the exception of a few short chapters and articles, scholarly material on Wilson is confined to brief discussions in more wide-ranging texts.[5] This volume begins the work of evaluating Wilson's contribution to children's literature in more detail.

Becoming Wilson

Jacqueline Wilson is indelibly associated with one of Britain's most successful teenage magazines, D. C. Thompson's *Jackie*. Although the often-repeated claim that she was the inspiration for the magazine's title is inaccurate, the relationship between the two is significant. Wilson's professional writing career began after she submitted an article to D. C. Thompson in response to an advertisement seeking material for their new teenage magazine. Several more articles followed, and shortly thereafter Wilson accepted a staff job with D. C. Thompson. It was an auspicious moment to become involved with the company: *Jackie* magazine was at the forefront of a new way of writing for young people, offering a connection with the concerns of teenagers in a way that was largely absent from the children's books of the period. When it launched in 1964, it included fashion tips, pin-ups of Elvis Presley and The Beatles and an article on 'The Art of Being Kissable'. By contrast, the 1964 list of Puffin's Peacock Books – the first British imprint specifically for teenagers – included Rosemary Sutcliff's historical novel *The Rider of the White Horse*, L. M. Montgomery's classic *Anne of Green Gables* and Geoffrey Household's 1939 spy thriller *Rogue Male*. While Wilson chafed at the house style of the magazine – she recollects that she 'had a very different approach to being a teenager [...] and tended to poke fun at things' – magazine publishing offered an alternative to the kind of fiction Wilson had encountered during her own childhood, which 'just didn't seem to reflect life the way I knew it'.[6] As a staff writer for D. C. Thompson she had the opportunity to write about issues which were just beginning to emerge in fiction for teenagers, not only in articles for *Jackie* – where the realism was constrained by the desire to 'nurture [readers'] romantic dreams' – but also on the women's magazine *Red Letter*, where Wilson answered readers' letters and produced articles on pregnancy and babies. This early experience in writing about real-life issues which lay well outside her own personal experience was a good preparation for Wilson's later work, which would see her engaging imaginatively with issues such as the lives of looked-after children.

D. C. Thompson's decision to offer Wilson a staff position reflected their interest in finding new voices which would appeal to the new market they were trying to reach. However, it almost certainly also owed much to the fact that Wilson had quickly shown she would be able to meet the demands of magazine publishing, following her initial article with a series of others in order to show, as she put it, 'that I wasn't a one-trick wonder'.[7] During her time with the magazine she not only produced a steady stream of writing for immediate publication, but also worked on developing her own voice. Although her writing was a good fit for D. C. Thompson's publications, this work was a means to an end: she recollects, 'I wrote endless short stories not only in my teens but in my twenties and thirties for magazines simply to make money whilst I was actually writing proper books as well.'[8] In 1972 her first 'proper book' was published: *Hide and Seek* appeared on Macmillan's crime list. Although it was not a novel for children, it was centred on child characters, as were the four adult novels which followed. Shortly after *Hide and Seek* Wilson's first book for children was published: *Ricky's Birthday* appeared in Macmillan Education's *Nippers* series in 1973.[9] These two early books represent two types of writing which were to come together in Wilson's later work: *Hide and Seek*, which deals with the kidnapping of two little girls, shows Wilson's ability to deal with difficult topics sympathetically. *Ricky's Birthday*, a 32-page picture book for beginner readers, steers clear of difficult issues but combines humour and understanding of the child's experience of the world with a realistic portrayal of a working-class family.

Although Macmillan had published both *Ricky's Birthday* and her early crime novels, they declined her first efforts for teenagers. These eventually found a home with Oxford University Press (OUP). Wilson has suggested that the subject matter of *Nobody's Perfect* (1982) struck a chord with OUP editor Ron Heapy, but OUP's acceptance of the novel also indicates that Wilson's years of writing had paid off. Writing for magazines, she had been conscious that 'it was no use putting in long passages of description or trying to use metaphors or similes, or striving to give my writing a little bit of sparkle or originality or humour'.[10] By contrast, OUP positioned themselves on the literary side of the market and offered more scope for the kind of writing Wilson had been working to develop. Wilson's reputation as a leading writer of social realism for children often leads to a focus on her subject matter rather than her style, but her writing is also complex and at times highly literary. Her move into writing for young people attracted immediate recognition: *Nobody's Perfect* was a runner-up for the 1982 Young Observer / Rank Organisation Fiction Prize. Although it was ultimately judged 'too slight', its appearance on a shortlist which included Jan Mark's challenging work of science fiction *Aquarius* and Aidan Chambers's complex postmodern novel *Dance on My Grave* (1982) indicates the success of Wilson's shift into a more literary genre.[11]

OUP offered Wilson the space to extend her literary style, but her breakthrough into novel writing also enabled her to begin developing the social realism with which she has become so closely associated. Writing for D. C. Thompson, she had been constrained by the need to offer romantic fantasies, but at OUP there was room for her to take a more unflinching approach to topics such as teenage pregnancy (*Amber*, 1986), suicide (*Falling Apart*, 1989) and drug use (*The Dream Palace*, 1991). This willingness to tackle difficult issues was to become a hallmark of Wilson's fiction: her novels for younger readers have addressed a range of challenging topics.

Humour had been a feature of Wilson's books from the beginning, but the OUP novels were relatively serious in tone. By the late 1980s, however, she was beginning to develop the style which would allow her to write so successfully for younger readers. Her *Stevie Day* series (*Stevie Day: Super Sleuth*, 1987; *Stevie Day: Lonely Hearts*, 1987; *Stevie Day: Vampire*, 1988; and *Stevie Day: Rat Race*, 1988) shows some of the stylistic characteristics which would reappear in Wilson's later work, notably in the use of a first-person narrator with a tendency for exaggeration. The jackets of the *Stevie Day* books also included a questionnaire purportedly filled out by Stevie, giving name, sex, age and details of family; a device which Wilson would deploy to much greater effect in *The Story of Tracy Beaker*. These books, which have a more light-hearted tone than Wilson's work for older teenagers, were published not by OUP but by Collins Armada, a paperback series which aimed at the more popular end of the market (Enid Blyton was one of Armada's key authors). *Books for Keeps'* review of the first two titles characterises them as 'Harmless escapism for the younger reader with more quality in the writing than one normally expects from this genre'.[12] Even in these books, it is clear that Wilson was interested in more than harmless escapism: *Stevie Day: Vampire*, for example, tackles both heroin addiction and badger baiting. However, she had not yet achieved a perfect balance between humour and a more thoughtful approach, and both themes are the fodder for an exciting adventure rather than part of a deeply felt experience for Stevie.

Wilson's appearance on the more popular Armada list reflects a shift in her sense of the kind of writing she was producing. An article in *Books for Keeps* commenting on *Nobody's Perfect* had expressed a wish 'for writers and editors who recognise that those reading books at this level will not, by and large, react when reference is made to Spare Rib, Laura Ashley, Durer, the Brontes etc. etc'.[13] In her early books for teenagers Wilson was not seeking to attract teenagers 'at large'; she 'deliberately aimed at the odd ones out, the quirky and imaginative and awkward' and − by default − at the kind of 'literary' reader who *would* react to references to feminist magazine *Spare Rib* and the Brontës.[14] Writing for this kind of reader allowed scope for the kind of literary writing she had not been able to produce when writing for magazines. By the late 80s, though, her position as a writer for young people was well established and she was beginning to receive invitations to speak at schools, where she encountered many children who were decidedly *not* 'literary' and 'started to think it might be good to try to interest the sort of kids who said they thought reading boring'.[15] At the same time, children's publishing was shifting, and the distinction between the 'literary' and the popular was becoming less pronounced. It was with a new publisher – Transworld – that she would combine elements of her earlier work to produce a style of writing which appealed to a much wider range of readers.

Beaker and beyond

Wilson's 'breakthrough book', *The Story of Tracy Beaker*, appeared just three years after *Stevie Day: Vampire*, but unlike the earlier novel it displays all the richness of Wilson's long apprenticeship. It is notable that the book appeared on a new list edited by David Fickling, who had worked on some of Wilson's OUP novels and suggested that she might like to try writing for a younger audience. Fickling's approach to children's publishing embraces the blend of the literary and the popular which had characterised Jacqueline Wilson's career up until that point. He 'discovered' Philip Pullman while working at OUP and was to go on to publish literary and demanding books under his own imprint David Fickling Books (now an independent publishing house). At the same time he is keenly aware of the need for children's books to compete with other popular media, pointing out that 'Books stand cheek by jowl with computers, computer games and music. Children watch "Pop Idol", E4 and the Cartoon Network as well as reading our books.'[16] This eclectic approach to children's books made Fickling receptive to Wilson's suggestion that she should write a different sort of book which would include plenty of illustrations to break up the text and attract more reluctant readers. Fickling suggested that Nick Sharratt might be a suitable illustrator, launching a partnership which has endured through the 25 years since.

Nick Sharratt's illustrations certainly made Wilson's text more eye-catching and appealing; combined with her innovative use of a diary style they also enabled a new shift in her writing style. The *Stevie Day* books had been light-hearted and humorous, but had lacked the emotional depth of her work for teenagers. In *Tracy Beaker*, Wilson uses Tracy's first-person narrative to balance these two elements. As a child in foster care, Tracy is completing her 'book about me' as a means of recording important information about herself. It therefore functions simultaneously as a personal, private record of her identity and a potential source of information for future carers. This allows for an intimate narrative that nevertheless withholds some important details and emotions. Tracy is always aware of her potential reader, and while she is keen to express her criticisms of the care system she is also concerned with putting on a brave face. Thus the reader is asked to infer many of the more potentially disturbing aspects of the narrative: while it is clear that Tracy's mother has essentially abandoned her, for example, this is partially masked by Tracy's creative excuses for her mother's absence and her insistence that she will eventually be reclaimed. Nick Sharratt's illustrations sometimes work to expose the gap between Tracy's version of events and the reality, but also add humour to the text, leavening the more serious themes. The result was favourably received: a review in the *Guardian* described it as 'an appealing mix of events and reactions that are both entertaining and moving. A book that lingers in the mind long after it is put down', and the book was highly commended for the Carnegie Medal.[17]

Wilson had found her voice with *Tracy Beaker*, and her subsequent works employed many of the same strategies to similar effect. She has often used the collaboration with Nick Sharratt to support more demanding literary strategies or to soften the impact of challenging or upsetting material. In *Double Act*, which was highly commended for the Carnegie Medal and won both the Nestlé Smarties Book Prize and the Red House Children's Book Award, Wilson's doubled narrative, which alternates between the voices of her twin protagonists, is visually represented by the use of separate illustrators: Ruby and Garnett are drawn by Nick Sharratt and Sue Heap respectively, underlining the fact that they are 'similar but different'. In *The Illustrated Mum*, the style of Sharratt's drawings encourages the child reader to view the eponymous character's tattoos as appealing rather than threatening or weird. Sharratt's illustrations thus help Wilson to avoid some of the constraints which might otherwise be associated with writing for 8–12-year-olds.

Jacqueline Wilson's most notable contribution has been to literature for 'middle-grade' readers: although her post-*Tracy Beaker* works range from books for children as young as five (*The Dinosaur's Packed Lunch*, 1995; *The Monster Story Teller*, 1997) through to novels for the early teens (the *Girls* trilogy, 1998, 1999, 2002; *Love Lessons*, 2005), she has never returned to writing for older teenagers, and the vast majority of her work has been for the 8–12 category. Within this category, she has pioneered a distinctive form of social realism. Part of the broad appeal of Wilson's fiction lies in her avoidance of the middle-class settings which used to dominate children's books. Her novels consistently feature children from working-class and sometimes deprived backgrounds, and often draw a contrast between their lives and those of more affluent children. In *Secrets* (2002), for example, Treasure lives on a 'vast tower-block council estate', 'very big, very bleak and very tough', while India lives on a 'luxury complex', but both girls have

problematic families.[18] Similarly, in *Diamond Girls* (2004) Dixie lives
on the deprived Planet Estate and her family rely on benefits, but
although her family is chaotic, it is middle-class Mary who is revealed
to be suffering from abuse. Wilson consistently shows that families
who live on benefits, feed their children junk food and are regarded
by more affluent people as 'feckless single mums on drugs and gangs
of drop-outs' are just as loving as middle-class families, and she writes
about the experiences of working-class children from the perspective
of an insider.[19] Within this setting she is willing to tackle challenging issues: the balance between humour and seriousness which she
established in *Tracy Beaker* has enabled her to write about a range
of difficult topics, including the experiences of looked-after children (*Dustbin Baby*, 2001, as well as the *Tracy Beaker* novels), unstable
accommodation (*The Bed and Breakfast Star*, 1994), mental illness (*The
Illustrated Mum*, 1999), bereavement (*Vicky Angel*, 2000) and domestic
violence (*Lola Rose*, 2003).

By writing realistically about such topics, Wilson has sometimes
provoked discomfort: when interviewed, she often comments on the
wariness she has encountered from parents about the content matter
of her books.[20] A *Daily Mail* article from 2008 exemplifies the kinds
of criticism Wilson has attracted: Winifred Robinson complains that
'the form Wilson pioneers [...] accounts for a good deal of the tension in otherwise stable middle-class homes' and 'opens the door to
experiences from which [children] should be protected for as long as
possible'.[21] Given her prominence in the children's market, however,
it is striking how *little* controversy she has engendered: it is difficult
to find extant news articles which criticise her approach. Even the
Daily Mail has frequently praised Wilson for her handling of difficult issues: *Bad Girls*, which features bullying, shoplifting and foster
care, was reviewed as 'a clear and sensitive book about very common
problems', and *The Illustrated Mum* was recommended as the best of
the 2000 Carnegie shortlist.[22] This reflects the striking achievement
of Wilson's post-*Tracy Beaker* writing, which introduces a note of
optimism which is less prominent in the earlier teenage novels. As a
young fan responding to Winifred Robinson's criticisms in the *Daily
Mail* pointed out, 'Her bestselling books aren't particularly graphic, or
malign; they introduce children to such issues in a subtle way.'[23] This
subtle and sympathetic handling of difficult issues has enabled Wilson
to establish a special connection with young readers. As she has wryly
commented, 'I never set out to be an agony aunt but I seem somehow to have become one. I get hundreds of letters and emails from
children telling me about their problems.'[24] The fact that even today

Wilson answers many such letters personally illustrates another reason for her popularity.

Given her prominence in the British market, it is no surprise that Wilson has also made her mark internationally. Her books have been translated into over 30 languages, including Chinese, French, German, Hungarian and Japanese. She has been well received in Australia, where one of her early teenage novels, *Falling Apart*, was recently brought back into print (none of these novels are currently in print in the UK). It is striking, however, that although Wilson has been well reviewed in the USA, she has not attracted the level of acclaim she has enjoyed in the UK. Whereas British fantasy has thrived in the US, spurred along by the Harry Potter phenomenon, realistic fiction has always been slower to cross the Atlantic. The relatively limited recognition of Wilson's books in the US can perhaps also be partially accounted for by the much weaker branding of the US editions: many of the earlier US editions were rejacketed with new cover illustrations, setting a different (and usually more serious) tone and disrupting the strong recognition factor which has aided Wilson in the UK market.[25] The revisions made to the US edition of *The Bed and Breakfast Star*, which was retitled *Elsa, Star of the Shelter!* and equipped with humorous footnotes explaining some of the British details, also indicate the possible cultural barriers in place for American readers. Wilson's very distinctiveness and nuanced depiction of the lives of British children may be less appealing to American readers with access to a wide range of home-grown social realism.

In recent years Jacqueline Wilson has moved away from contemporary social realism into historical fiction. Her first historical novel, *Hetty Feather* (2010), arose out of her time as Coram Fellow with the Foundling Hospital and follows the life of a Victorian foundling. Three more novels about Hetty followed: *Sapphire Battersea* (2011), *Emerald Star* (2012) and *Diamond* (2013) (told from the point of view of another character).[26] Wilson has also explored the Edwardian period in *Four Children and It* (2012) and *Opal Plumstead* (2014), and has tackled more recent history in *Queenie* (2013), which is set at the time of Queen Elizabeth's coronation. These novels feature many of the elements which have made Wilson's contemporary work so popular, including strong and characterful heroines and challenging social themes, but the historical context has allowed Wilson scope to develop her style in new directions. It is this versatility which has enabled Wilson to maintain her freshness and success after over 100 novels. Perhaps the move away from contemporary social realism will also open up new markets: *Katy*, her 2015 adaptation of Susan

Coolidge's *What Katy Did*, seems likely to catch the attention of fans
of this American classic.

The essays in this casebook

This volume examines many of the issues touched upon above. The
first two chapters of the volume consider Jacqueline Wilson's early
career and the way both her writing and her 'brand' have developed.
Julia Eccleshare's chapter sets Wilson's books in the wider context of
the children's market and shows how her talent and experience as
a writer, her engagement with her child readers and a combination
of publishing and marketing decisions have combined to help make
Wilson the household name she is today. Ika Willis also looks back at
Wilson's apprenticeship as a writer: her chapter explores the novels
published by OUP in detail and shows how they laid a foundation for
much of Wilson's later work. As Jacqueline Wilson herself has observed,
her books take place within a world as distinctive as that of Anita
Brookner or Anne Tyler; a world which 'is always going to be about
misunderstood girls: shy ones, bookish ones, lonely ones, naughty ones,
fierce ones'.[27] Willis shows how the OUP novels work to establish this
world, not only with respect to Wilson's characters, but also in terms of
her thematic concerns, settings and distinctive language.

The middle chapters of this volume consider Jacqueline Wilson's
contribution as a writer of social realism, examining how her books
have engaged with issues relating to gender and family, and how she
has responded to the question of children's books as 'bibliotherapy'.
Lucy Pearson shows how Wilson's approach to the latter issue has
evolved over the course of her career, comparing her approach to
fantasy and escapism in her OUP novel *The Other Side* (1984) with
that in her later work *The Illustrated Mum* (1999). Pearson sets these
works in the wider context of debates around fantasy and realism in
children's literature, showing that Wilson's early work reflects some of
the ideas about children's need for realistic fiction which were current in the 1970s and 1980s, while her later writing develops a more
nuanced approach to fantasy which reflects her pioneering approach
to writing social realism for younger readers.

Kay Waddilove's chapter deals with the issue which Wilson herself
has identified as the one which is at the heart of her work: girlhood.
The OUP novels are explicit in their exploration of gender issues: the
heroine of *Nobody's Perfect* reads *Spare Rib* and reflects ruefully, 'I still
wanted to be a feminist – but I wanted to look pretty too.'[28] Changes
in social context and in Wilson's intended readership mean that later

books engage with feminism less directly, but Kay Waddilove's chapter on Wilson's 'feisty girls and fearful boys' shows that they continue to grapple with issues of gender. Waddilove suggests that while Wilson has created a gallery of strong female characters whose emotional, and sometimes physical, survival is contingent upon their cussedness, her books do not simply offer a reversal of gender expectations. Instead, they engage in current debates on gender and the family by offering representations of girls and boys, women and men, which transcend concepts of masculine–feminine polarities.

One gendered issue to which Jacqueline Wilson has repeatedly returned is the question of motherhood. She has created a series of heroines with absent, neglectful or simply unconventional mothers, from Sandra in *Nobody's Perfect*, whose early life included a period in care due to the mental breakdown of her single mother, through to the eponymous heroine of *Hetty Feather* (2010), abandoned by her mother at the Foundling Hospital. As the short story Wilson wrote for an anthology on mothers suggests, however, although mothers may be absent or problematic they are not dispensable: Wilson's story was titled 'No One Else Will Do'.[29] Helen Limon explores Wilson's representation of mothers and mothering, arguing that her books show both the importance and the ambivalence of the mothering role. Limon shows that Wilson's representation of 'distributed' mothering practices acknowledges that carer–child relationships are not always perfect, but also offers the possibility of a wider range of nurturant relationships which can offer 'good enough' care regardless of sex or age. While acknowledging the importance of the mothering role, Wilson shows that someone else *will* do, and that children can thrive even when offered incomplete care.

The later chapters of this volume focus more closely on Wilson's literary strategies. Her status as a literary writer is often obscured by her reputation as a writer of social realism, but her writing is playful, complex and often innovative. Her successful use of an unreliable narrator in her most famous book, *The Story of Tracy Beaker*, is indicative of the innovation Wilson has brought to writing for younger readers. Unreliable narration is a feature more commonly associated with books for young adults but, as Helen Day's chapter shows, *Tracy Beaker* successfully deploys this technique for much younger readers. Day considers *Tracy Beaker* in the context of cognitive and rhetorical approaches to unreliability, showing how Wilson's text and Nick Sharratt's illustrations work together to give Tracy's lies psychological realism and enable the child reader to engage with her unreliable narration. By contrast, the popular BBC television adaptation sacrifices some of the complexity of Tracy's unreliable narration in favour of a clearer distinction between fantasy and realism, a choice which Day suggests offers less to the developing child audience.

Like her fellow OUP authors Jane Gardam and Geraldine McCaughrean, Jacqueline Wilson frequently employs metafictive strategies, and often writes about characters who are themselves writers or storytellers. Clémentine Beauvais looks at the recurrent motif of the double, twin, replica or döppelganger in Jacqueline Wilson's metafictional works, in particular *Double Act, The Lottie Project* (1997) and *Four Children and It* (2012). In these three novels, the figure of the young female writer (or writers, in the case of *Double Act*) is markedly accompanied by the shadow presence of another self very much like her own, and yet distanced from her by the creative act of writing. Beauvais's chapter offers a literary critical analysis of some of the same concerns explored in Pearson's chapter on bibliotherapy, showing how the 'doubling' of the self in the young writer allows for the opening up of a parallel world of 'illusion' and the consequent escape into a 'copy' of reality marked by 'duality'. Beauvais suggests that the preservation of narrative and psychological duality in these texts is precarious, and frequently collapses as, to put it colloquially, 'reality calls'. Only in these moments of heightened tension can we be sure that, for instance, it is Charlie who is 'writing Lottie' in *The Lottie Project*. In *Double Act*, it is when Ruby and Garnet part ways, each writing into their own notebook, that Garnet finally confirms to herself and to the reader that she can now 'write about me' and 'not about us', that she is not a creation of Ruby, despite being her double. Such lapses into unicity provide gateways for the teenage female reader to project herself outside of the innumerable, literary 'doubles' of herself which Jacqueline Wilson's books offer. By counterbalancing the comfort of having a double – an alternative self – with the unsettling realisation that this dual relationship always falls back on itself and reveals unicity, Jacqueline Wilson forbids closure. Beauvais suggests that this strategy ensures that the young reader is able to project herself into the story, but ultimately escape complete identification with the characters and their worlds.

Sheena Wilkinson also considers Wilson's use of metafictive strategies, showing how the series of historical novels which begins with *Hetty Feather* traces the coming of age of its heroine as both a young woman and a writer. Wilkinson argues that Wilson's move into historical fiction, which is heavily influenced by her own reading of Victorian novels, enables her to employ a more complex literary style and to follow her heroine from childhood to the cusp of womanhood without alienating young readers. Wilkinson's chapter offers a useful understanding of how Wilson has retained her appeal for the tween-age and early teen audience at a point when she is no longer confident about portraying contemporary teenage life.[30]

The final critical chapter in this volume takes a broader view of Jacqueline Wilson's position as a writer for children and young teens, situating her work in a comparative context. Rebecca Morris's chapter locates Wilson's contributions within the broader context of the problem novel genre in Anglophone literature for children and teens, with a particular focus on how Wilson's work compares to that of American writer Judy Blume. Morris's analysis perhaps sheds light on the different reception of Wilson in the US. She argues that despite the tendency to view Wilson as the 'British Blume', Wilson's work deviates from that of her American counterpart in its less reassuring tone, especially with regard to the treatment of sexuality, which is more dangerous and less comfortable than in Blume's novels. Despite the temptation to draw parallels between the two authors, Morris suggests that this divergence reflects their differing approaches to the problem genre, and thus signals their separate contributions to the development of the genre as a whole.

The volume concludes with the words of Jacqueline Wilson herself. Pearson's 2014 interview with Wilson explores the author's perspective on many of the issues tackled by the critical chapters, including her early career and publishing history, her relationship to her child readers and her recent shift into historical fiction.

As the range of chapters in this volume attest, Jacqueline Wilson's immense popularity and accessible writing belies the range and complexity of her work. It is difficult to do justice to a career which has spanned 40 years and over 100 novels, and there is much more to explore, but we hope that this volume has begun to illuminate Wilson's contribution to British children's literature.

Notes

1 Public Lending Right, 'Most Borrowed Authors July 1997–June 1998', https://www.plr.uk.com/mediaCentre/mostBorrowedAuthors/top20Authors/1997-1998Top20Authors.pdf [accessed 31 March 2015]; Public Lending Right, 'Most Borrowed Authors July 2002–June 2003', https://www.plr.uk.com/mediaCentre/mostBorrowedAuthors/top20Authors/2002-2003Top20Authors.pdf [accessed 31 March 2015]. Wilson maintained her number one spot for five years before being ousted by James Patterson in 2006. Public Lending Right, 'Most Borrowed

Authors July 2006–June 2007', https://www.plr.uk.com/mediaCentre/
mostBorrowedAuthors/top20Authors/2006-2007Top20Authors.pdf
[accessed 31 March 2015].

2 Brian MacArthur, 'Best-selling Authors of the Decade'. *Telegraph* 22
December 2009, http://www.telegraph.co.uk/culture/books/6866648/
Bestselling-authors-of-the-decade.html [accessed 31 March 2015];
http://core.ac.uk/download/pdf/244281.pdf.

3 Guinness rejected the nomination on the grounds that the event had
not been formally monitored. John Ezard, 'Book Signing Lasts 8 Hours'.
Guardian 10 March 2004, http://www.theguardian.com/uk/2004/
mar/10/booksforchildrenandteenagers.books [accessed 31 March 2015].

4 Wilson first appears on PLR's list of most-borrowed authors in 1996/1997,
debuting at number 91. Public Lending Right, 'Most Borrowed Authors
July 1996–June 1997 (Adults and children combined)', https://www.plr.
uk.com/mediaCentre/mostBorrowedAuthors/top250Authors/1996-
1997Top100Authors.pdf [accessed 23 March 2015].

5 See the Further Reading section of this volume for a survey of existing
material on Wilson.

6 Interview with Jacqueline Wilson in this volume.

7 Ibid.

8 Ibid.

9 Although the publication of *Ricky's Birthday* post-dates that of *Hide and
Seek*, it seems that it was actually the first book Wilson had accepted for
publication. Wilson herself identifies *Ricky's Birthday* as her first book,
stating, 'Although it was only a little paperback and it certainly wasn't
widely distributed, it meant so much because this was a book which was
published. That had been my ambition right from when I was a small
girl' (interview in this volume). The account she gives of encountering
the Nippers series when her own daughter was a toddler and writing
a book to match the format is consonant with the idea that *Ricky's
Birthday* pre-dated *Hide and Seek*, since Wilson's daughter was born in
1967. The relatively limited output of the Nippers series – all edited by
Leila Berg – makes it not unlikely that it took several years for the book
to actually appear.

10 Interview with Jacqueline Wilson in this volume.

11 The prize was jointly awarded to Jan Mark's *Aquarius* and Mary
Melwood's *The Watcher Bee* (1982). Melwood's current obscurity is
an interesting reflection of the limitations of book awards. Pat Triggs,
'Teenage Fiction Award'. *Books For Keeps* 18 (January 1983), p. 14.

12 Val Randall, 'Stevie Day: Super Sleuth ¦ Stevie Day: Lonely Hearts'.
Books for Keeps 50 (May 1988) http://booksforkeeps.co.uk/issue/50/
childrens-books/reviews/stevie-day-super-sleuth-%C2%A6-stevie-day-
lonely-hearts [accessed 20 March 2015].

13 Steve Bowles, 'Teenage Fiction: Another Uninspired Year'. *Books for
Keeps* 18 (January 1983), p. 16.

14 Interview with Jacqueline Wilson in this volume.
15 Ibid.
16 David Fickling, quoted in Rod Stewart, 'The Fickling Factor'. *The Bookseller* 14 February 2002, http://www.thebookseller.com/feature/fickling-factor [accessed 13 February 2015].
17 Margo Halcrow, 'Children's Books: Romance and a Rake's Progress – Junior Comedy'. *The Guardian* 20 June 1991, http://www.nexis.com/docview/getDocForCuiReq?lni=40FN-KFH0-00VY-83XH&csi=138620&oc=00240&perma=true.
18 Jacqueline Wilson, *Secrets* (London: Corgi Yearling, 2003), p. 63; p. 64.
19 Ibid., p. 64.
20 Interview with Jacqueline Wilson in this volume.
21 Winifred Robinson, 'The Hypocritical Ms Wilson: Why Children's Authors are to Blame for Loss of Innocence'. *Daily Mail Online* 4 March 2008, http://www.dailymail.co.uk/news/article-526369/The-hypocritical-Ms-Wilson-Why-childrens-writers-hugely-blame-loss-innocence.html [accessed 15 March 2015].
22 Michelle Hanson, 'Michelle Hanson is Intrigued by the Bizarre and a Bazaar in Stories for Eight to 10 Year Olds'. *Night and Day: Mail on Sunday* 14 July 1996, http://www.nexis.com/docview/getDocForCuiReq?lni=3TD9-V9F0-0074-D1RW&csi=138794&oc=00240&perma=true [accessed 15 March 2015]; Susan Elkin, 'They're All Right in Our Book'. *Daily Mail* 4 July 2000, http://www.nexis.com/docview/getDocForCuiReq?lni=40NB-YWT0-0074-D0WS&csi=138794&oc=00240&perma=true [accessed 15 March 2015].
23 Letter from Kathy Brown, 'Child's Fiction Which Tackles the Facts'. *Daily Mail* 13 March 2008, http://www.nexis.com/docview/getDocForCuiReq?lni=4S25-22T0-TX4S-P0HG&csi=138794&oc=00240&perma=true [accessed 15 March 2015].
24 Interview with Jacqueline Wilson in this volume.
25 More recent editions have retained or restored the Nick Sharratt jackets, signalling the growing importance of Sharratt to the Wilson 'brand'.
26 2015 saw the publication of another novel in the series, *Little Stars*.
27 Interview with Jacqueline Wilson in this volume.
28 Jacqueline Wilson, *Nobody's Perfect* (London: Fontana Lions, 1983), p. 13.
29 Jacqueline Wilson, 'No One Else Will Do' in Miriam Hodgson (ed.), *Mother's Day: Stories of Mothers and Daughters* (London: Methuen, 1992), pp. 128–137.
30 Interview with Jacqueline Wilson in this volume.

1

A Publishing Phenomenon: The Marketing and Branding of Jacqueline Wilson

Julia Eccleshare

Jacqueline Wilson's writing career has been long, extremely productive and outstandingly successful. She has made an unparalleled
contribution to children's literature in two major respects: she has
brought an unusually large number of children to reading because
they so love her books, and she has pushed forward the frontiers of
what it is possible to write about. In doing so she has not only created
a particular niche for herself which can be defined as the Jacqueline
Wilson 'brand', but she has also had a long-lasting effect on what can
loosely be defined as 'family fiction'. For any single author to have
such an impact is unusual; it gives both Wilson's books and her very
public role an exceptional status and power in twentieth- and twenty-
first-century children's literature.

From the current vantage point, it would be easy to assume
that Wilson's success was assured from the outset. That would be a
misreading of the facts. The exceptional place that Wilson holds in
children's books and her very long tenure of that place was created
by a number of factors which, just because their impact has been
so remarkable, should not be thought of as pre-determined or even
assured. What may now look like a well-planned path to success took
hold slowly. Most importantly, its origins lie in Wilson's quality and
integrity as an author: without the appeal of her books none of it
would have happened. That, allied to her tenacity of purpose and
the exceptional energy which led to an unusually large output, is the
starting point of her success. But those attributes alone might not
have been sufficient to have given Wilson the role she has attained. As
with most exceptions to rules, her unique status can never be readily
replicated or even entirely explained. It was shaped by a combination

of deliberate actions by Wilson herself, her publishers and some critics; and by the special opportunities presented by the publishing and
educational context of the time.

At the outset Wilson had no blueprint to follow in building her
career, although with the benefit of hindsight it can be seen that it
was forged in a number of ways: her ability to set her work in an
entirely contemporary context, the needs of the readers at the time
and Wilson's fulfilment of those needs, the role her publisher played
in understanding the special quality of her books and positioning
them in the market accordingly, and finally, the burgeoning of children's literature in the UK which took place during the time that
she was writing. Her own work and reactions to it from both readers
and commentators contribute to an understanding of how that came
about and the role she and others played in creating the identity
which led to her being marketable as a 'brand' in ways that reached
far beyond the usual confines of a children's author.

Wilson's writing career and the publishing context in which it
was developed is well-documented in her autobiography and has also
been much discussed by her during her very many media appearances.[1] In all these accounts, she describes a solitary childhood which
she enlivened by 'inventing' play companions and by writing stories.
'The Maggotts', written in an exercise book in her neatly formed, if
somewhat loopy, nine-year-old hand, could be called the beginning
of her career as a writer; Wilson certainly attributes her interest in
her future career to that book and other childish attempts at writing.
Her career began more formally and for wider public consumption
with her first job as a writer for D. C. Thomson, the Dundee-based
newspaper and magazine publishers. Seeing an advertisement calling
for submissions, Wilson got the job on the strength of a piece she
sent them describing the experience and feelings of a luckless girl at a
disco. She was 17 and still at technical college but keen to leave home
and to get into writing. She worked on the woman's magazine *Red
Letter* contributing short stories, horoscopes and articles about pregnancy and babies, and also writing the readers' letters as there were
never enough sent in. As Wilson said in *Talking Books*,

> I was eighteen and had never been pregnant. It's amazing what you can
> do with a bit of research and imagination! It was an invaluable training,
> because it taught me not to be precious about writing, to be adaptable,
> to turn my hand to anything and to write whenever it was needed.[2]

Wilson arrived at D. C. Thomson shortly before the company
launched *Jackie* in January 1964. A weekly magazine filled with stories,

'real-life experiences', fashion tips and celebrity gossip, *Jackie* was the most influential magazine for teenage girls for almost three decades. *Jackie* launched with a circulation of 350,000 copies a week and peaked with sales figures of almost 606,000 copies a week before closing in 1993. Following Wilson's enormous success with the same age group an apocryphal story that the magazine had been named after her seemed highly plausible and was widely adopted. However, in an interview in the *Observer* (23 March 2014) Wilson set the record straight:

> The men in charge were Mr Cuthbert and Mr Tate, and on Friday mornings I had to take them their coffee and give them a report of what I'd been doing. On one of these mornings they told me they'd named it after me, and I was charmed. But later on, someone else said it had been nothing to do with me: the name was in the air thanks to Jackie O.[3]

Jackie Onassis, formerly Jackie Kennedy, wife of the then US president, was herself one of the female icons of the time. Despite the lack of absolute truth in it, Wilson went on to say that she continued to bring the story out as it is such a good one and *Jackie*, the magazine, had been read by all the mothers of the girls who loved her books.

From such a vantage point within teen culture it could look surprising that apart from a single children's title, *Ricky's Birthday* (1973), a story about inner-city children which was published in the Nippers series for beginner readers, Wilson's first books were adult crime novels and a couple of radio plays. But a look at the market for teenage fiction at the time shows that the impulse to write for it would have been considerably less strong than it would be today. While magazines for teenagers thrived, teenage fiction in the UK was in its infancy; even over a decade later the entry on Teenage Novels in *The Oxford Companion to Children's Literature* (1984) reads, 'Teenage novels, often described as "young adult" or "adolescent" fiction, are, generally speaking, a modern phenomenon.'[4] It identified this phenomenon as a largely US strand of publishing which, as it had developed from J. D. Salinger's *The Catcher in the Rye* (1951), naturally led authors such as Paul Zindel, Judy Blume and Robert Cormier to create 'Holden Caulfields of their own, with comic self-regarding attitudes and complicated feelings about the adult world.'[5] Carpenter and Prichard's examples of British authors in this category include K. M. Peyton, whose Flambards series and Pennington novels are lightly dismissed as belonging to the well-established genres of romantic fiction and school stories respectively. It concludes with Jill Paton Walsh and John Rowe Townsend who are described as typical of their generation in 'producing "adolescent" books which deal with their heroes' quests for personal identity, but do so in a reflective "interior" manner derived from the mainstream of the English novel rather than from Salinger'.[6]

Definitions like this reflected the widespread view of UK critics in the 1970s and 1980s most of whom were slow to value the UK's own 'realist' teenage novel. The result was that the UK market was dominated by the US authors Carpenter names above, who were imported alongside titles from Sweden such as Gunnel Beckman's *The Girl Without a Name* (1967), a story of contemporary teenage life, and *Mia Alone* (1973), which airs the dilemmas of a young girl facing an abortion, while the UK authors were paid less attention. Blume − to whom Wilson is most often compared, as both speak directly to teenage girls about their complex inner emotions − was quickly a bestselling author achieving widespread praise as early as 1970 when *Are You There, God? It's Me, Margaret* was named as Outstanding Book of the Year in the *New York Times*.[7] With the publication of *Forever* (1975), her groundbreaking title which is cited as the first title for teenagers to describe intercourse overtly, Blume became a household name as well as one of the most banned authors in schools and libraries.

It was against that background and its implicit expectations about what British teenagers would read that Wilson's first 'children's' books were published. The switch from writing for adults to writing for younger readers was not as extreme as it might look, as Wilson's characters in the later titles were 15-year-olds who, in those days, were on the edge of leaving school if not deemed 'clever' and so were facing the tensions around the ending of childhood and the step into adulthood. Although these books were categorised so differently in the market and therefore involved a repositioning of Wilson in readers' minds, Wilson herself saw the switch as a natural one given that each of her adult titles had a prominent child character in it. The move to writing for and about children also fitted with her own often-repeated accounts of how she wrote stories as a child and the games she created to play with the child characters she imagined.

Unrelated in terms of character or specific content but closely linked in terms of style and subject matter, the six early novels are: *Nobody's Perfect* (1982), *Waiting for the Sky to Fall* (1983), *The Other Side* (1984), *Amber* (1986), *The Power of the Shade* (1987) and *This Girl* (1988). These books are dark stories with rough edges and unhappiness bubbling not far below the surface. They all centre round a girl although there are boys in them − necessary where love is burgeoning as in *Nobody's Perfect* and *Amber*. As Ika Willis's essay in this volume shows, they all contain much that is recognisable in Wilson's later and more successful stories, but the telling of them is bleaker and pitched at teenagers rather than younger readers. Well-constructed stories with believable characters, they are about family, friends, class, sex, identity – all the issues of adolescence which the characters tackled in a convincing if a rather too sober way. While in terms of subject matter they were close to contemporaneous titles such as Robert Westall's *The Scarecrows* (1981), an angry story of family breakdown as seen through the eyes of a teenage boy which won the 1981 Carnegie Medal, and *Madame Doubtfire* (1987), Anne Fine's wildly humorous but nonetheless hard-hitting story on the same subject, they lacked a distinctive enough voice to make Wilson either a prize winner or readily identifiable to consumers. Critics were, however, noticing this newcomer. In *Children's Books of the Year 1986*, Julia Eccleshare selected *Amber* for inclusion and in its annotated entry praised Wilson's ability to recognise contemporary lives – in this case Amber's rejection of her hippy parents: 'At last a book which sets today's teenagers in a proper context, with parents whose experiences reflect the particular time they lived through rather than some generalised idea of "parent" or "adult".'[8] However, the books were not of enough significance as a body of work to earn Wilson a place in the 1987 revised edition of *Written for Children*, for example.[9]

In the 1980s that omission was not so remarkable and it partly reflects the state of the publishing and distribution of children's books at the time. The way children's books reached the market was slow. It involved many adult intermediaries – parents, teachers and librarians, booksellers – and a laboriously constructed information system of print-based reviews and a handful of prizes. Only three years later, Wilson's books had gained wider critical respect individually, and her work overall could be identified by common themes. Writing an entry for her in *Twentieth-Century Children's Writers* based largely on those titles, Robert Leeson, a children's writer who was himself a well-respected chronicler of contemporary children's lives, describes this substantial contribution to teenage fiction in this way: 'Wilson is one of those authors who can show from the inside how teenagers feel and who prove that British children's literature no longer depends upon American authors for credible stories in this age group.'[10] Wilson's books already included the core elements she was later to distil more sharply, which led Leeson to describe her work as 'contemporary [...] with a strong emphasis on dialogue and inner feelings'[11]

While Wilson's teen titles were beginning to attract critical success, they were not making a significant impact on the readers in shops.

Fortunately, even as she was publishing the above titles, she was also writing in other ways and for other readers. Unusual for Wilson in having a boy as the main character, *The Killer Tadpole* (1984) was a light-hearted story for those embarking on solo reading. Pitched just a bit older, *How to Survive Summer Camp* (1985) revealed Wilson's unerring ability to understand the critical importance of friendship for pre-teens. Capturing the different voices of her characters through first-person narration and speaking directly to her readers, it is here that the origins of what was to become her trademark voice lie (it is no coincidence that this is the only one of her early titles to remain in print). Other titles from the same period such as *Glubbslyme* (1987) showed other skills; her ability to write about magic, for example.

Published in paperback with attractive covers, these titles were the ones which began to put Wilson directly into the hands of her readers. They were funny and easy to read, a perfect combination for the difficult 'middle-grade' area of the market. In terms of reading age and complexity of characterisation at the time they seemed slight compared with Wilson's teen novels. As her writing developed and her success began to be established, these stories with their perky tone and light touch are clearly as central to her writing as the darker tones of her teenage novels. By the end of the 1980s, Wilson was displaying two different but related styles in her writing, which between them were attracting critical notice and a loyal following of readers. Also evident was the creative energy and ability to write at speed that was to characterise her years of prodigious success.

Breakthrough book

Those almost two decades of Wilson's writing and the very different way in which her books were received are frequently forgotten by the contemporary headlines that surround Wilson today. This long apprenticeship must be noted, however, as it is evidence that whatever the inherent quality of an author's work there can be no assurance of success and the attendant fame. Other factors always play a significant part. Knowing of the existence of these early titles raises the question of why and how Wilson achieved her reputation and the status that accompanies it, and it provides the opportunity to look at what changed for Wilson in terms of her own writing, how she was published and how childhood was changing in Britain at the time. *The Story of Tracy Beaker*, the book that is universally cited as Wilson's breakthrough title, was published in 1991. The book was the first of her titles to be published by Transworld on the Doubleday list, which was expanding under the editorial direction of David Fickling who had edited Wilson's previous novels while at Oxford University Press. By the time it was published Wilson had already been writing for over 20 years. A decade later Nicholas Tucker writes, 'Wilson's first great success, *The Story of Tracy Beaker* (1991), describes as if from her own experience the life of a disturbed but endearing ten-year-old child living in care after being abandoned by her parents.'[12] The point of such an apparently simplistic description was to convey both the directness of Wilson's child-voice and the comparatively unusual central character. Brought together here it marks out what, with many permutations in terms of the difficulties faced by both the children and the parents in her stories, was to become typical of Wilson's stories.

This career-defining change of combining some of the inter-family struggles of her books for teenagers with the direct, first-person narration of her younger novels in a style that was warm-hearted but did not shy away from difficulties was a gamble. This new approach was potentially difficult to promote, since Wilson did not have the advantage of being a new voice – which anyway, in the pre-J. K. Rowling days of 1991, was not the kind of advantage which it is today – nor was she well known enough in the middle-grade market to be sure of a following. The gamble was to try something that would help her to reach a wider audience. The risk was that in doing so she could alienate her followers at the younger end of the market by offering a far more challenging story. The change that followed was a fortunate coming together of Wilson's deliberate decision to change how she wrote and Wilson's new publisher's endeavour to make books for 8–12 years far more appealing than they had previously been.

Wilson wrote *The Story of Tracy Beaker* for a new list of titles for 8–11s which David Fickling, who had edited Wilson previously, was creating at Doubleday. Her new kind of writing and the fresh way it had of telling the story fitted his passionate commitment to giving younger readers freshly told stories which would kindle a lifelong interest in them. In an interview in June 2013 Annie Eaton, the current editorial director of Doubleday who was then working on the list, remembers her reaction to reading the manuscript as one of feeling she had 'never read anything quite like this'. Unusually, it also required little editorial work, the finished book being published with almost no changes from the manuscript.[13]

To match its originality Fickling, who wanted illustrations which would equally capture contemporary readers directly, turned to an illustrator with whom he had worked at Oxford University Press. Nick Sharratt's interpretation proved perfect: his cover rough picked up the key themes from the book and matched the mood exactly. More subtly and more significantly, his illustrations inside often told a different story to the one that Tracy herself was busily relating about her behaviour as, for example, when she is trying to make herself attractive to prospective adopters.[14] As Kate Agnew notes,

> The book is written as if the heroine were filling in 'my book about me' and Nick Sharratt's illustrations subtly show her untruths, so that while Tracy claims 'she sort of clung a bit' when a visitor returns her to the home, the illustrations show her having to be prised away.[15]

The decision to publish *The Story of Tracy Beaker* with illustrations was part of a general initiative about making books for younger readers more attractive. As it turned out, although Sharratt drew the illustrations without discussion with Wilson, his careful and sensitive reading of the text embellished Wilson's creativity rather than merely reflecting it. The success of the pairing of Sharratt with Wilson was evident in *The Story of Tracy Beaker*, and it laid down the foundation of what was to become the 'branding' of Wilson which, in itself, was an important feature in the shaping of her career as a writer.

The difference between *Tracy Beaker* and Wilson's earlier books lay more in the way Wilson wrote than in her choice of subject. It was a difference that she had deliberately adopted having recognised sooner than most of her contemporaries that the reading tastes of contemporary children were changing.

> Nowadays, even kids from arty, literary homes want more immediacy in a text. They want to get sucked in straightaway, they don't want to work too hard at things. If it is not immediately grabbing their attention, children will dismiss it, say 'This is boring' and put it down.[16]

To counter this and in a clear stylistic break from her previous work, Wilson changed her writing style: 'I began writing in the first person, broke up the text more and made my writing more jokey.'[17] In adopting this new style, which was a kind of written replication of speech, Wilson made a break from her contemporaries such as Anne Fine, Anne Pilling or Jan Mark, all of whom were also writing dark family stories ameliorated by their humorous telling but within more literary conventions.

Wilson's own definition of how she reshaped her writing is significant. Her recognition of the need to re-think how to write for readers at the end of the millennium in ways that reflected their own lives and her intelligent approach to doing so are an integral part of her subsequent success. It reflects her sharp and seemingly instinctive ability to know her readers, which became a hallmark of the Jacqueline Wilson brand. Too often it is thought that she was innovative in terms of subject matter, but it was her way of telling the stories, beyond the use of a first-person narrative, rather than their content which really marked her out.

The theme of children living without parents for any number of reasons is a standard trope within children's literature from folk stories onwards, with every generation adapting the reason for abandonment to reflect contemporary circumstances. By the early 1990s it was neither unusual nor wholly original to be writing about children facing extreme family difficulties. Typically, these stories recorded the very obvious changes to families of the time, particularly in terms of the rising rate of divorce which left so many young children managing lives split between two homes and two parents, and often included the anguish of moving home and school as well as attendant problems of poverty. Throughout the previous decade and even before, authors such as Robert Westall and Anne Fine had written stories directly reflecting contemporary children's lives. Fine, like Wilson, was notable for her ability to show challenging and even potentially tragic circumstances for children living outside the context of the traditional model of a happy, stable family home in an entertaining and upbeat way. Her satirical stories such as *Madame Doubtfire* (1987) and *Goggle Eyes* (1989) were both highly regarded, the latter winning the 1989 Carnegie Medal and the former being subsequently turned into the popular film *Mrs. Doubtfire*.

In terms of its story of dysfunctional family life, *Tracy Beaker* fitted into that tradition. Wilson was aware of the trends in contemporary publishing and later, in an interview for *Talking Books*, she described what her books were about: 'They're realistic modern books about children with problems. They sometimes deal with very sad subjects like divorce and bullying but the children always find a way of dealing with these issues.'[18]

However, although well within that tradition, Wilson did push the boundaries forward and stepped into more challenging territory. Children living in care do not feature frequently in children's fiction but Tracy Beaker's home has become so fractured that there is nowhere for her to live with a parent. Instead, she lives in a children's home, has had failed placements with foster parents and can only dream of contact with her real mother as none actually exists. Wilson pulls no punches about Tracy's distress and how it manifests itself in difficult behaviour but, because the story is told by Tracy herself, the whole effect is un-judgemental and free from preachiness. Tracy describes her inner struggle as she oscillates between outraged despair and hopeless, unfounded optimism, and readers recognise her anguish and feel it too. Wilson's use of the first-person narrative, a trademark way of telling the stories that allows her to speak so directly to her readers, conveys all the emotions poignantly while also allowing for some make-believe which could not go unchecked by an outside narrator. As Nicholas Tucker writes, '*The Story of Tracy Beaker* ends on a hopelessly unrealistic note, but this is deliberate, since it is Tracy's voice that is speaking and her own hopes that are so patently and characteristically deluded.'[19]

How Wilson and her publishers capitalised on the success of The Story of Tracy Beaker

The combination of Wilson's thoughtfully created and instantly appealing first-person narrative and the striking presentation of a book that looked and felt attractive enough to make an instant impact on the existing market took *The Story of Tracy Beaker* into the hands of readers. Wilson appealed directly to children, becoming classroom currency, while the adult opinion – formers and gatekeepers were largely bypassed: an unusual achievement and one that lay at the heart of Wilson's success.

Recognising the popularity of the book with the readers for whom it was intended, Doubleday and Wilson were quick to capitalise on it. At the time, the big 'brands' were the series titles – typically US imports – among the most famous of which were The Babysitters' Club and the Point Horror series. While the latter did have an author, R. L. Stine, it was the series rather than the author that was accentuated. Uniformly published with an instantly 'collectible' feel, they dominated the children's shelves in the bookshop chains. Fickling, as the publisher at Scholastic in the UK, had worked closely on both series. He understood the power of brands and how they needed to be kept both ever-present and refreshed.

With that in mind, and given that *The Story of Tracy Beaker* had so quickly achieved success, Fickling set the Wilson output rolling. *The Story of Tracy Beaker* was followed by *The Suitcase Kid* (1992), *The Bed and Breakfast Star* (1994), *Double Act* (1995) and *Bad Girls* (1996). The publication of one new Wilson title a year kept the increasingly enthralled readers supplied, while Wilson herself varied the subject matter enough to make them all different while maintaining a familiar and distinctive narrative voice. By 1997, following an agreement between Wilson and Doubleday, that output had been doubled.

Wilson produced an astonishing two books a year and sometimes more from 1997 onwards. She needed little encouragement from her publishers, and it seems likely that her early work on magazines made her well-attuned to the need for regular new instalments of any story to keep the readers committed. It was an unusually focused output for an author of her stature.

While each title had a very obviously different subject matter, the key ingredients and, in particular, the steadfastly child-centric view of the world remained constant. Although adult readers frequently judged the titles on the subject matter and so mistakenly assumed they were a fictional version of a 'misery memoir' offering a dispiriting kind of literary voyeurism, the children who flocked to read Wilson knew better. The simple style and grim subject matter have hidden depths. As Nicholas Tucker says, 'She invites compassion from readers rather than shock-horror responses, encouraging them to read between the psychological lines when trying to make sense of a particular child's aberrant behaviour.'[20]

Doubleday's unswerving backing of Wilson and their calculation that the market could take such an output was justified from the outset. Wilson's output, even at that rate, remained remarkably consistent, as did Sharratt's illustrations. Sharratt's contribution of illustrations which had enough cartoon qualities about them to make them attractive to the age of the readers gave the stories a coherent and readily recognisable appeal which, like Wilson's writing, cleverly combined a deceptively simple look with subtle depth. Instantly recognisable on the shelves and attractive enough to be both impulse buys and 'collectibles', the look of the books played a significant part in giving Wilson her visible place in bookshops.

The building of an author as a brand was by no means new, nor was the pairing of an author and an illustrator. Roald Dahl, the most successful children's writer of the second half of the twentieth century, had been given an immediately dramatic and also long-lasting boost by the re-illustration of his titles by Quentin Blake who gave all readers an image of Dahl's best-loved characters such as the BFG and Matilda. The success of the Dahl titles provided a useful model, particularly since Dahl had initially been very much an author who appealed to children rather than adults in much the same way as Wilson had. While very different stylistically, both authors champion children in ways that children adore and adults can find threatening. For both authors, appealing directly to the child as purchaser was vital to success: hence the importance of their illustrators both of whom themselves had a childish appeal.

The timing of Wilson's first 'branded' title was fortunate. Dahl died in 1992 having dominated the children's book market for 20 years, getting evermore instant popularity and acclaim. *Matilda*, published in 1988 at the end of Dahl's life, had the kind of immediate 'must-read' appeal that was later replicated on a far bigger scale by J. K. Rowling's Harry Potter titles. Even with no new Dahl titles (bar the few shorter posthumous ones) the extent of Dahl's dominance of the market is shown in a Waterstones poll of Top Ten Children's Books in 1997, in which *Matilda* and six other Dahl titles took the bulk of the spaces, and in the BBC Radio 4 'Treasure Islands' poll of 'favourite modern children's authors' of the following year, in which he was still the top favourite. Despite that long legacy, it was obvious that Dahl's death left a gap in the market; publishers and booksellers were open about the need for 'an heir to Dahl'. Wilson, with her new-look titles, began to fill it. In the two polls mentioned above, Wilson's *Double Act* took tenth and fourth place respectively. R. L. Stine's Point Horror series continued to feature significantly as did Dick King-Smith with *The Sheep-Pig* (1983) in particular.

Building the brand

With Wilson's books achieving high volume sales and winning awards – typically those selected by children rather than adults, such as the 1993 Children's Book Award for *The Suitcase Kid* and 1995 Nestlé Smarties Prize for *Double Act* – Wilson was establishing herself as an author with a clear appeal and an eager readership.

In general, the early 1990s were not a particularly propitious time for children's books. That was changed by the publication of *Northern Lights*, the first part of Philip Pullman's 'His Dark Materials', in 1995 and J. K. Rowling's *Harry Potter and the Philosopher's Stone* in 1997, which can now be seen as a watershed in children's literature. However, its impact was not felt until a few years later when Pullman won the Whitbread Book Prize for *The Amber Spyglass* against all other categories – a first for a children's book – and the Harry Potter titles became a publishing phenomenon and redefined forever the size of the children's books market. Before that, what children read was of little interest to any except those with a professional involvement including publishers, librarians and teachers, and parents who took an interest in what their children were reading at any given time. Parents were quick to know what they didn't like – and Wilson was an author they took a long time to understand – but, as children's books were firmly 'for children' and the idea of 'crossover titles' was still some way off, they didn't know what they *did* like as they rarely read children's books at all.

Wilson's awards brought prominence in bookshops generally and especially in the specialist children's books outlets, helping to bring her to the attention of those with an interest in children's books. Additionally, Wilson played an active role in promoting herself. At the beginning of the 1990s, ways to reach readers and influence them beyond their experience of reading the book were far fewer than today. School visits and literary festivals existed, but they were on a small scale. Building the personal brand of the author by making face-to-face contact, which is now so widely seen as a vital way of building up an author's readership, was relatively under-explored. Wilson was a pioneer in this respect. From the publication of *The Story of Tracy Beaker* onwards Wilson visited schools tirelessly. It was something she enjoyed – 'I like meeting lots of children and it's fun hearing what they think of my books' – and she instinctively understood that by talking directly to her readers she could build up loyalty to her books.[21]

Wilson's pleasure in listening to children was reflected in her ability to talk naturally to any child between about 5 and 13 – mostly girls, as might be expected, but also boys. All found in her someone unstuffy and un-judgemental.

Despite the time it took from writing, Wilson was unusually generous in visiting schools in return for nothing more than the gift of some chocolate buns to take home. From the first she actively enjoyed meeting children. Striking in appearance, she managed to be a 'granny' figure while also being obviously 'cool'. Dressed always in the neatest of black with appealing shoes to match and adorned with large-scale silver jewellery, she was instantly recognisable and stylish. Wilson's looks and her ability to speak to the children was as direct and personal in the flesh as it was in her books; those present felt she knew them personally and understood exactly how they were feeling.

Initially, the rewards were intangible. There were few or no book sales directly on the back of the visits but through these, and her equally assiduous response to readers' letters, Wilson built up a personal following which was essential to her subsequent sales success. She, almost as much as the books, became an integral part of the reader's enjoyment of them. As Wilson's fame and success grew she continued to nurture this personal relationship with her readers even though the fan base became too large to manage on such a personal level.

When the market for children's books changed beyond recognition after the publication of *Harry Potter and the Philosopher's Stone*, Wilson was already an award-winning and highly successful author in the minds of the children on whose enthusiasm her reputation was built. This was especially remarkable given that all the time she was gaining this success she was also the subject of criticism in the media for 'spoiling' childhood by writing about its darker side, and was still under-valued by adult readers – even librarians who, surprisingly, never awarded her the Carnegie Medal.

With 'His Dark Materials', the sequence of Harry Potter titles and many other successful children's books becoming 'crossover' books and thus part of adult as well as children's reading, Wilson, too, began to be read by a wider group of adults. It was lucky timing that *The Illustrated Mum*, the story of a mother with manic depression and one of Wilson's most powerful titles, was published in 1999. Although stylistically very like Wilson's previous titles, her sensitive portrayal of the deeply damaged Mum of the title added additional qualities, and it achieved recognition by adults when it won Wilson the *Guardian* Children's Book Award. Far from depressing children or presenting a false and unduly grim picture of the world it was now clear that Wilson's books were magnets to children who not only wanted a good story but also fictional characters who could help them to manage the increasingly complex and chaotic lives they might be experiencing. Although the wider media still carped, critics, librarians and teachers all began to see the point. In his review of it in the *Independent*, in which he described *The Illustrated Mum* as Wilson's darkest, perhaps most brilliant novel, Nicholas Tucker wrote, 'The message is that some people are never going to fit in, simply because they can't rather than because they won't. Anyone, including government ministers, should after finishing this story come out understanding a little more and condemning a little less, whatever their preconceptions.'[22]

If school visits – speaking to a class of 30 at a time – launched Wilson behind the scenes, her truly public profile really took off at literary festivals. At the biggest festivals such as Hay, which she supported from very early on, and also Cheltenham and Edinburgh, she was soon capable of attracting an enthralled audience to the biggest tents of all. To the chagrin of many adult authors, Wilson quickly won herself the reputation as the most queued-for author at a signing session as children, with their reluctant parents in tow, were willing to stand for up to a record-breaking seven hours to get their books signed and have the chance of a word with the creator of their heroines.

'Most queued-for author at a festival' was one of Wilson's first records and it marked the beginning of many more. In public Wilson was rapidly becoming an instantly recognisable celebrity with all the additional attention and honours that it attracted. But she did not let that detract from her writing. Through the 2000s and 2010s, Wilson was writing her two books a year, the publications of which were increasingly lavishly promoted with launches in Claridges and advertising campaigns on London taxis. The media coverage now matched the output and Wilson soon had other records: in the 2003 'The Big Read' poll, which the BBC conducted, Wilson had four titles in the 100 most popular books in Britain; in 2004 she replaced Catherine Cookson as the most borrowed author from UK public libraries, a place she held until 2008; in 2002 she was awarded the OBE for her services to literacy in schools, an honour which was capped in 2008 when, following her time as Children's Laureate, she was appointed Dame Commander of the Order of the British Empire, the first ever Dame among the children's authors in the UK.

Wilson had built her career throughout the 1990s and the 2000s and, as a result of her popularity and influence, she was an obvious choice for the role of Children's Laureate in 2005. Curiously, having once been vilified in the media, Wilson became a national treasure. Gradually adults came to see that her books were not subversive and destructive but rather, they provided an invaluable picture of the world against which children could make sense of their own lives. Wilson's tireless generosity to the children themselves and her thoughtful contribution to discussions combined with her commitment to campaigns to improve literary standards such as the Get London Reading Campaign orchestrated by the *London Evening Standard*, of which she became an ambassador, all played a part in changing public perception of her.

Already highly visible to her core readers and all those who worked with children and books, she now assumed a much wider profile. What children had already learnt about Wilson's gifts of enthralling those who met her was now evident to readers of all ages. Wilson's skills as a broadcaster and commentator made her an excellent subject of such programmes as BBC Radio 4's *Desert Island Discs*, which she recorded in 2005, and the *South Bank Show*, which was devoted to her life and work in 2006, alongside contributing to media debates on many aspects of literacy learning and childhood in general.

Beyond all her book and reader activities, Wilson's major contribution to children's books in her time as Children's Laureate was her passion for reading aloud. Believing it to be the most effective way of encouraging all children to become readers, Wilson, who was handsomely supported by her publisher in this, created Great Books to Read Aloud, a heavily subsidised resource for which she selected and annotated 70 suitable titles. In the foreword to the book she wrote, 'Reading aloud is the best way to get your children hooked on books for life. It's great for children to be read to every day – but it's also great for those who get to do the reading too!'[23] Her legacy also included 'Daydreams and Diaries: the story of Jacqueline Wilson', an exhibition on Wilson's life and writing for children curated by Seven Stories, National Centre for Children's Books, Newcastle, and opened there in 2013.

Outside of books but still very related to children Wilson became the first Fellow of the children's charity, Coram. Her compassion for children experiencing family difficulties – an experience common to all the children who had entered the Foundling Hospital at Coram Fields – made her a natural fit for the post. It also proved to be fruitful to Wilson as a spur to writing *Hetty Feather* (2009), the story of a little girl who is abandoned by her mother in the Foundling Hospital in the nineteenth century. Wilson's stories set in the past, which were also illustrated by Nick Sharratt and so shared the same branding as those set in the present, showed an ability to make the past come alive that gave a new dimension to Wilson's writing. Still directly addressing her readers in her writing and still writing about family problems, she showed that it was her ability to capture how people feel rather than her portrayal of any particular time or place that made her books so appealing. The historical novels soon proved to be as popular as those in the present – even to Wilson herself who in answer to questions at festivals told children that Hetty Feather was now her favourite character – and a Hetty Feather series took shape.

After her years as Children's Laureate Wilson's profile remained as high as ever, and she continued to gather sales and prizes for her books as well as honours such as becoming the Chancellor of the University of Roehampton in 2014. The strong link forged with Nick Sharratt in the 1990s proved to be of great use as Wilson became widely known around the world through her website www.jacquelinewilson.co.uk. The visually powerful brand created in the 1990s by Sharratt's covers was as compelling in drawing readers into the website as they had been when the books first went on sale. Sharratt also created an instantly recognisable image of Wilson herself, allowing her to preside over her website and engage with the children who use it as they browse her books, her life and much more. The result is that through the website, Wilson's books can still be enhanced by the sense of being in touch with Wilson herself, which has become such a powerful part of the Jacqueline Wilson story. Knowing how important this is, it is something Wilson herself plays on in her books such as *Clean Break* (2005) in which a girl gets to meet her favourite author, one Jenna Williams, whose books bear a striking similarity to Wilson's own. Just in case any readers fail to make the connection between the authors and their near-identical titles, Wilson herself is instantly recognisable in Sharratt's illustrations.

Wilson had been writing for 20 years before she transformed herself with her publisher's support into a widely recognisable brand making a significant contribution to children's reading. While instant success was uncommon at the time – Philip Pullman's career trajectory was not dissimilar in terms of the length before and after success – the transformation of Wilson into such a recognisable and marketable brand was remarkable and influential. As such, while the Jacqueline Wilson brand remains unique, as does Wilson's status as a writer, it has also paved the way for her followers. Wilson showed the enormous market value of appealing directly to children through stories that reflect their lives. By capturing such a large market share with her stories she gave books of that kind a significant space in children's literature.

Notes

1 Jacqueline Wilson, *Jacky Daydream* (London: Doubleday, 2012).

2 James Carter, 'Jacqueline Wilson' in *Talking Books: Children's Writers Talk About the Craft, Creativity and Process of Writing* (London: Routledge, 1999), pp. 232–255, pp. 239–240.

3 Jacqueline Wilson, quoted in Rachel Cooke, 'The Story of Jacqueline Wilson', *Observer* 23 March 2014, http://www.theguardian.com/books/2014/mar/23/the-story-of-jacqueline-wilson [accessed 30/3/15].

4 Humphrey Carpenter and Mari Prichard, 'Teenage Novels' in *The Oxford Companion to Children's Literature* (Oxford: Oxford University Press, 1984), pp. 518–519, p. 518.

5 Ibid.

6 Ibid.

7 Rebecca Morris examines the comparison between Wilson and Blume in her chapter for this volume.

8 Julia Eccleshare (ed.), *Children's Books of the Year 1986* (London: National Book League, 1986), p. 136.

9 John Rowe Townsend, *Written for Children* 3rd rev. edn. (London: Penguin, 1987).

10 Robert Leeson, 'Jacqueline Wilson' in Tracy Chevalier (ed.), *Twentieth-Century Children's Writers* (Chicago and London: St James Press, 1989), pp. 1057–1058 .

11 Ibid.

12 Nicholas Tucker, 'Jacqueline Wilson' in Nicholas Tucker and Nikki Gamble (eds.), *Family Fictions* (London and New York: Continuum, 2001), pp. 68–84, p. 74.

13 Interview with Julia Eccleshare, London, September 2013.
14 Helen Day explores this effect further in her chapter for this volume.
15 Kate Agnew, 'Jacqueline Wilson' in Victor Watson (ed.), *The Cambridge Companion to Children's Literature* (Cambridge: Cambridge University Press, 2001), p. 761.
16 James Carter, 'Jacqueline Wilson', p. 242.
17 Ibid.
18 Ibid., p. 233.
19 Nicholas Tucker, 'Jacqueline Wilson', p. 75.
20 Ibid., p.72.
21 James Carter, 'Jacqueline Wilson', p. 234.
22 Nicholas Tucker, 'Mums, Mafia and Magic', *The Independent* 17 July 1999, p. 10.
23 Jacqueline Wilson, *Great Books to Read Aloud* (London: Corgi, 2006), n.p.

2

From Realism to Romance: The Early Novels

Ika Willis

The story of Jacqueline Wilson's career is much rehearsed. In her own biographical notes and in two book-length biographies for children (Parker 2003; Bankston 2013), we learn that she has been writing professionally since the age of 17. She has written magazine fiction, adult crime novels, books for older reluctant readers and fiction for children of all ages, from beginning readers to young adults, writing solely for children and young adults since 1982. In tension with this story of prolific and varied output is the fact that Wilson's name is now associated with one particular and well-defined set of works, her post-1991 full-length books illustrated by Nick Sharratt (I will refer to these as 'the Sharratt books'). These are clearly marked off from her earlier books, both in branding/marketing – the Sharratt books have remained consistent in appearance across more than 20 years of changing fashions in book design – and in the narrative of her career, which positions the publication of *The Story of Tracy Beaker* (1991, hereafter *Tracy Beaker*) as a turning point.[1]

Before *Tracy Beaker*, Wilson wrote nine teenage novels for Oxford University Press (OUP), from 1982 to 1993, which gradually fell (and remain) out of print in the UK: *Nobody's Perfect* (1982), *Waiting for the Sky to Fall* (1983), *The Other Side* (1984), *Amber* (1986), *The Power of the Shade* (1987), *This Girl* (1988), *Falling Apart* (1989), *The Dream Palace* (1991) and *Deep Blue* (1993).[2] (I will refer to these as 'the OUP novels'.) *The Dream Palace* came out in the same year as *Tracy Beaker*; *Deep Blue* appeared two years later, and was republished by Puffin in 1995, by which time four of the Sharratt books were already in print (*Tracy Beaker*, *The Suitcase Kid* [1992], *The Bed and Breakfast Star* [1994] and *Double Act* [1995]). The two sets of books thus overlap, and I will argue in this chapter that the overlap is more than simply chrono- logical. The OUP novels are classic examples of the realist adolescent problem novel, while the Sharratt books, written for a younger readership, have a very different focus and tone: nonetheless, the Sharratt books constantly return to and rework characters, themes and material introduced in the OUP novels.

In this chapter, I will first summarise the OUP novels, on the basis that they will be unfamiliar to most readers, and then compare them to the Sharratt books, arguing that Wilson's hard-to-classify but wildly popular Sharratt books rework themes and motifs from the adolescent problem novel in the mode of romance. The appeal of the Sharratt books, I will conclude, lies not in their realism, but in their creation of a self-contained and satisfying alternative reality.

Nobody's Perfect (1982)

Wilson's first novel for young adults tells the story of 15-year-old Sandra, who lives with her respectable mother, her irritable stepfather and her outgoing and cheerful half-sister. In the course of the book, Sandra forms a friendship with a clever but geeky younger boy, Michael, and tracks down her real father, who lives nearby with his new family and is not interested in getting to know her. Sandra's real-life experience is contrasted to a romanticised story she writes for a magazine competition about a girl named Rosamund finding her father. The novel thus reflects metatextually on the competing modes of realism and romance within teenage literature, positioning itself squarely on the side of realism: at the end, Sandra's story is published but, she says, 'they'd left out all my poetic bits … They'd even changed the heroine's name. She wasn't Rosamund any more. They'd called her Sandra!'[3]

Nobody's Perfect introduces four characters who were to become recurring types in Wilson's work. Sandra, a shy, creative girl who is not interested in dating and finds it hard to sustain friendships with her peers, is the first in a long line of such protagonists, including Katherine in Waiting for the Sky To Fall (1983), Andy in The Suitcase Kid (1992), Mandy in Bad Girls (1996), Dolphin in The Illustrated Mum (1999), Violet in Midnight (2004), Floss in Candyfloss (2006), Sylvie in Kiss (2007) and Beauty in Cookie (2008). An absent, uncaring father and/or unsatisfactory stepfather will recur in three OUP novels (The Other Side [1984], Amber [1986], The Dream Palace [1989]) and eight Sharratt books: The Bed and Breakfast Star (1994), The Lottie Project (1997), The Illustrated Mum (1999), Secrets (2002), Lola Rose (2003), The Diamond Girls (2004), Little Darlings (2010) and Lily Alone (2011). Julie, Sandra's 'cutie-pie half-sister'[4] in Nobody's Perfect − a confident performer, cuter, more outgoing and (the protagonist fears) more lovable than her big sister – will reappear as Rosa in *The Other Side*, then as Katie (the nastiest version of this type) in *The Suitcase Kid* (1992); as Natasha (Nadine's 'horrible little showy-offy sister'[5]) in the *Girls* series (1997–2002); and as Patsy (the most sympathetic version) in *Secrets* (2002). Finally, Michael, the clever, geeky, highly articulate boy who both charms and irritates Sandra, is the prototype of a character who we will see again as a friend or boyfriend to the protagonist in *The Other Side*'s Andrew (1984), *Amber*'s Justin (1986), *Falling Apart*'s Adam (1989), *Deep Blue*'s Luke (1993), *Bad Girls*'s Arthur (1996), *The Lottie Project*'s Jamie (1997), *Girls In Love*'s Dan (1997) and *The Illustrated Mum*'s Owly/Oliver (1999).

Waiting for the Sky to Fall (1983)

Wilson's second OUP novel tells the story of one summer in the life of 15-year-old, lower-middle-class Katherine as she awaits her O-Level results. Her anxiety over her results is the focus for the novel's emotional dynamic, while the narrative follows her secret romance with a working-class boy, Richard; her attempt to pull away from her younger sister, Nicola, and the imaginary games they used to share; and her conflict with her parents. Again, this novel introduces some character types who went on to populate later books: Katherine's domineering shopkeeper father and her fat, downtrodden mother. This couple reappears in a very different narrative context in *Love Lessons* (2005); the bullying father appears with a different wife in *Deep Blue* (1993) and *Cookie* (2008).

The Other Side (1984)

The Other Side's protagonist, 12-year-old Ali, comes home from school to find that her mother Maureen is having a breakdown. When Maureen is hospitalised, Ali and her little brother Chrissie (a sensitive little boy with a liking for dolls and a tendency to regress into baby talk, like Kenny in *Lola Rose* [2003]) have to move in with their father, his new wife and their cutie-pie half-sister Rosa. Ali starts at a new school, where she befriends geeky Andrew. Under the pressure of the new family and school environment, as well as her continuing grief over the recent death of her beloved Nan, Ali begins lucid dreaming/ hallucinating that she can fly at night. At the end of the book, she sleepwalks out of her window and has to be rescued by her father;

this physical rescue seems to pull her psychologically back into reality, and the novel ends with an ambivalent encounter between Ali and her mother, still hospitalised for an unnamed mental illness. *The Other Side* is a clear forerunner of *The Illustrated Mum*, as is Wilson's next novel, *Amber*.

Amber (1986)

Amber has been raised in communes by her hippy mother, Jay. Like Star in *The Illustrated Mum*, she resents her mother, blaming her for her lack of education and failure to fit in, and strives to dress and 'act ordinary at school'.[6] *Amber* opens and closes with encounters between Amber and Jay, suggesting that the emotional heart of the narrative is their mother–daughter relationship. However, the story in the foreground of the novel is that Amber has taken to her bed in a state of emotional overwhelm (as Ali tries to do in *The Other Side*). This is the first of Wilson's OUP novels to use non-chronological narrative: through a series of flashbacks we follow the development of Amber's friendship with Justin, an odd, clever, posh boy who talks like Michael in *Nobody's Perfect*, this time through a quasi-puppet, Sleeve, made out of the sleeve of his jumper. Although it looks as though this friendship might turn into a romance, we eventually learn that Amber has, instead, slept with Justin's more conventionally attractive and popular brother, Jonty, and fears she is pregnant by him. In the final section, Davie, an ex-boyfriend of Jay's, returns and offers to live with Amber and 'look after [her] and the baby'.[7] It is unclear whether he envisages a parental or a romantic relationship with Amber; in any case, he moves on again after her period starts, making way for a fragile peace between Amber and Jay.

The Power of the Shade (1987)

The Power of the Shade is a multi-stranded book and thus difficult to summarise. Its heroine, May, is being raised by her grandparents and great-aunt; her mother Amy, an artist, died in childbirth, and her father committed suicide soon afterwards. May's grandparents and great-aunt idealise Amy, and expect May to become an artist like her. May has a close but fraught friendship with the beautiful, charming and malicious Selina, the neglected daughter of two actors and a clear prototype of *Midnight*'s Jasmine (2004), who initiates May as a white witch in a highly eroticised ritual.[8]

Meanwhile, May is also developing a close relationship with her new English teacher, Rob, a plotline which returns in *Love Lessons* (2005). May writes a series of fairy tales for Rob, which are interspersed throughout the novel and relate symbolically to her own life, functioning like the illustrations from the fictional Casper Dream books in *Midnight*. Through her relationship with Rob, and his encouragement of her writing, May begins to detach herself both from her grandparents' expectations of her and from the image of her dead mother. She also learns that the woman she calls her great-aunt is in fact her grandmother (her mother's mother, who had an affair with her sister's husband). Convinced that she has magical powers, she believes (like *Love Lessons*'s Prue and *Deep Blue*'s Barbara) that she has caused her grandfather's heart attack. In a climactic, hallucinatory scene at the end of the novel she also believes that she has burnt down Rob's flat, but discovers that she has not. This dramatic moment of physical danger brings about her psychological return to reality, as with Ali in *The Other Side*.

This Girl (1988)

This Girl tells the story of Coral, a dreamy girl who feels out of place on her council estate and in her working-class family, and escapes into fantasies about the Victorian period. These fantasies are counterposed to her experience in a real Victorian house, working as an au pair to a posh couple, Toby and Isabel. Coral takes the children, Freddy and Ada (names which will be reused for two of the Victorian children in *The Lottie Project* [1997]), to the park, where she meets and befriends Deb, a young single mother. The novel ends when Coral rejects Isabel's exploitation and moves in to 'cohabit' with Deb in her new council flat.[9] The novel manages to be both unambiguous and oblique about the sexual relationship between Coral and Deb, which perhaps explains the failure of critics and readers to recognise the lesbian content in *This Girl*, 16 years before Julie Burchill's *Sugar Rush* (2004) was 'flagged as the first lesbian teen novel'.[10]

Falling Apart (1989)

Falling Apart returns to the heterosexual cross-class romance featured in *Waiting for the Sky to Fall* and *Amber*, this time between working-class Tina and posh Simon. Tina is 15; her twin brother, Tim, died at the age of seven. The novel makes it clear that Tina's fixation on the doomed romance with Simon is a way of escaping her unresolved grief: 'She can't give up on Simon now. She's felt so sad ever since Tim died but now she's found happiness again, and she's going to hang on to it.'[11] Tina takes an overdose in the first chapter, and the bulk of the novel flashes back to the story of her relationship with Simon. Simon seems also to be in a relationship with his spiteful gay best friend Adam, although Wilson's use of circumlocution, innuendo and implication to convey homosexual content in this book, in contrast to *This Girl*, makes the exact nature of their relationship hard to decipher. In any case, Simon eventually leaves Tina for a girl of his own class ('we've got so much more in common … Caroline and I even went to the same Latin summer school a couple of years ago'[12]), triggering Tina's overdose. In the last chapter, Tina's stomach is pumped and she recovers. She confesses her feelings of guilt over Tim's death to her sisters, watches Simon and Adam walk away through the hospital window, and 'then notices her own reflection in the glass, looking back at her. The other side of herself. So maybe she's been a whole person all along.'[13]

Like *Amber*, this novel tells the story of a cross-class heterosexual romance in flashback, with a frame narrative, but this time the stakes are higher. The protagonist of *Falling Apart* is no longer a girl who has taken to her bed over a mistaken pregnancy scare, but a girl attempting suicide. This raising of the stakes begins in *The Power of the Shade*, and in *Falling Apart*, Wilson continues to intensify her narrative and emotional lines and to provide more dramatic situations and resolutions.

The Dream Palace (1991)

The Dream Palace marks the climax of this intensification, having the most adult (or at least young adult) content in Wilson's entire oeuvre: stabbings, heroin deals, hepatitis-related deaths, homelessness and prostitution, both female and male ('I can go down the amusement arcades and try peddling my arse, but I'm too old and I'm not even pretty. So we'd better get you where the action is, little Lolly. King's Cross?'[14]).

The protagonist of *The Dream Palace* is Lolly (short for Loretta), an imaginative teenager who disconcerts her more conventional, boy-crazy friend Lynn with her darker flights of fancy, like Violet in *Midnight* or Dolphin in *The Illustrated Mum*. Lolly's father died soon after leaving her mother, and she is fixated on a memory of him taking her to afternoon tea at the then-posh Palace Hotel, now abandoned and squatted by a group of hippies.[15] The hippies seem romantic to Lolly, especially one couple, Greg and Rosamond. (Not coincidentally, Rosamund is the name Sandra gives the fictional, romanticised version of herself in *Nobody's Perfect*.) Lolly starts a relationship with Greg, who attempts to rescue her from her unsatisfactory stepfather by stabbing him with bacon scissors. Lolly and Greg go on the run to London on a motorbike borrowed from a friend of Greg's in return for drugs. Lolly eventually realises she cannot sustain a criminal lifestyle and returns home. She informs on Greg to the police, but remains in love with him. The novel ends with her looking out to sea and fantasising hopelessly about Greg's return.

Deep Blue (1993)

Wilson's final novel for OUP, *Deep Blue*, retreats from the urban/criminal landscape of *The Dream Palace* to the suburban setting of Kingtown. *Deep Blue* features a familiar cast of characters, including a domineering father and a posh boyfriend. It also has a familiar storyline, in which Barbara (like May in *The Power of the Shade* and Tina in *Falling Apart*) struggles to find her own identity, under pressure both from her ex-diver father's image of her as an Olympic-standard diver and from her Barbie-collecting mother's image of her as a pretty, feminine girl. Like Ellie in *Girls Under Pressure* (whom she otherwise does not resemble), Barbara becomes briefly anorexic during the course of the novel but recovers without outside intervention.

    Deep Blue incorporates a cross-class romance with posh Luke, who is a disappointment to his father in the same way, and for the same reasons, as Michael in *Nobody's Perfect* (Michael says, 'I can't catch a ball, I can't hit a ball. Consequently my father thinks I haven't *got* any balls';[16] Luke says, 'I was this little weedy kid who didn't want to kick a ball about with Daddy and be one of the lads. My dad's practically given up on me'[17]). Luke's brother Danny is the first of Jacqueline Wilson's characters with Down's syndrome, followed by Poppy in *Dustbin Baby* (2001) and Sarah in *Love Lessons*, all of whom befriend protagonists who otherwise have difficulty forming healthy friendships with peers. Barbara's domineering father suffers a sudden life-threatening attack after a row, like Prue's father in *Love Lessons* (Barbara's father has a heart attack, Prue's a stroke). Barbara copes by bargaining, making a promise to do the thing she most fears; 'I'll do anything, but don't let my dad die. I'll dive again. I'll go up on the highboard ... just don't let Dad die.'[18] Successful bargaining will recur in *Lola Rose* (2003), when Lola's mum, Victoria, is very ill with an

infection following surgery for breast cancer, and Lola, who is terri-
fied of sharks, bargains for her recovery by staying by the shark tank
at the aquarium for an hour.[19]

Reworkings

There are, then, significant continuities between the OUP novels and
the Sharratt books, as well as important differences. The same character types populate both sets of books, and all the books are recognisably set in the same world: the very first OUP novel, *Nobody's Perfect*,
is set in Kingtown (a fictionalised version of Kingston-upon-Thames,
where Wilson grew up and lives), as are the majority of both the OUP
novels and the Sharratt books. Additionally, a great deal of material
from the OUP novels is reworked in the Sharratt books.

This reworking is of a particular kind. None of the Sharratt novels is a straightforward rewriting of a single OUP book. The closest
Wilson comes to this is *Midnight*, which, like *The Power of the Shade*,
combines a revelation about a family secret with a fraught relationship
between the protagonist and a magical girl. In *The Power of the Shade*,
Selina invites May over for a sophisticated supper, including white
wine, and initiates her as a white witch; in a closely parallel scene,
Midnight's Jasmine invites Violet for supper with wine and claims to
be a 'white witch … with amazing occult powers'.[20] As for the family
secret, May learns that her grandmother is really her great-aunt and
vice versa; Violet learns that her beloved but difficult brother Will
was adopted.

However, *The Power of the Shade* also contains several elements
which do not appear in *Midnight* but were reworked in other novels.
The romance with a teacher recurs in *Love Lessons*, while the doomed
romance as a way of acting out and/or working through a bereavement recurs in *Falling Apart*. The idea of Anne Frank as an imaginary
friend, mentioned in passing in *The Power of the Shade* ('I've thought
about Anne so much I feel I know her. She's far more of a friend to
me than Selina'[21]), becomes a structuring element in *Secrets*, where
India writes, 'I feel Anne and I are soul sisters', and refers to Anne as
a 'fictional friend'.[22]

This is typical of the way that Wilson reworks material across
several books, returning to and re-examining particular characters,
themes and narratives. Sometimes she reworks a particular narrative
strand several times from different perspectives and in different ways.
The clearest example of this is the father-romance, which enters the
Wilson world as a central narrative concern in the very first OUP

novel, *Nobody's Perfect*, and is then reworked and re-examined in *Amber* and *The Dream Palace* before appearing for the last time in *The Illustrated Mum*.

In *Nobody's Perfect*, Sandra's magazine story starts out as a romance: 'My fifteen-year-old heroine … was going to run away from her coarse, cruel stepfather and indifferent mother. She would roam London, living in assorted squalid squats, then fall in love with a drug addict, a lean, dark-eyed, wild-haired poet, and they would have a passionate affair before his tragic death from an overdose.'[23] As she writes and rewrites the story, the plot about the heroine's search for her father becomes more and more central, and the final version of the story ends with their reunion: '[Rosamund's] father smiled back at her. The sun shone on his thick greying curls, his lean tanned face … "You don't know just how much I've longed for this moment", he said in his attractively husky voice.'[24] In *Amber*, Amber has a similarly complicated mixture of daughterly and erotic feelings towards her mother's ex-boyfriend, Davie. At the end of the novel, Amber frames herself as in direct competition with her mother for Davie's affections. Jay asks her, 'Do you think [Davie] loves me just a little?' and Amber thinks, 'He comes for *me* … He wants me. How can she be such a fool?'[25]

In *The Dream Palace*, the father-romance is developed and intensified. Greg both idealises and infantilises Lolly, calling her 'the most special little girl in all the world',[26] and preferring her to wear girlish clothes or school uniform. He takes on an increasingly paternal role when they run away to London, trying to take Lolly out for tea at a hotel in a failed attempt to replay her favourite memory of her real father,[27] and then going to Hamleys, where 'he leads [her] round shelf after shelf of cuddly toys' and buys her 'the biggest rabbit in the whole of Hamleys', while Lolly 'act[s] up to him, little girl loving Daddy'.[28] Through Greg's 'grisly Daddy parody',[29] Lolly comes to realise that her real father was not as perfect as she remembers.

This narrative strand finds its final and most successful form in *The Illustrated Mum*. The much-tattooed mother of the title, Marigold, has been raising her daughters, Star and Dolphin, alone. She remains hopelessly in love with Star's father, Micky, a mythic figure in the girls' lives. After meeting Micky again at a gig, Marigold believes that she will be romantically reunited with him; he, meanwhile, is not interested in her, but is enchanted to find that he has a daughter. Star and Marigold are thus in direct competition over Micky, and Star's words to Dolphin about Micky closely recall Amber's thoughts about Davie: 'He doesn't want to see her [Marigold] … He only stayed the other night because of me … Micky thinks I'm special … It's just magic between us.'[30] Like Greg, Micky takes Star to Hamleys, but unlike Amber and Lolly, Star has no erotic feelings for her father-figure, and the 'magic' between them is not sexualised – a change consonant with the fact that the readership of *The Illustrated Mum*, with its ten-year-old protagonist/narrator, is younger than those of the OUP novels. Rather than being a constraint on the storyline, though, the change in readership seems to have enabled Wilson to find an effective use for this narrative strand. Instead of being part of Star's own psychosexual development, as in the earlier books, the 'romance' between her and her father is seen from ten-year-old Dolphin's point of view and remains metaphorical. It is used structurally to draw a satisfying contrast between the glamorous, feckless Micky and Dolphin's dull but ultimately reliable father, Michael.

The Illustrated Mum also incorporates and reworks material from two more OUP novels, combining the mothers from *Amber* and *The Other Side* into Marigold, who is nonconformist and feckless like Jay (*Amber*), and whose breakdown is very like Maureen's (*The Other Side*). Two key incidents in *The Illustrated Mum* directly rework scenes from earlier novels. The structure and many details of the scenes where Owly helps Dolphin track her father down recall Michael helping Sandra find her father in *Nobody's Perfect*;[31] the scene two-thirds of the way through *The Illustrated Mum* in which Dolphin finally has to admit that she cannot cope with her mother's illness closely recalls the opening scene of *The Other Side*. Comparing the two versions of this scene illuminates some of the differences between the OUP novels and the Sharratt books.

In *The Other Side*, Ali comes home from school to find her mother, Maureen, sitting at the kitchen table and refusing to move or eat. Maureen is low-energy and irritable, interpreting her daughter's words over-literally and punning:

'Mum, have you got the sack?'
'The sack? What do you mean?' Mum did a little pantomime of looking.
'What sack? A rubbish sack? A potato sack? Father Christmas's sack?'[32]

In the equivalent scene in *The Illustrated Mum*, Dolphin wakes up in the night to find Marigold in the bathroom, painted all over with white gloss paint, and exhibiting the pressured, accelerated speech and flight of ideas which characterise manic episodes: 'It will dry and so will I. And then I'll be right. I'll be white … no more tattoos, Star hated them, she hated me, but now they're gone, until the laser, could

I use a razor? No, too red, I want white, pure light, that's right...'[33] Both Ali and Dolphin are unable to get their mothers to bed; both go to sleep themselves. In the morning, Maureen is still at the kitchen table; Marigold is still standing on the lino in the bathroom. Neither of them are speaking or responding. Ali phones her best friend's mother, who calls a doctor, who has Maureen hospitalised; Dolphin calls an ambulance.

The scenes are closely parallel, but with some important differences. Marigold's attempt to erase her tattoos with white gloss paint is a visual metaphor, underlined by her verbal flight of ideas around purity, light and rightness, and by Dolphin's competing metaphor of her mother as 'a ghost' or 'ghostly'.[34] There is no equivalent use of visual imagery to unify or intensify the scene in *The Other Side*. *The Illustrated Mum* is also both more extreme and simpler, narratively and emotionally. The scene in *The Other Side* lasts for nearly 20 pages[35] and involves Ali's little brother Chrissie, her best friend's mother, Maureen's ex-boyfriend Michael, and a doctor, as well as a description of the flat and a lengthy digression about the clichéd expectations of school English teachers while Ali does her homework.[36] In *The Illustrated Mum,* the scene lasts for eight pages, including two illustrations, and involves only Dolphin and Marigold.[37] Ali's feelings are unclear, ambivalent and seldom named, conveyed instead through dialogue or physical sensations. She tells her mother 'I hate you!', and then 'I didn't mean it. I love you, Mum'.[38] When she feels pride, she 'glow[s]'; when she feels fear, she 'suddenly [feels] sick'; when she feels shame, she 'burn[s]'.[39] In contrast, the scene in *The Illustrated Mum* is saturated with Dolphin's intense, clearly named feelings: 'I was shaking ... I was so scared ... I felt I was betraying Marigold'.[40]

The differences between *The Other Side* and *The Illustrated Mum* are typical of the broad differences between the OUP novels and the Sharratt books. *The Illustrated Mum* is simpler and clearer in its emotional landscape and its narrative lines; it is also much more concrete and visual in its imagery. Although both the Sharratt books and the OUP books deal with 'difficult' material, like a mother's mental illness, the Sharratt books contain much less of the 'adult' material which would make it difficult to market the OUP books to younger readers – for example, the references to drugs and prostitution in *The Dream Palace* and the detailed suicide attempt in *Falling Apart*.

The Sharratt books are also, in general, much more optimistic than the OUP novels, as instanced by their respective constructions of fantasy and of girl–girl friendships. In *This Girl*, Coral's imaginary games are seen as a problem: her mother even takes her to the doctor, saying that she hears voices. At the end of the novel, Coral converts her fantasy investment in the Victorian period into a pragmatic use of her knowledge for profit, working on an antiques stall to support Deb and Pete.

Fantasy is also construed as a problem, and as something to be left behind, for Katherine in *Waiting for the Sky to Fall*, May in *The Power of the* Shade and, especially, Ali in *The Other Side*, whose lucid dreaming eventually threatens her physical safety and her life. In the Sharratt books, by contrast, while fantasising does not solve the characters' problems, it does not usually lead them into danger. In general, it is seen as a comforting and benign coping strategy, as in *The Illustrated Mum*, where Dolphin's witchy fantasies and imaginary friends help her cope with bullying and with her own difficult feelings.

Similarly, *This Girl* is the only one of the OUP novels where a relationship between girls is portrayed as positive and sustaining, rather than as something dangerously seductive which must be outgrown. Although a few of the Sharratt books present girl–girl friendships as difficult, fraught, or dangerous – notably *Vicky Angel* (2000) – a much larger number view female friendship as important, positive and central to the lives of girls: *Bad Girls* (1996), the *Girls* series (1997–2002), *Dustbin Baby* (2001), *Secrets* (2002), *Best Friends* (2004), *The Diamond Girls* (2004) and *Little Darlings* (2010).

An even clearer and more significant example of the OUP novels' pessimism and the Sharratt books' optimism, however, is their treatment of class. The romance between middle-class Katherine and working-class Richard in *Waiting for the Sky to Fall* is portrayed as doomed; in *Falling Apart* the class difference between Tina and Simon is equally insurmountable and much more tragic in its consequences. The most sustained treatment of class in the OUP novels is in *This Girl*, where Wilson uses comparisons between the Victorian period and the present day to develop an argument about the persistence of class division. Twenty years later, in *The Lottie Project* (1997), she revisits this material to very different effect.

In *This Girl*, Coral takes a live-in job as an au pair in a Victorian house which her employer, Isabel, has kept largely in period. Isabel teaches a 'Herstory' course about the Victorian period, and describes that 'intelligent women denied a decent education, imprisoned in their ludicrous corsets, lying on their *chaise longues* and sighing their lives away … while other women *lace* those corsets, dust the *chaises longues*…'[41] She harangues Coral about the 'servant situation': 'Young girls treated like dirt, forced to bob and curtsy and slave from dawn to dusk for their so-called betters!'[42] As the novel progresses, we realise, along with Coral, that although the style of interaction between employers and servants may have changed, the essential inequality has not. Coral's own position is shown to be very similar to that of a Victorian servant, culminating in a confrontation with Isabel: 'I thought we were meant to be equals nowadays? Oh no, you want me to bow and scrape to you just as much as the Victorian ladies.'[43]

The Lottie Project's protagonist, Charlie, forms a prickly friendship with a middle-class boy, Jamie, who lives in a Victorian house which, like Isabel's, is kept in period. The physical setting of the house again enables comparisons between contemporary and Victorian life to be made. When Charlie's mum, Jo, loses her job, she takes on a cleaning job in Oxford Terrace, where Jamie lives, prompting a fantasy from Charlie which echoes Isabel's vision of Victorian women on their chaise longues: 'I could just imagine Jamie lounging on a velvet chaise-longue in his posh William Morris-papered parlour, snapping his fingers imperiously at Jo.'[44]

The narrative of *This Girl* intertwines the story of Coral's personal growth with social commentary, and the turning point of the novel comes when Coral consciously identifies and names the power dynamics between herself and her middle-class employers, enabling her to start an independent life as a market trader and the head of a family. She realises that true friendship between herself and Isabel is impossible, because of the insurmountable barrier of class. In strong contrast, *The Lottie Project* ends with Charlie successfully achieving a friendship with posh Jamie Edwards *despite* the class barrier. In Sharratt books, class difference typically functions as a potential barrier to friendship which can be overcome through mutual tolerance, understanding, courage and negotiation. We see this in *The Lottie Project*, but also in the friendships between Mandy and Tanya in *Bad Girls* and between India and Treasure in *Secrets*.

Returns

So far I have dealt with instances where Wilson revisits particular ideas or themes from the OUP novels, reworking them in a clearer and more optimistic mode, suitable for the younger audience of the Sharratt books. But there is another way in which the Sharratt books relate to the OUP novels, this time through returns rather than reworking. By 'returns' I refer to the way in which concrete incidents and motifs from the OUP novels reappear in the Sharratt books, unchanged in their details but situated in different contexts, associated with different characters, and serving different narrative functions. The unwanted giant rabbit is a typical example. It first appears in *The Dream Palace*, where 'Greg presses a huge snowy monstrosity into my arms, and insists it has to be this one because it's the biggest rabbit in the whole of Hamleys';[45] it returns in *Cookie* (2008) as a birthday gift to Beauty from her actual father Gerry. Here it is again described as a 'monster' (three times) and Gerry uses Greg's words: 'Biggest in the whole of Hamleys!'[46] Similarly, the act of drinking hot chocolate at a swimming pool café first appears in *Deep Blue* and then returns in *Girls Under Pressure*, in both cases as a symbolic affirmation of the protagonist's recovery from anorexia.[47] The location makes sense for *Deep Blue*'s Barbara, who is a diver, but is notably less appropriate for Ellie. In *The Power of the Shade*, May and Selina attempt to make a voodoo doll by baking a biscuit in the shape of Selina's ex-boyfriend Bruno, but the biscuit bloats and distorts, like the angel biscuits Marigold tries to make in *The Illustrated Mum*, although there are no other similarities between the characters or the narratives of the two books.[48]

Perhaps the most striking example of a return is the reappearance of the ending of *The Dream Palace* in *Love Lessons*. *The Dream Palace* establishes a parallel between Lolly's romance with Greg and the long-ago doomed romance between another unsuitable boy (a 'dirty tinker'[49]) and Annie, an old woman with dementia in the care home where Lolly works. After Lolly has turned Greg over to the police, the novel ends with a conversation between Lolly and Annie about looking out to sea and hopelessly awaiting the return of their lovers.[50]

At the end of *Love Lessons*, where Prue has been separated from her equally unsuitable teacher boyfriend, Rax, Wilson not only reworks one of the plotlines of *The Power of the Shade* but, more oddly, returns to the seaside setting of *The Dream Palace*. Prue says, 'I could make for the seaside ... I could walk along the sands every day. It would be desperately lonely but I could think about Rax.'[51] The novel ends with Prue walking past Rax's house in the definitively landlocked suburb of Kingtown, and the very last line is: 'I walked and walked and walked, slowly, dreamily, as if I was strolling along the seashore...'[52] As with the swimming pool café at the end of *Girls Under Pressure*, there is no real reason within the world of *Love Lessons* for Prue to associate her hopeless longing with the seashore: these concrete motifs simply return, like the bloated biscuits which appear in both *The Power of the Shade* and *The Illustrated Mum*.

This reuse of material should not, however, be seen as a failure of creativity on Wilson's part. Rather, it is part and parcel of the way in which Wilson has mapped out an astonishingly consistent emotional and material landscape across both the OUP novels and the Sharratt books, which, I argue, is key to her appeal.

Wilson's world

Reworking particular themes and returning to particular motifs, Wilson's books create a coherent and self-consistent world, populated by familiar characters and oriented around familiar concerns. Her novels have a distinctive 'feel', blending a detailed physical environment into the protagonists' imaginary worlds of artistic creation, fears and fantasies. Small, affectively charged objects – toys, cuddle blankets, gel pens – are intensely present in all the novels: a complete set of Caran D'Ache crayons or felt-tip pens is a persistent object of desire for 20 years, from *The Other Side* ('Perhaps … he'd buy her a huge tin of Caran D'Ache crayons like Claire's') through *The Illustrated Mum* ('Owly Morris … [has] got this giant set of Caran D'Ache') to *Clean Break* ('He helped Maxie unwrap an enormous set of expensive Caran d'Ache colouring pens').[53]

Pleasurable and unpleasurable eating experiences, and food as a marker of class, are part of all the books' sensual universes, from Selina's sophisticated supper of 'sparkling white wine still misty from the fridge' and 'a festive cake on a white fluted plate', so 'wondrously different' from the 'surfeit of stale chocolate log' available at May's house in *The Power of the Shade*, to Dolphin's unpleasant first encounter with mushrooms on pizza in *The Illustrated Mum*, and, in *Lily Alone* (2011), Lily's delicious stolen fruit: 'enormous strawberries … soft downy peaches and smooth purple plums', which 'we ate in awe. We had fruit at home sometimes but it was only ever apples, and perhaps little oranges at Christmas.'[54]

Protagonists fantasise about luxurious, white, private places to live. A throwaway line in *Nobody's Perfect* ('I often design my dream flat and all its furniture and imagine myself living there … I shall live alone') is elaborated into the 'wonderfully white' house Amber imagines; into Tracy Beaker's fantasised mother's dressing rooms ('She has white velvet sofas … and a white rug so soft she sinks into it up to her ankles'); into the fabulous penthouse apartment imagined by Mandy and Tanya in *Bad Girls*, 'with white furniture and white carpets and a heart-shaped white bed and a huge swimming pool on the roof with real dolphins'; and, finally, into Lily's imaginary bedroom in *Lily Alone*: 'a pure white, utterly sound-proof bedroom [with] white walls and white carpet so soft it was like fur … I sat on a white velvet stool.'[55]

This affectively and materially coherent world is first created in the OUP novels, which set the parameters for the emotional, narrative and material possibilities of Wilson's later books. Even *Tracy Beaker*, framed as a turning point in Wilson's work, in fact reworks material from the OUP novels. *Tracy Beaker* is the first of Wilson's novels to be actually set in a care home, but in the very first of her OUP novels, *Nobody's Perfect*, we learn almost parenthetically that Sandra was in care for ten weeks when she was five. What she remembers of the experience is bad food, fear of bedwetting, fear of smacking and unsatisfactory cuddles[56] – precisely the elements that structure characters' experiences, fears and fantasies of care in the Sharratt novels. In *The Illustrated Mum*, Dolphin's mother Marigold 'was in one foster home where the mother used to put the sheets over [her] head if [she] wet them'.[57] Dolphin's own fears about foster care centre on smacking and bedwetting,[58] and although her experience is contrasted to Marigold's and shown to be much more benign,[59] the contrast still focuses on cuddles ('cuddled in close like I was one of the babies'); bedwetting (her foster mother is 'not the littlest weeniest bit cross' when Dolphin wets the bed); and food (Dolphin mistakes Marmite for chocolate spread but 'Aunty Jane was sympathetic even though I spat my mouthful right out … She understood').[60] *Tracy Beaker*, too, retains these co-ordinates: Tracy's own foster mother Aunty Peggy 'smacks hard and serves up frogspawn for … pudding', and her friend Peter wets himself.[61]

The remarkable consistency and coherence across the OUP and the Sharratt novels is reflected in and operated through the books' style. Wilson's vocabulary is highly distinctive. Throughout her work, she has a fondness for certain unusual, old-fashioned adjectives and verbs and certain archaic usages, including 'wondrous', 'fingered', 'peeped', 'fashioned' (meaning 'made/created'), 'fancied' (meaning 'imagined', rather than 'was sexually attracted to'), and the conjunction 'and yet'. These striking words are not used to position particular characters or types as old-fashioned or upper-class: they are used both in the narrative voice and in dialogue, by characters of different ages, sexes and classes, across both the OUP books and the Sharratt novels. Similarly, Wilson regularly uses striking and old-fashioned adverbs and alliteration, often in combination: 'utterly obsolete' (*Amber*), 'positively perverted' (*The Power of the Shade*), 'positively paranoiac' (*The Dream Palace*) and 'amazingly atrocious' (*The Lottie Project*).[62]

Although her characters speak colloquially, the slang they use is an idiosyncratic mixture of words from multiple decades, classes and subcultures. Roy, a boy who works as a fitter at the Fulwell works in *Nobody's Perfect*, says, 'You're a right nosy bird, aren't you?' and 'the engine's just all to cock', but also 'She's got a smashing personality, your friend.'[63] Similarly, *The Illustrated Mum*'s Dolphin says 'goody-goody wimpy little brainbox Oliver' and 'he's dumped you on the Social' but also 'blub' ('You'll think I blub all the time') and 'absolutely super-duper'.[64] As with the old-fashioned verbs and adverbs listed above, these slang terms are used by characters of all ages, sexes and classes: Dolphin says 'blub', but so does Barbara's taxi-driving father in *Deep Blue*.

Wilson seems to have solved the problem of writing contemporary novels for children in a fast-changing linguistic landscape without becoming dated very quickly by developing her own undatable, stylised language, an idiolect which mixes archaicising words with words of more recent vintage and which remains remarkably stable over the 32 years between *Nobody's Perfect* and the time of writing this book. Some words do appear and disappear according to the changing speech patterns of contemporary children ('blub' is not used after *The Illustrated Mum*), but 'ultra' first appears in the second OUP novel, *Waiting for the Sky to Fall*, and is still in use in the most recent Sharratt book, *Four Children and It* (2012). It appears in her autobiography, *Jacky Daydream*, and her novel *Queenie*, which are set in the 1950s; it even appears in *Hetty Feather*, which is set in the nineteenth century, underlining the lack of connection between Wilson's stable idiolect and the changing speech patterns of real-life children.[65]

Wilson's idiosyncratic but coherent style, and especially the language spoken by her characters, thus serves not to mark her works as realistic reflections of an extratextual world but, on the contrary, to create a stable and internally consistent textual world. It is here that both the continuity and the difference between the OUP novels and the Sharratt books ultimately lie.

Conclusion: From realism to romance

In the OUP books, Wilson discovered her material, which is that of the adolescent problem novel: working-class characters, absent, violent and/or domineering fathers, inadequate mothers, blended families, half- and step-siblings, foster care, illness in the family, difficult friendships, peer pressure, bullying. The adolescent problem novel is very strongly associated with realism as a genre or mode, and Wilson begins her work for OUP, as noted above, with a metatextual commitment to realism over romance. The Sharratt books, however, are problem novels in the mode of romance. They employ the iconography and the subject matter of the problem novel, but their optimistic narratives are structured around emotional states and interpersonal relationships, rather than around social systems and moral dilemmas, like the OUP novels. In the Sharratt books, the world Wilson created in the OUP novels is freed from the constraints of realism to become an alternative reality, which its readers can inhabit and enjoy on its own terms and for its own pleasures.

This is a striking intervention into the conventions of the adolescent problem novel, which has traditionally legitimated itself by its reference to a 'reality' left unaddressed by other children's literary genres.[66] The pleasure and value of Wilson's work, however, lies elsewhere: in her development of a stylised world and a stylised language. This is precisely what Evelyn Waugh valued in the work of P. G. Wodehouse, writing, 'Mr Wodehouse's characters ... live in their own universe like the characters of a fairy story ... their language has never been heard on human lips. It is a world that cannot become dated because it has never existed.'[67] Like Wodehouse, Wilson has 'made a world for us to live in and delight in'.[68] Its iconography and characters are drawn from the traditionally realist world of the adolescent problem novel, but it is a fantasy world nonetheless. The Sharratt books give us sustained access to this world, and allow us to enjoy it on its own terms: it was the OUP novels, however, that built the Wilson world.

Notes

1 Vic Parker, *All About: Jacqueline Wilson* (Oxford: Heinemann Library, 2003), p. 22; John Bankston, *Jacqueline Wilson* (New York: Chelsea Press, 2013), n.p.

2 One of the OUP novels, *Falling Apart*, was republished in Australia in 2011. The Australian teen magazine *Girlfriend* wrote: 'After years out of print, we're glad to see this popular read return for a new generation of fans!' (http://textpublishing.com.au/books-and-authors/book/falling-apart/); the rhetoric highlights just how striking it is that the other eight OUP novels have *not* returned for Jacqueline Wilson's 'new' fans.

3 Jacqueline Wilson, *Nobody's Perfect* (Oxford: Oxford University Press, 1982), p. 104.

4 Ibid., p. 97.

5 Jacqueline Wilson, *Girls Under Pressure* 3rd edn. (London: Corgi, 2003), p. 171.

6 Jacqueline Wilson, *Amber* (Oxford: Oxford University Press, 1986), p. 45.

7 Ibid., p. 152.

8 Selina both acknowledges and disavows the erotic elements of their magic when May asks her to send away two visiting boys so that 'we could do some more – you know...', and Selina responds, 'Really, May. You sound positively perverted' (128). Similarly, when Violet first sees Jasmine she says, 'I fell in love with her instantly' (59), but when she is asked who she would choose for a love affair, she says, 'I thought of Jasmine. I loved her, but not in that way' (147). Jacqueline Wilson, *The Power of the Shade* (Oxford: Oxford University Press, 1987).

9 Jacqueline Wilson, *This Girl* (Oxford: Oxford University Press, 1988), p. 178.

10 Adèle Geras, 'Short and Sweet/Review: *Sugar Rush*, by Julie Burchill'. *Guardian* 13 November 2004, http://www.theguardian.com/books/2004 /nov/13/booksforchildrenandteenagers [accessed 30 March 2015]. Presumably this meant the first British lesbian teen novel; Nancy Garden's *Annie On My Mind* was published in the US in 1982, and Jenny Pausacker's *What Are Ya?* in Australia in 1987. *What Are Ya?* was published as *Get a Life!* in the UK in 1990, two years after *This Girl* and 14 years before *Sugar Rush*. Tamzin Cook suggests that the obliquity of Wilson's references might be a consequence of the notorious Section 28 of the Local Government Act (1988), which prohibited the promotion of homosexuality in schools (personal conversation, 2014).

11 Jacqueline Wilson, *Falling Apart* 2nd edn. (Melbourne: Text, 2001), p. 78.

12 Ibid., pp. 238–239.

13 Jacqueline Wilson, *Falling Apart*, p. 277.

14 Jacqueline Wilson, *The Dream Palace* (Oxford: Oxford University Press, 1991), p. 233.

15 Greg and the other squatters are consistently called 'hippies' in *The Dream Palace*, although I think they would have been called 'New Age travellers' or 'crusties' in the UK in 1991. Wilson's use of slang is discussed below.

16 Jacqueline Wilson, *Nobody's Perfect*, p. 86.

17 Jacqueline Wilson, *Deep Blue* 2nd edn. (London: Puffin, 1995), p. 155.

18 Ibid., p. 148.

19 Jacqueline Wilson, *Lola Rose* 4th edn. (London: Corgi, 2013), p. 298.

20 Jacqueline Wilson, *Jacky Daydream* 2nd edn. (London: Corgi, 2008), p. 79.

21 Jacqueline Wilson, *The Power of the Shade*, p. 20.

22 Jacqueline Wilson, *Secrets* 3rd edn. (London: Corgi, 2007), p. 18, p. 215.

23 Jacqueline Wilson, *Nobody's Perfect*, p. 1. The story that Wilson gently parodies here bears a striking resemblance to the actual plot of *The Dream Palace*, which also features a romanticised 'Rosamund'.

24 Jacqueline Wilson, *Nobody's Perfect*, p. 27.

25 Jacqueline Wilson, *Amber*, p. 173.

26 Jacqueline Wilson, *The Dream Palace*, p. 103.

27 Ibid., p. 236.

28 Ibid., p. 237.

29 Ibid., p. 249.
30 Jacqueline Wilson, *The Illustrated Mum* 2nd edn. (London: Corgi, 2000), p. 123.
31 Ibid., pp. 175–181; *Nobody's Perfect*, pp. 53–55.
32 Jacqueline Wilson, *The Other Side* 2nd edn. (London: Fontana Lions, 1986), pp. 12–13.
33 Jacqueline Wilson, *The Illustrated Mum* 2nd edn. (London: Corgi, 2000), p. 158.
34 Ibid., p. 157, p. 159.
35 Jacqueline Wilson, *The Other Side*, pp. 11–29.
36 Ibid., pp. 15–16.
37 Jacqueline Wilson, *The Illustrated Mum*, pp. 157–164.
38 Jacqueline Wilson, *The Other Side*, pp. 19–20.
39 Ibid., p. 29.
40 Jacqueline Wilson, *The Illustrated Mum*, pp. 159–164.
41 Jacqueline Wilson, *This Girl*, pp. 76–77. Emphases in the original.
42 Ibid., p. 150.
43 Ibid., p. 165.
44 Jacqueline Wilson, *The Lottie Project* 2nd edn. (London: Corgi, 1998), p. 62.
45 Jacqueline Wilson, *The Dream Palace*, p. 237.
46 Jacqueline Wilson, *Cookie* 2nd edn. (London: Corgi, 2009), pp. 143–144.
47 Jacqueline Wilson, *Deep Blue*, pp. 168–169; *Girls Under Pressure*, p. 201.
48 Jacqueline Wilson, *The Power of the Shade*, p. 188; *The Illustrated Mum*, p. 38.
49 Jacqueline Wilson, *The Dream Palace*, p. 61.
50 Ibid., pp. 272–273.
51 Jacqueline Wilson, *Love Lessons* (London: Doubleday, 2005), p. 253.
52 Ibid., p. 264. Ellipses original.
53 Jacqueline Wilson, *The Other Side*, p. 16; *The Illustrated Mum*, p. 54; *Clean Break* (London: Doubleday, 2005), p. 17.
54 Jacqueline Wilson, *The Power of the Shade*, p. 8; *The Illustrated Mum*, p. 90; *Lily Alone* (London: Doubleday, 2011), pp. 240–242.
55 Jacqueline Wilson, *Nobody's Perfect*, p. 4; *Amber*, pp. 9–11; *The Story of Tracy Beaker* 2nd edn. (London: Corgi, 1992), p. 205; *Bad Girls* 2nd edn. (London: Corgi, 1997), p. 117; *Lily Alone*, p. 137.
56 Jacqueline Wilson, *Nobody's Perfect*, p. 6.
57 Jacqueline Wilson, *The Illustrated Mum*, p. 56.
58 Ibid., p. 198.
59 As Lucy Pearson pointed out to me in her extremely helpful editorial comments to a draft of this chapter (personal communication, 2014).
60 Jacqueline Wilson, *The Illustrated Mum*, p. 203, 203, 210.
61 Jacqueline Wilson, *The Story of Tracy Beaker*, p. 45, p. 54.
62 Jacqueline Wilson, *Amber*, p. 25; *The Power of the Shade*, p. 128; *The Dream Palace*, p. 175; *The Lottie Project*, p. 173.
63 Jacqueline Wilson, *Nobody's Perfect*, pp. 21–23.

64 Jacqueline Wilson, *The Illustrated Mum*, p. 280, p. 219, p. 195, p. 42.
65 Jacqueline Wilson, *Midnight* 3rd edn. (London: Corgi, 2008), p. 168, p. 237, p. 321, p. 342; *Queenie* (London: Doubleday, 2013), p. 6, p. 90, p. 327; *Hetty Feather* 2nd edn. (London: Corgi, 2010), p. 22, p. 119.
66 Michael Cart, *From Romance to Realism: 50 Years of Growth and Change in Young Adult Literature* (New York: HarperCollins, 1996); Alleen Pace Nilsen, and Kenneth L. Donelson, *Literature for Today's Young Adults* 4th edn. (New York: HarperCollins College Publishing, 1993), pp. 100–139.
67 Evelyn Waugh, 'An Angelic Doctor: The Work of Mr P. G. Wodehouse'. *The Tablet* 17 June 1939, 786–787.
68 Evelyn Waugh, 'An Act of Homage and Reparation to P. G. Wodehouse'. *Sunday Times* 16 July 1961.

3

'This Started Like a Fairy Story': Fantasy, Realism and Bibliotherapy in Jacqueline Wilson

Lucy Pearson

> *This started like a fairy story. And it's going to finish like one too. Happily Ever After.*
>
> −*The Story of Tracy Beaker* (1992)

Tracy Beaker's characterisation of her own life as 'a fairy story' may seem at odds with Jacqueline Wilson's reputation as a realist writer. Both Wilson's champions and her critics comment on lack of easy 'happily ever afters' in Wilson's books and her willingness to 'lift the curtain on subjects once seldom discussed in literature aimed at the young'.[1] Proponents of her work often praise these qualities in terms which emphasise their potentially therapeutic value for young readers: her novels frequently appear on lists of recommended titles for children experiencing problems in their own lives. Such lists are premised on the assumption that 'reading about experiences which mirror aspects of their own experience can help them feel less isolated and more able to think about what is happening'.[2] This assumption also underpins a more formal understanding of 'bibliotherapy' which seeks to use books in a therapeutic context to enable both children and adults to grapple with particular problems.[3] This approach suggests that books which deal with particular problems are both necessary and important; nevertheless, Wilson's realistic portrayal of topics such as bereavement, family breakups and child abuse has provoked discomfort in some critics. Winifred Robinson, writing for the *Daily Mail*, explicitly contrasted Wilson's realistic handling of such themes with fairy tales, commenting, 'children's horror stories were once set in fantasy worlds which bore scant relation to their own [...] The problem with realistic settings is that the horrors, too, are that much more real.'[4] As Tracy Beaker's telling of her own story indicates, however, Wilson is not unaware of the tensions between fairy-tale optimism and realistic narrative. On the contrary, across her career she has repeatedly returned to the theme of fairy tales and romance, exploring the boundaries between fantasy and realism and examining the therapeutic qualities of each. While her early novels make the case for realistic fiction by positioning fantasy as potentially problematic, her more recent works show a more nuanced negotiation of the tensions between the two. This chapter will explore this progression. It sets Wilson's early career in the context of key trends in children's literature, before examining the shift in approaches to realism and fantasy in two key texts: Wilson's early teenage novel *The Other Side* (1984), which deals with the impact of a mother's mental illness on her teenage daughter, and *The Illustrated Mum* (1999), which reworks this theme for younger readers.[5] While the two novels share common preoccupations, the strategies Wilson employs in the later work provide a richer and more complex portrayal of the role of narrative in children's lives.

New stories for real children: Jacqueline Wilson's early career

Jacqueline Wilson embarked on her career as a writer during a period characterised by a new emphasis on the importance of realistic fiction for children. The 1960s and 1970s saw a new generation of writers and critics who were critical of the predominately white, middle-class world of children's books, arguing that children from all backgrounds needed books which reflected their own lives.[6] One key proponent of this view was the writer and activist Leila Berg, who argued,

> The majority of children who now read, cannot read anything about themselves. For with very few exceptions, the children who exist in books are middle-class children. [...] Even in the books they get in school, which are often the only books they handle, they see no recognition, no reflection of themselves, nothing that tells them they belong in this world; they grow up feeling they have no right to exist.[7]

Berg sought to address this gap with the Nippers series of early readers, intended as an alternative to series such as Ladybird's popular 'Key Words Reading Scheme' (better known as the 'Peter and Jane' books after their main protagonists). Nippers were 'for kids from working-class homes, with a strong though not necessarily respectable sense of family, a sense of humour, an ear for realistic situations, and colloquial language'.[8] For anyone familiar with Wilson's books, it is unsurprising that this ethos resonated with her: she recounts that the stories in Nippers as 'just seemed [her] sort of territory'.[9] She acted on the inspiration, evaluating the format of the Nippers books in her local library and submitting a manuscript to Leila Berg. The venture paid off, and Wilson's first book for children, *Ricky's Birthday*, was published in Nippers in 1973. This short picture book, which centres around a small boy's requests for his birthday, does not feature any of the more challenging topics for which Wilson was to become well known. Nevertheless, it lays the foundation for her later work in its use of colloquial language and its realistic portrayal of a close working-class family, as in this scene with Ricky and his teenage sister:

'Here, Pam, tea's ready.'
Pam was putting on hair spray. She was seeing her boyfriend, Ted, after tea. Ted had a motorbike.
'Watch with that spray. Did you know it's my birthday next week?' said Ricky.
'Oh yes', said Pam. 'Stop mucking about with that scent.'
'I want a motorbike like your Ted's for my birthday', said Ricky.
'Some hopes', said Pam.[10]

The story exemplifies many of the characteristics fans of Wilson's later work would enjoy. The characters are recognisably working class and are depicted in realistic situations (it is hard to imagine Peter and Jane encountering an older sibling preparing to meet her boyfriend). Small details in Margaret Belsky's illustrations contribute to the realism of the portrayal: in the picture of the kitchen, mum is buttering the end of the unsliced loaf. Although the story is atypical for Wilson in terms of the age of its target audience, her later writing retained the Nippers ethos, offering children who did not come from two-parent, middle-class homes the opportunity to see a 'reflection of themselves' in books.

Nippers attracted some criticism for their realistic portrayal of low-income families, but this series for very young readers was largely optimistic in tone and avoided difficult themes.[11] Social problems and challenging issues were very much present in books for older readers, however; the so-called 'problem novel' had become a staple genre for teenage fiction, which had begun to emerge as a distinctive category in the late 1960s. American writers such as Paul Zindel, Robert Cormier and Judy Blume had become known for books which tackled quotidian topics such as puberty and emerging sexuality alongside more hard-hitting issues like drugs, abortion and racism. When Wilson returned to writing for younger readers – almost a decade after the publication of *Ricky's Birthday* – it was within this tradition. Her first novel for teenagers, *Nobody's Perfect* (1982), addresses the theme of parental abandonment; subsequent novels tackled a range of issues including menarche and anorexia (*Deep Blue*), bereavement and suicide (*Falling Apart*), and teenage pregnancy (*Amber*).[12] Writing within this tradition positioned Wilson more firmly as a writer of 'therapeutic' novels: her sympathetic approach to difficult topics has led many children to regard her as a sort of de facto agony aunt, and her correspondence for young readers includes many letters about the issues they are facing in their own lives. While Wilson notes that she writes what she is interested in rather than seeking to address specific issues, she has spoken of the sense of privilege inherent in realising that one of her books has helped a child in a difficult situation and – despite the volume of mail she now receives from child readers – she still tries to respond to letters 'from children who are worried or ill'.[13] In this context, the realism of her fiction justifies itself by its strong sense of purpose: hard-hitting issues are included not to shock, but to reassure the reader.

The move towards more social realism and the portrayal of more challenging social issues was a key trend of the 1970s, but during the same period a new emphasis on the value of fairy tales was also emerging. The influential essay collection *The Cool Web* emphasises the role of story and fantasy in children's lives;[14] James Britton's article is characteristic in its argument that fantasy offers children 'symbols which may and embody and work upon the hate and love that are part of a close, dependent relationship' and thus enables them to work towards 'a more harmonious relationship between inner needs and external demands'.[15] In the same volume, Betty Bacon criticised the pessimism of the social realism being offered to children, arguing that 'children are left defenceless and alone in a world which they do not understand and with which they cannot deal unaided'.[16] By contrast, Bruno Bettelheim's seminal 1976 work *The Uses of Enchantment* suggested that fairy tales could be a means of aiding children in coping with difficult emotions. Bettelheim made a significant contribution to ideas about children and fantasy with his claim that fairy tales could play a unique role in the psychological development of the child.[17] He argued that 'By dealing with universal human problems, particularly those which preoccupy the child's mind, these stories speak to his budding ego and encourage its development, while at the same time relieving preconscious and unconscious pressures.'[18] Central to Bettelheim's argument was the belief that fairy tales were a better means of addressing difficult issues than realistic fiction; he argued that while the latter could reassure children about their ability to overcome specific problems, it could also cause frustration in children who applied its lessons too literally to their own lives. By contrast, he argued, fairy tales offered symbolic victories that resonated with the child on a subconscious level and offered a safe space for working out difficult feelings, without providing too literal a model. Bettelheim also saw happy endings as crucial to the therapeutic role of fairy tales, arguing that children need to engage in 'optimistic fantasies'.[19] Winifred Robinson's 2008 article on Jacqueline Wilson is clearly informed by similar assumptions: she characterises fairy tales as a space 'Where fear can be experienced safely'.[20] Bettelheim's work has not been without its critics, however. As early as 1976, Jack Zipes argued,

> [A]ssuming there is some validity to using fairy tales therapeutically in educating children, one must still question the manner in which Bettelheim imposes meaning on the tales as well as his indiscriminate application of their meaning to children of all ages, sexes, and class backgrounds [...] The immanent meaning of the tales has little to do with providing suitable direction for a contemporary child's life.[21]

Jacqueline Wilson engages with precisely these concerns in her realistic fiction. The importance of fantasy and imagination is a recurring theme in both her teenage and children's fiction, much of which features creative characters: the protagonists of *Nobody's Perfect* (1983), *The Power of the Shade* (1987), *The Lottie Project* (1997), *Four Children and It* (2012) are all creative writers; *Amber* (1986) and *Midnight* (2004) feature protagonists who sew; and Ellie in *Girls in Love* (1997) and Dolphin in *The Illustrated Mum* (1999) are talented artists. However, the way in which this theme is represented has evolved significantly. Wilson's early novels emphasise the need for realistic stories and position fantasy as problematic. Writing for magazines, she had been constrained by the need to 'nurture [teenagers'] romantic dreams'; as Ika Willis notes in her chapter for this volume, Wilson's first teenage novel, *Nobody's Perfect*, centres around the contrast between such romanticised stories and real teenage experience.[22] Some of Wilson's other novels for teenagers went further in emphasising the need to grow beyond romanticised stories and engage with real life: in *Falling Apart* (1989) escapism is presented as potentially fatal. The book's protagonist Tina retreats from the difficulties of her real life into a romanticised fantasy about her own death: as she prepares to commit suicide she imagines how she will be 'reverently laid in the silk-lined coffin [... with] a little spray of forget-me-knots in her lifeless hands', reflecting as she begins to swallow pills that 'it's almost as if she's watching herself on television'.[23] By contrast, Wilson's later work displays a more sophisticated sense of narrative as a coping strategy and therapeutic tool: a sceptical reader may question Tracy Beaker's assertion that her story will end 'Happily ever after' but there is no sense that Tracy's fairy tales are damaging in the way that Tina's fantasies are. A close comparison of Wilson's early novel *The Other Side* and her later work *The Illustrated Mum* illustrates the increasing nuance in Wilson's representation of realism and fantasy.

Revisioning fairy tales: From *The Other Side* to *The Illustrated Mum*

The Illustrated Mum (1999), for which Wilson won the *Guardian* Award, reworks some key features of *The Other Side* (1984), her third novel for teenagers. While some significant elements appear in both books, the ways in which they are reworked in *The Illustrated Mum* is indicative of Wilson's evolving understanding of narrative and fantasy. Both books feature a mentally ill single mother who is hospitalised in the course of the narrative: in *The Other Side*, the book opens with her mental breakdown, while in *The Illustrated Mum*, it forms the central crisis point of the novel. Both Alison in *The Other Side* and Dolphin in *The Illustrated Mum* use fantasy to help them negotiate their traumatic experiences; however, only Dolphin is able to do so in a fully productive way.

In *The Other Side*, Wilson invokes fairy tales early in the narrative. Alison is sent to live with her father following the mental breakdown of her mother, only to discover he now lives with a new partner:

> 'Hi, I'm Briony. I suppose I'm your stepmother', she said, giggling. 'Watch out for the poisoned apple, Alison.'
> Alison thought of her old book of fairy-tales. She remembered the illustration of Snow White's stepmother, her face contorted as she stamped her pointed slipper in front of the mirror. But Briony obviously didn't need to feel jealous. Alison felt fatter than ever.[24]

Whereas Bettelheim argued that fairy tales enable children to successfully negotiate family dynamics, this exchange demonstrates that the roles offered by fairy tales are unhelpful to Alison. *Snow White* appears to offer an imaginative structure which could allow Alison to forgive her own mother for her temporary abandonment and project her own feelings of resentment and loss onto her stepmother, safely cast in the fairy tale as a 'worthy' recipient of negative feelings. Bettelheim suggests that in *Snow White*, the stepmother's jealousy is a safe expression of the child's jealousy of the mother: 'The feeling of inferiority is defensively turned into a feeling of superiority.'[25] Prior to her breakdown, Alison's mother has encouraged this dynamic, portraying Alison's father as a 'villain' who abandoned his family. Alison's recognition of Briony's beauty and her negative view of her own body disturb her imaginative identification with the fairy tale, however, since she does not 'fit' the pattern in which beauty and goodness are aligned. In fact, the comparison highlights the fact that *she* feels jealous of Briony, who is not only more beautiful than her but also holds the affection of Alison's father and enjoys a fairly comfortable middle-class lifestyle. Fairy-tale logic suggests that this is not simply circumstantial: Alison is *undeserving* of her father's affection because she does not fit the model of the fairy-tale princess. More threateningly still, Briony's failure to live up to the role of wicked stepmother implicitly serves to transfer this role to Alison's own mother. Tellingly, Alison's fear of disloyalty to her own mother prompts her to try to cast Briony in the wicked stepmother role by resisting Briony's overtures of kindness.

Following her rejection of the Snow White story, Alison 'tries on' a series of literary narratives throughout the book. In each case, Wilson reflects the limitations of the stories available to Alison in helping her make sense of her own situation. Early in the novel, shortly after Alison has come to live with her father, she sifts through the books on offer at a jumble sale:

> [A]t the bottom of a pile she found a picturebook called *Pookie*. It was rather a silly story about a white rabbit with wings. He was very unhappy because his family were horrible to him so he flew away, and after some very worrying adventures he lived happily ever after with Belinda, the woodcutter's daughter. Alison had owned her own copy of *Pookie* years ago, but she'd thrown it away, considering it too babyish even for Chrissie. But now she turned the pages wistfully and bought it for five pence. (p. 63)

The significance of the story for Alison is obvious, and the episode serves to subtly emphasise the fact that social realism is not the only genre which can offer child readers support in difficult situations. She reads and rereads *Pookie*, which successfully provides a refuge from her difficult emotions. This episode is interestingly reminiscent of a

1970 article by Elaine Moss, who was among the most vocal proponents of the need for literature which reflected the lives of child
readers. In 'The "Peppermint" Lesson', Moss recounts her puzzlement
at her daughter's fondness for what Moss perceived as a rather poor-
quality book, featuring 'a white kitten […], sad-eyed, pink-eared, and
bewhiskered' rejected when all the other kittens of its litter are purchased.[26] Eventually Moss realised that the resolution of the story, in
which the kitten is adopted and cherished by a loving owner, had a
deep emotional resonance for her daughter, who was herself adopted.
The similarity between the two episodes may be coincidental, but it
is indicative of Wilson's sense of the nature of the debates surrounding
children's literature at the time she was writing.[27]

   Alison's experience of reading a more realistic novel is more ambivalent: although she enjoys reading Judy Blume's *Are You There, God?
It's Me, Margaret,* 'she thought Margaret made a lot of fuss about nothing. She had a wonderful mother, a wonderful father, even wonderful
grandparents.' (p. 73) When she reflects that her friend Claire enjoys a
similarly close relationship with her mother, Alison's feelings of envy
overcome her and she rips the book in half. Blume is one of the leading writers of realistic fiction for adolescents (and was certainly the
most prominent in 1984, when *The Other Side* was published). Like
Wilson, her books have often been praised for their bibliotherapeutic
qualities, but while they negotiate challenging issues such as bereavement, they typically do so within a particular set of parameters which
include the presence of at least one (more usually two) reliable and
loving parents within a loving middle-class household. Blume's books
offered the kind of reassurance which Betty Bacon (in *The Cool Web*)
had complained that many novels for teenagers lacked; it is significant,
then, that Wilson's novel actively engages with the limitations of these
books. Alison's reaction to *Are You There, God? It's Me, Margaret* implicitly makes the case that for children in more difficult circumstances,
the kind of social realism offered by Blume is insufficient.

   Since fiction for children fails in offering Alison a framework for
negotiating her situation, she turns to nineteenth-century narratives
about young women. She is 'captivated' by Austen's *Mansfield Park*
(1814), a book which offers a more sophisticated version of the same
escapist fantasy she has already found in *Pookie*: ill in bed with glandular
fever, it is easy for Alison to imagine herself as the ailing and oppressed
Fanny. Unlike *Pookie,* the book also offers Alison a model of female
behaviour: Fanny's 'goody-goody' behaviour is appealing because
'Alison was so used to being a baddy-baddy that Fanny's behaviour
seemed attractively novel' (p. 74). Later, when she is ill, Alison finds that

Fanny's meek behaviour also has subversive potential, reflecting that 'She'd been a fool herself to waste all this time being rude and difficult. It was much more fun being good and outwitting them all' (p. 80). Reframing her own resistant behaviour as counter-productive helps to pave the way for Alison to accept Briony's overtures of friendship, establishing a more positive relationship between the two. However, both Fanny's meek demeanour and the self-aggrandising fantasy which *Mansfield Park* provides prove insufficient as ways of helping Alison cope with her own situation, which has no easy resolution.

Jane Eyre provides Alison with a similar fantasy of oppression and resolution, but whereas Fanny offers Alison a model of 'good' behaviour which is ultimately impossible for her to live up to, Jane offers a more disruptive model of female behaviour. It is notable that Alison identifies the text as offering an alternative to traditional narratives: 'She loved the way Jane set out to rescue Rochester from his misery. It was like a fairytale turned upside down. Fierce little Jane fought her way through the brambles and turned the wretched wounded beast back into her dark prince' (p. 123). The empowering potential of *Jane Eyre* is disrupted, however, by Bertha, who intrudes into Alison's fantasies both as a symbol for her mother – whose mental illness aligns her with Bertha – and as a focus for Alison's anxieties about her own identity:

> Alison still slept in the box-room at the top of the house even though she had officially recovered from her glandular fever. Alison in the attic. Alison getting up in the middle of the night with her long, white night-gown. Loony Alison. Madness is hereditary. Bertha's mother was insane … Alison's mother was insane. (p. 122)

Here the symbolic value of Bertha as Jane's 'shadow-self' is complicated by Alison's real-life experience of mental illness. She cannot read the eventual destruction of Bertha as a symbolic victory over unstable aspects of the self, since it denies the possibility of a positive outcome for her own mentally ill mother.

The process of trying on and discarding narratives which can help her understand her own experiences in *The Other Side* suggests the need for narratives which might more effectively engage with the kind of situation Alison faces. Ultimately, however, the novel problematises the idea of stories as a means of coping with trauma by its depiction of Alison's increasing retreat into fantasy. Alison begins to experience lucid dreams of flying – so vivid that she believes they are real – in which she gradually becomes more and more invested.

This fantasy space offers her the same kinds of easy resolutions to her anxieties she has found in the escapist fiction she has read: in one dream she visits her former best friend, Claire, and easily resumes their close friendship. In the final, most vivid dream, Alison imagines that her grandmother is still alive and creates a perfect birthday visit to her in which all the tensions of her real life are erased. The fundamental unreality of this fantasy is hinted in the description of the landscape in which Alison finds her Nan's house, '*little scarlet roofs and whitewashed walls, trees with careful little green curls and neat little blobs of apples* [emphasis in the original]' (p. 142), which she later recognises as a 'crayoned cottage' (p. 162). Even the photos in the photo album portray only Alison and her grandmother: the more problematic figures of her mother and father have vanished. The details of the dream also add meaning to Alison's earlier escapism: a letter in the album thanks Nan for Alison's birthday present, noting 'I LIKED YOUR POOKIE BOOK BESTEST OF ALL' (p. 152). Although the two are celebrating Alison's 13th birthday, the episode reflects Alison's desire to retreat into the simplicity of her early childhood experiences: her Nan baths and dries her, and cuddles Alison in her lap 'the way she always did when I was little' (p. 149). This escapism is not healing, however, but dangerous: Alison is awoken by her brother to find that she has been sleepwalking and is on the verge of falling from her attic window.

The intertextual references throughout *The Other Side* illustrate the psychological importance of fantasy, but the novel ultimately suggests that Alison must move beyond fantasy and accept reality in order to grow. This transition is crucial to the book's ending, in which Alison is reunited with her mother. The reunion is relentlessly quotidian: Alison 'waited for Mum to come rushing forward, to throw her arms around her, to beg her forgiveness' (p. 165), but like Jane Eyre she is denied this moment of vindication. Her mother is the same prickly, often judgemental personality she was before her mental breakdown, and although she expresses a desire for Alison and her brother to return to living with her, she is unable to articulate her feelings for Alison. Alison's character growth at the end of the novel is signalled by her willingness to offer the forgiveness that her mother is unable to ask for:

Alison struggled. It wasn't fair. Why should she?
'It's all right, Mum', she said, 'I understand. I still love you.'
Mum groaned and then stumbled forward and took Alison in her arms. (p. 168)

This resolution echoes Jane Eyre's 'full and free forgiveness' of Mrs Reed, but the shift from Alison's fantasy escapism to her engagement with reality is a bleak one. The challenging nature of this resolution is underlined in Jacqueline Wilson's afterword to the 1990 edition of the book, in which she reflects,

> Maybe her Mum'll never be able to mother Alison properly and meet all her needs, but I think Alison will manage somehow. She's always been very good at mothering Chrissie. She's starting to learn that she might have to mother her own mother. She'll have to grow big enough to mother herself too. (pp. 171–172)[28]

While Alison has worked through some of the issues she has been struggling with, then, the ultimate resolution of the book is predicated on her need to recognise and accept the reality of her situation. Letting go of her fantasy of family life does have positive consequences for Alison – for example, in allowing her to accept the love and support of her father and stepmother – but by closing on this difficult resolution with her mother, Wilson implies that the realistic narrative is inevitably a more difficult one. This is underscored by Alison's choice of reading material at the end of the novel: she selects *Jude the Obscure*, by far the bleakest of the nineteenth-century novels she has engaged with throughout the book.[29]

The Other Side engages closely with the therapeutic role of books, but while it acknowledges the role of fantasy in reassuring and comforting the child reader, it ultimately positions this as regressive. The case it makes for realistic fiction for children, then, is that its role is in encouraging children to *accept* difficult situations rather than necessarily guide them in *resolving* them. While acceptance has been a core strand of, for example, books about divorce and stepfamilies, such narratives frequently also work to reassure the child that the situation is not as bad as it may initially have appeared. *The Other Side*, by contrast, works to guide both Alison and the reader to the understanding that the difficult situation may never be ameliorated, without asking them to regard it as positive in and of itself.

The Illustrated Mum returns to these themes; however, in the intervening two decades Wilson can be seen to have radically renegotiated her understanding of bibliotherapy and the role of fantasy and narrative in children's lives. While the book reiterates the need for moving beyond escapist fantasy, it does so not by rejecting it outright, but instead offers parameters within which the narrative can be retold.

The Illustrated Mum is aimed at younger readers than *The Other Side*, but offers a more detailed and sustained portrait of a parent's mental illness than the earlier novel.[30] Whereas Alison's mother suffers a sudden mental breakdown and is hospitalised within the first few chapters of the novel, in *The Illustrated Mum* it is clear that Dolphin and Star have lived with their mother's mental illness for most of their lives, and she is not hospitalised until more than halfway through the narrative. As in *The Other Side*, Wilson introduces the fairy-tale motif early in the narrative, but her focus on a wider cast of characters allows for a more sophisticated presentation of fantasy. Whereas *The Other Side* focuses on Alison's attempts to negotiate her experiences through a series of different narratives, *The Illustrated Mum* shows a range of responses to fantasy from Dolphin, her sister Star and her mother Marigold. Crucially, the character who is most dominated by escapist fantasies is not Dolphin, but Marigold, who is 'magic at making things up' (p. 59). Marigold continually constructs positive narratives for herself, many of which centre around the idea of a reunion with Star's father, Micky. Star scoffs at Marigold's conviction that she will attain a fairy-tale happy ending, "'Like she's stupid Cinderella. In search of putrid Prince Charming'" (p. 75), and although Marigold does reunite with Micky her fantasy is clearly presented as unrealistic. As the novel progresses, her storytelling moves from optimistic to delusional: she dismisses the revelation that Micky has a new girlfriend, insisting, "'I'm the one he went looking for. I'm the mother of his *child*'" (p. 104). As in *The Other Side*, this retreat into escapist fantasy ultimately proves dangerous: Marigold's attempt to seek out Micky and recreate her imagined family unit precipitates the mental health crisis which is the major turning point in the book's narrative. Marigold's refusal to accept the reality of the problems that she faces and her attempts to retreat into fantasy are destructive not only for herself, but also for her children.

For the first third of the book, Star represents the antithesis of Marigold's delusional fantasy. Her scorn for Marigold's Cinderella fantasy is indicative of her rejection of escapist narratives: 'Star would rarely play pretend games nowadays. She said she couldn't do it properly any more. She'd try to pretend but she'd just feel a fool. She couldn't believe it any more' (p. 59). Star offers an alternative narrative of their lives which focuses on 'gritty realism', rejecting Dolphin's impulse to narrate their lives in more positive terms. When Dolphin reflects on the 'wonderful' occasion on which Marigold bought nothing but ice cream, for example, Star emphasises the more unpleasant consequences of Marigold's irresponsible spending.[31] Star voices the connection between realism and maturity which is implicit in *The*

Other Side: when Dolphin laments that Star has changed and is no longer willing to see her family as 'colourful', Star responds, "'that's what I'm supposed to do. Grow up. [...] *She's* the only one who won't do anything about growing up'" (p. 46). The narrative arc of the novel to some extent supports the notion that maturity entails moving beyond fantasy to accept realistic experience. The optimistic narrative of Marigold as 'different' rather than 'mad' enables Star and Dolphin to conceal her neglectful and erratic behaviour, and Dolphin's recognition that Marigold is really ill and needs professional help is a major turning point in the novel. However, whereas *The Other Side* concludes with Alison's painful recognition of the reality of her situation, *The Illustrated Mum* offers a more nuanced understanding of fantasy. As Star's assertion that she *can't* play pretend games implies, a complete rejection of fantasy entails a loss, one which has been forced on Star prematurely because of the imbalance between Marigold and her children. Dolphin's experience offers a more positive negotiation of the liminal space between Marigold's fantasies and Star's brutal realism.

Dolphin's struggle to negotiate fantasy is explored through explicit reference to fairy tales.

Significantly, it is Marigold who introduces the fairy-tale theme. Scattering crumbs from the cakes she has baked during a manic episode, she is reminded of the story of Hansel and Gretel: "'What's that story where the children get lost in a wood and leave a trail of crumbs?" she said. "It was in some fairy tale book. I had it when I was your age"'.[32] The story's themes of poverty and parental abandonment have obvious relevance to Marigold's life: she has spent her childhood in care after her own mother abandoned her, and this episode follows one in which she fails to return home to her own children after a night out. Bettelheim's reading of the story, which presents Hansel and Gretel's success in rescuing themselves as a means by which the child can imaginatively transcend 'his [*sic*] immature dependence on his parents', signals the potentially consolatory nature of this narrative for Marigold. Since her instability leads her to depend on her own children, the ending of the story – in which Hansel and Gretel are able to provide support for their own family – has an obvious appeal. Dolphin's response to the fairy-tale narrative, however, is less optimistic: "'I don't like fairy stories. The good things happen to the beautiful people and the ugly ones are always the baddies'" (p. 53). She is only partially reassured by Marigold's assertion that she is beautiful, regarding it as a 'fib' (p. 53). Like Alison, Dolphin's engagement with fantasy is disrupted by her sense that fairy-tale rules mean that she will be denied a happy ending.

Dolphin's ability to embrace the consolatory fantasy of the fairy tale is more fundamentally disrupted by the nature of the happy ending itself. Marigold's remembered enthusiasm for the witch 'with her big hooky nose and her wild hair and her long gnarled fingers' and her suggestion that they build their own 'fairytale gingerbread cottage' (p. 55) makes explicit a link between Marigold and the witch which has already been signalled elsewhere in the novel. Marigold has green 'Witch's eyes' (p. 27), a 'magical musky smell' (p. 10) and is – in Dolphin's eyes – 'the most magic mother in the whole world' (p. 38). As a consequence, the ending of *Hansel and Gretel* is problematic for Dolphin, who argues,

> The witch wasn't really the scary bit. It was the mother and father at the beginning. They took Hansel and Gretel [...] they deliberately led them into the wood and got them lost on purpose. And yet at the end, it was supposed to be a *happy* end, Hansel and Gretel got away from the wicked witch and got all the way home to their mum and dad and it was like, wow, we're together again, one big happy family. (55)

Marigold's response – 'I'd never leave you and Star' (p. 55) – indicates her recognition that Dolphin's discomfort with the ending of the story stems from a real fear of parental abandonment. Unlike Marigold, whose recollection that she primarily enjoyed the pictures in her book of fairy tales (p. 53) indicates her tendency to focus on the outward appearance of the narrative, Dolphin engages more closely with the implications of the narrative. Dolphin's reading of the story is also revealing in a number of other ways. Although she remembers it as a narrative which restores the nuclear family, in the Grimms' version of the story Hansel and Gretel return home to find that their stepmother has died in their absence. Dolphin's misremembering of the story, then, indicates her inability to contemplate the destruction of the mother: in her own life she has experienced abandonment by several father figures, while her mother has remained a constant – if unreliable – presence. Her attempt to solve this problem by retaining both parents at the end of the story is hindered by her identification of Marigold with the witch, who must be destroyed in order to achieve the happy ending.

Carolyn Daniels reads this episode in a way which is consonant with Bettelheim's interpretation of the Hansel and Gretel story, arguing that Marigold's dependence on her daughters prevents the separation from the parent which Bettelheim suggests is imaginatively achieved through the narrative.[33] Although Marigold's neediness is certainly presented as problematic, and the novel does ultimately show that the survival of the family depends on acceptance of the need for separation, Wilson is engaged in a more complex interrogation of fairy-tale narrative than Daniels' reading suggests. Dolphin's resistance to the Hansel and Gretel story does not simply reflect the dysfunctional nature of her own family; it serves to highlight the limitations of the available narratives through which she can interpret her life. Although she remakes the Grimms' narrative, she is unable to imagine a version which does not entail the death of the witch, and instead superimposes a conventional nuclear family onto the traditional ending. The unsatisfactory nature of this ending for Dolphin is reinforced later in the novel, when Star's father Micky offers to take in both children and form a conventional family unit with his new girlfriend. Dolphin reflects,

> It was like one of the fairy tales. No, you don't have to stay locked up with the wicked witch. This handsome prince has come along and he's turned the two little beggar girls into princesses, even the scraggy ugly one, and they can all live in a new fairy castle together. Only Marigold wasn't a wicked witch. She was our mum. (p. 121)

Fairy tales are troubling not only because they erase the significance of earlier hardship, but also because the price of a happy ending is too high. Although it is possible for Dolphin to envisage a 'fairy-tale ending' which includes her, the consolatory potential of the narrative is diminished because it cannot accommodate Marigold. Bettelheim reads the violence of the fairy tale symbolically, arguing that fantasy provides a safe space for children to deal with difficult emotions, but Wilson highlights the degree to which this depends on the relative safety of the child reader.

The treatment of fairy tales in *The Illustrated Mum* makes explicit a broader tension around fantasy and realism. Despite Marigold's insistence that she '[doesn't] want to be normal' (p. 13) she is unable to reconcile her identity as someone who has 'lived [...] on the outside edge' with a happy ending. Instead, her fantasies all follow a conventional pattern: she imagines their family with Micky as comprising 'my new lucky number, four, the perfect balanced number' (p. 89). Marigold's recollection that 'it was really the pictures I liked' in her book of fairy tales highlights her tendency to focus on the surface narrative: she fails to recognise that it is her erratic behaviour which causes problems for her children and instead tries to achieve a happy ending through attempts to *look* like a conventional mother, first by concealing her tattoos under conventional clothing (p. 134) and then by painting over her tattoos. Just as Dolphin cannot imagine an ending to Hansel and Gretel which does not involve the death of the witch, Marigold's attempt to remake herself into a 'good mother and a good lover' by erasing her tattoos (p. 158) reflects an assumption that these roles entail a symbolic death of her countercultural identity. Marigold is an escapist, but Wilson makes it clear that her focus on happy endings is problematic not just because it entails a turning away from the real world but also because conforming to these narratives entails an act of violence against the self. This tension is similar to the one explored in *The Other Side* through the *Jane Eyre* narrative; however, in *The Illustrated Mum* Wilson goes further in exploring the problems with more apparently realistic narratives. Marigold's linking of her physical appearance with her status as a good mother reflects the wider cultural narrative to which Marigold and her children are subject throughout the novel: more conventional characters see Marigold's tattoos as 'dead common' (p. 65) and Dolphin is teased for her unusual clothes and colourful mother (28). Star's social success is predicated on her ability to conform: she customises her uniform 'the way all the wilder girls in her class altered their uniform' (28) and emphasises her desire for Marigold to behave like 'Any old mother' (41). Wilson shows how common cultural narratives around mental illness shape the lives of Marigold and her family: Dolphin imagines Marigold's brain as 'bright pink and purple, glowing inside her head', (p. 40) and both Marigold and her children believe that treatment for Marigold's problems will erase her creativity as well as her erratic behaviour. Dolphin's resistance to seeking help has also been shaped by the realistic narratives provided to her by Marigold, who recounts her own difficult experiences in foster care, such as a home 'where the mother used to put the sheets over my head if I'd wet them' (p. 56). Wilson uses these stories to subtly suggest the limitations of social realism: while they may accurately reflect Marigold's experience, they also limit Dolphin's ability to imagine an outcome for her own life which is both realistic and positive.

In *The Other Side*, Wilson suggests that Alison's problems can be resolved only by a willingness to face reality. The climax of *The Illustrated Mum*, in which Dolphin recognises that Marigold needs medical help and she herself needs an adult's help, seems to suggest a similar message. However, the way Wilson handles this narrative is much more nuanced. Dolphin's first encounter with foster care is strongly reminiscent of Alison's fantasy about her grandmother:

> It was a small terraced house with a postbox-red door and window frames, yellow curtains downstairs, blue upstairs. There was a green hedge

and an untidy front garden with daisies and dandelions all over the long grass. It didn't look at all the sort of place the Foster Mother would live in. It looked like the sort of house I drew with my coloured crayons. (p. 199)

For Alison, the crayon house exists only in fantasy. In *The Illustrated Mum*, Wilson raises the possibility that the positive elements of fantasy are not simply escapist: they can exist in real life. Dolphin's foster mother Aunty Jane, 'small and fat and old [...] rather ugly [...] with a big nose that was almost purple' (p. 200), resembles Hansel and Gretel's witch, but although she feeds Dolphin on 'rounds of buttery toast spread with her own home-made strawberry jam' (210), the sweet food does not foreshadow malign intent. Aunty Jane disrupts both the fairy-tale logic which equates beauty with goodness, and the 'realistic' narratives Dolphin has absorbed about foster care. Instead, she offers the possibility of combining both: when Dolphin voices the fear that her own creativity may be a sign that she shares Marigold's mental illness, Aunty Jane draws a crucial distinction between escapism and storytelling, suggesting 'I think your legs are planted too firmly on the ground for you to lose your head' (210). The distinction between the image of fantasy here and the harmful escapism Alison indulges in in *The Other Side* is clear: Alison's fantasies literally lift her feet off the ground.

In *The Other Side*, Alison must turn away from fantasy and acknowledge the reality of her own life. By contrast, Aunty Jane's reassurance that Dolphin has 'her feet planted firmly on the ground' frees Dolphin to pursue her own creativity. When she returns to school after she has been placed with Aunty Jane, she wins a gold star for a story she writes with her friend Owly, 'the first star I'd ever been given for anything at school' (p. 207). The stories the other children tell are clearly wish fulfilment, centring around dreams of being rich and famous. Significantly, Dolphin's story is neither pure escapism nor fully realistic: 'I decided to be the only survivor of a tragic accident at sea. I made out I was in hospital and talked all about my horrendous injuries, and how I felt so lonely and guilty being the only one on the ship still left living' (p. 206). Dolphin's story clearly offers her a means of expressing the guilt and loneliness she is experiencing at a time when she has been separated from the other members of her own family. Although melodramatic rather than realistic, it illustrates the therapeutic value of unhappy stories. More importantly, however, this is the first point in the novel at which Dolphin is able to take full control of a narrative. The story is therapeutic because she is in control. Similarly, by the end of the story Wilson shows that Marigold has also been able to take control of her creativity in a positive way. Her fear that receiving treatment for her illness will erase her creative self proves unfounded; on the contrary, creative practice is part of her treatment. The regressive nature of her creativity at the start of the book is symbolised by her tattoos, which turn her creativity inwards. By contrast, at the end of the book Marigold deploys a needle for sewing rather than tattooing, symbolically turning her creativity towards the outside world. The fact that she is sewing a 'crazy quilt' (p. 222) indicates that she is engaging with the reality of her life rather than using creativity in an escapist fashion.

The fact that Dolphin's story is co-written with her friend Owly is also significant for Wilson's representation of fantasy. In *The Other Side*, Alison's engagement with stories is almost exclusively solitary: for the majority of the book, she uses it as a means of *avoiding* social connections. By contrast, for Dolphin stories are frequently the focus for her connections with others, as in the Hansel and Gretel episode, where their shared storytelling enables Dolphin and Marigold to express some of their emotions about their own relationship. Despite Star's assertion that she can no longer play pretend games, collaborative storytelling also repeatedly functions as a source of connection and comfort for the sisters, as when they 'play television' (p. 20) because the rental company have repossessed theirs, and 'tell each other really really scary stories' to distract themselves from their real fears when Marigold fails to return home from her night out (p. 25). Thus narrative is not simply a means of turning outwards towards the world, it is a means of turning towards others. This allows for a much richer view of fantasy which positions it as part of a 'quilt' of narrative strategies which also includes – rather than opposing – realism.

This view is reflected in Wilson's narrative strategies for the book itself. The ending of *The Other Side* is unflinching in its realism, reinforcing the sense that fantasy must ultimately be abandoned. By contrast, *The Illustrated Mum* closes with a qualified happy ending: 'we'd always have our mum, Marigold. It didn't matter if she was mad or bad' (p. 223). This ending offers the possibility of a much more optimistic reading: Dolphin is sure that Marigold 'really did love me and Star' (p. 222). Her acknowledgement that Marigold may be 'mad or bad', however, signals that the family's future is still uncertain and places creative control over the ending in the hands of the reader. Wilson thus provides readers with the 'pieces' of the quilt and offers a collaborative mode of reading which allows different readers to 'choose' an optimistic reading or take a more 'realistic' view of the likely outcome for the family.

Conclusion: The child's own fairy tale

Throughout her career, Jacqueline Wilson has challenged the notion that children's literature should simply protect child readers from difficult emotions and experiences. A voracious child reader herself, she nevertheless felt that there was 'something missing' from the stories she encountered.[34] *The Other Side* and *The Illustrated Mum* reflect her sense of the pleasures of story, but also show the need for narratives which reflect the experiences of real child readers. Both Alison and Dolphin are alienated by simple happy endings which depend on the erasure of difficulties: Wilson recognises that the psychological satisfaction of slaying the witch or vanquishing the madwoman is complicated by the existence of real 'witches' in children's lives. Both books therefore make the case for the kind of writing Wilson herself offers child readers, which acknowledges that they may experience genuine difficulties which they will not necessarily be able to vanquish.

In *The Other Side* Wilson clearly engages with the 1970s and 1980s discourse about the value of realistic fiction. Like Wilson herself, Alison is a 'literary' child, but although Wilson makes it clear that fantasy provides reassurance and escape, the book ultimately makes a case for turning away from fantasy to embrace real life, even when it is difficult or painful. By the time Wilson wrote *The Illustrated Mum*, however, she had developed a more nuanced approach to fantasy, which is reflected in the nature of her own work. Although Marigold's inability to face her real-life responsibilities illustrates the danger of purely escapist narratives, neither Dolphin nor the child reader of *The Illustrated Mum* are forced to accept the kind of bleak realism which is present in *The Other Side*. Wilson has said that she feels more responsibility to provide an optimistic ending for younger readers; however, the optimism of *The Illustrated Mum* does not simply reflect the fact that Dolphin (and the book's readers) are much younger than Alison. Instead, Wilson shows that Dolphin needs to be able to envisage a range of narratives, both the realistic and the fantastic, in order to take control of her own story. These narratives are most productive when they are encountered within the context of a shared narrative experience, so that they facilitate social connection rather than escapism.

The sense that it is *how* stories are encountered rather than the *genre* of those stories reflects changing attitudes to children's literature. Since the publication of Wilson's first books for teenagers in the 1980s, the world of children's literature has expanded to reflect a much wider range of social experiences and issues.[35] Writers such as Anne Fine, Morris Gleitzman and Jacqueline Wilson herself have helped to establish social realism as a major genre in children's literature.[36] At the same time, formal understandings of bibliotherapy have shifted away from a focus on specific problems towards a deeper understanding of narrative. Research from reading charity The Reader Organisation and the University of Liverpool on the benefits of shared reading for mental health, for example, found that a 'rich, varied, non-prescriptive diet of serious literature' coupled with 'support and a sense of community' provided by a shared reading group had measurable benefits for mental well-being.[37] Not coincidentally, since the early 2000s Wilson herself has been closely involved in advocacy for shared reading: she is patron of the Reading Agency's Chatterbooks scheme, which supports children's reading groups, and during her time as Children's Laureate promoted shared reading with children, commenting that 'It's a wonderful way of bonding together and simultaneously entering the magic world of the imagination'.[38] This is the experience that she portrays within the narrative of *The Illustrated Mum*.

As a leading writer of social realism Jacqueline Wilson has offered more children the opportunity to 'see themselves' in stories, and thus to understand that they are not subject to a narrative framework in which 'the good things happen to the beautiful people and the ugly ones are always the baddies'. In *The Other Side* and her other early fiction, she makes a strong case for the necessity of providing children with books which acknowledge the real difficulties many readers will encounter, showing that simple escapism is damaging. This theme continues into her later work, but as Wilson herself has noted, her books for younger readers also embrace fairy-tale optimism: 'just like in a fairy tale, your princess or your swineherd or whatever has to fight through many, many battles but generally, at the end, there is a happy ending.'[39] By creating narratives which include optimism as well as stark realism, Wilson opens up new possibilities for envisaging happy endings. Crucially, these narrative possibilities are at their most productive when situated within a social context: Wilson shows that children not only need to see themselves in stories but they need to share them too.

Notes

1   Nicholas Tucker, 'Jacqueline Wilson' in Nicholas Tucker and Nikki Gamble (eds.), *Family Fictions* (London: Continuum, 2001), pp. 69–84, p. 72.

2   Rosemary Stones, 'Books for Anti-Bullying Week (15–19 November) and Beyond'. *Books for Keeps* 185 (2012), http://booksforkeeps.co.uk/issue/185/childrens-books/articles/other-articles/books-for-anti-bullying-week-15-19-november-and-be [accessed 12 May 2014].

3 See Hugh Crago, 'Healing Texts: Bibliotherapy and Psychology' in Peter Hunt (ed.), *Understanding Children's Literature* 2nd edn. (London: Routledge, 2005), pp. 86–102, p. 184.

4 Winifred Robinson, 'The Hypocritical Ms Wilson: Why Children's Writers are Hugely to Blame for Loss of Innocence', *Daily Mail* 4 March 2008, http://www.dailymail.co.uk/news/article-526369/The-hypocritical-Ms-Wilson-Why-childrens-writers-hugely-blame-loss-innocence.html [accessed 5 June 2014].

5 Ika Willis examines the way Wilson reworks material from her early teenage novels across much of her later work in her chapter for this volume.

6 For a survey of this movement, see Lucy Pearson, *The Making of Modern Children's Literature in Britain: Publishing and Criticism in the 1960s and 1970s* (Farnham: Ashgate, 2013), pp. 50–55. Wallace Hildick, Geoffrey Trease, Aidan Chambers, Bob Dixon, Elaine Moss and Sheila Ray were among the other important voices in this movement.

7 Leila Berg, *Reading and Loving* (London: Routledge, 1977), pp. 83–84.

8 http://www.aspects.net/~leilaberg/nipper1.htm.

9 Jacqueline Wilson, interviewed in this volume.

10 Jacqueline Wilson, *Ricky's Birthday* (Basingstoke and London: Macmillan, 1973), p. 3.

11 See Lucy Pearson, *The Making of Modern Children's Literature in Britain*, pp. 52–54.

12 Ika Willis's chapter for this volume discusses these titles in more detail.

13 Julia Eccleshare, 'Authorgraph No. 115: Jacqueline Wilson'. *Books for Keeps* 115, March 1995, http://booksforkeeps.co.uk/issue/115/child-rens-books/articles/authorgraph/authorgraph-no115-jacqueline-wilson [accessed 11 May 2014]; Jacqueline Wilson, quoted in Rachel Cooke, 'The Story of Jacqueline Wilson', *The Observer* 23 March 2014, http://www.theguardian.com/books/2014/mar/23/the-story-of-jacqueline-wilson [accessed 12 May 2014].

14 *The Cool Web* collects a range of essays on children and children's literature, bringing together material ranging from the nineteenth century through to the early 1970s. Although not published until 1977, the text was prepared in 1974 and therefore predates Bruno Bettelheim's influential text *The Uses of Enchantment*. (See Editors' note to Margaret Meek, Aidan Warlow and Griselda Barlow (eds.), *The Cool Web: The Pattern of Children's Reading* (London: The Bodley Head, 1977). The majority of the essays in the section on 'the reader' are relevant to the argument made here about fantasy, notably those by Dick Cate, Frances Hodgson Burnett, James Britton, K. Chukovsky and Arthur Applebee.

15 James Britton, 'The Role of Fantasy' in *The Cool Web*, pp. 40–47, p. 47.

16 Betty Bacon, 'From Now to 1984' in *The Cool Web*, pp. 129–133, p. 131.

17 This theory did not originate with Bettelheim, but his work was one of the most widely known and influential.

18 Bruno Bettelheim, *The Uses of Enchantment: The Meaning and Importance of Fairy Tales* (London: Penguin, 1991), p. 3.

19 Ibid., p. 126.

20 Winifred Robinson, 'The Hypocritical Ms Wilson'.

21 Jack Zipes, 'On the Uses and Abuses of Folk and Fairy Tales with Children' in *Breaking the Magic Spell: Radical Theories of Folk and Fairy Tales*, rev. and expanded edn. (Lexington: University Press of Kentucky, 2002), pp. 179–205, p. 191.

22 Interview with Jacqueline Wilson in this volume.

23 Jacqueline Wilson, *Falling Apart* (Oxford: Oxford University Press, 1989), p. 10.

24 Jacqueline Wilson, *The Other Side* (Oxford: Oxford University Press, 1990), p. 36. All further references in this chapter are taken from this edition and given in the text.

25 Bruno Bettelheim, *The Uses of Enchantment*, p. 204.

26 Elaine Moss, 'The "Peppermint" Lesson' in *Part of the Pattern: A Personal Journey Through the World of Children's Books, 1960–1985* (London: The Bodley Head, 1986), pp. 33–34, p. 34.

27 In her interview for this volume, Wilson states that she was not aware of the debate surrounding social realism which was taking place at the time she wrote *Ricky's Birthday*, suggesting that she was unlikely to have come across 'The "Peppermint" Lesson' on its first publication in the National Book League publication 'Books' in 1971. By the time she wrote *The Other Side*, however, she had written several other books for children and teenagers and was thus in a position to be more actively aware of the children's book world. Furthermore, children's books were well covered in the mainstream media during the 1970s: Elaine Moss wrote for the *Guardian* and the *Times* as well as for specialist children's books publications.

28 This afterword in fact leaves the reader with a much more optimistic vision of Alison's future than that offered by the end of the novel itself, which does not contain the same reassurance about her ability to cope. This reflects the shift in Wilson's approach to writing social realism that had already taken place by the time this edition of the book was published.

29 Significantly, Alison chooses *Jude the Obscure* because she believes it will attract the attention of Andrew, a boy with whom she has begun to develop a friendship based around shared reading. His suggestion earlier in the novel that 'old Bertha had a raw deal' (p. 121) in *Jane Eyre* subtly anticipates Alison's forgiveness of her mother at the end of the book. This more productive mode of *shared* reading is explored much more fully in *The Illustrated Mum*.

30 Wilson's website lists *The Illustrated Mum* in the 9–11 category.

31 This episode is discussed in more detail in Helen Limon's chapter for this book.

32 Jacqueline Wilson, *The Illustrated Mum* (London: Corgi Yearling, 2007), p. 53.

33 Carolyn Daniels, *Voracious Children: Who Eats Whom in Children's Literature* (London: Routledge, 2006), p. 102.
34 Interview with Jacqueline Wilson in this volume.
35 British black and ethnic minority communities are still significantly unrepresented in children's literature, both as protagonists and creators.
36 This shift was already well underway in the 1970s, but by the 1990s the work of these writers was much less contested than that of earlier authors of social realism for children.
37 Liverpool Health Inequalities Research Institute, 'An Investigation into the Therapeutic Benefits in Relation to Depression and Well-being'. November 2010, http://www.thereader.org.uk/media/72227/Therapeutic_benefits_of_reading_final_report_March_2011.pdf [accessed 12 March 2015].
38 The Reading Agency, 'Chatterbooks'. *The Reading Agency*, 2013, http://readingagency.org.uk/children/quick-guides/chatterbooks/ [accessed 10 March 2015]; Jacqueline Wilson, quoted in 'Jacqueline Wilson'. *The Children's Laureate*, 2015, http://www.childrenslaureate.org.uk/previous-laureates/jacqueline-wilson/ [accessed 12 March 2015].
39 Jacqueline Wilson, interview with Lucy Pearson, December 2014.

4

Feisty Girls and Fearful Boys? A Consideration of Gender Roles and Expectations in the Work of Jacqueline Wilson

Kay Waddilove

In more than two decades of prolific publishing, from the notably feisty heroine of *The Story of Tracy Beaker* (1991) to *Opal Plumstead* (2014), allegedly the 'most outspoken, fiery heroine yet', Jacqueline Wilson has become well known for her creation of a gallery of strong female characters, whose emotional, and sometimes physical survival is contingent upon their cussedness.[1] The determined female protagonist battling against adverse social circumstances is frequently contrasted with male supporting characters whose weaknesses apparently serve mainly to foreground the resilience of the heroine. This simple reversal of traditional gender expectations is often held to contribute to Wilson's popularity with female readers, who, not unnaturally, enjoy identifying with a powerful, if troubled, central character. Nevertheless, while both Tracy and the eponymous heroine of *Opal Plumstead* conform to the 'feisty' stereotype, her texts contain a variety of representations that go beyond a simple binary challenge to received gender positions. This chapter will examine such representations, both of the children she creates and of the adults who feature in their lives, with especial attention to fathers or father-substitutes. It postulates that, by offering a variety of subtle interpretations of female and male protagonists that transcend concepts of masculine–feminine polarities, Wilson engages in current debates on gender and the family and makes a significant contribution to this discourse. New historicism, with its 'integration of text and socio-historic context' has proved a useful theoretical approach here; Mitzi Myers's argument that literary practices can 'shape the psychic and moral consciousness of young readers' by 'legitimating or subverting dominant [...] gender ideologies'[2] accords with Margaret Meek's view that an academic study of children's literature should reflect the 'interactions of culture, history, language, literature, psychology [and] sociology'.[3] In adopting this perspective, I will locate Wilson's work within the socio-economic and cultural contexts of twentieth- and twenty-first-century changes in the family, and discuss her approach to gender roles in order to examine the ideological, social and psychological messages her books contain. These issues will be explored through a variety of texts, with particular reference to *Lola Rose* (2003), *Clean Break* (2005), *Candyfloss* (2006) and *Cookie* (2008).

The ideology of gender

> Writers for children are transmitters not of themselves uniquely, but of the worlds they share. The starting point must be a shared understanding of the present, and an actuality which the young reader believes in. Ideology is not something which is transferred to children; it is something they already possess, having drawn it from a mass of experiences far more powerful than literature.[4]

It is now widely accepted that there will be links between the prevailing ideologies of any society and the texts produced by it. Children's literature is no exception, and if it is to be accorded its due importance as a form, it has to reflect the changing world that children occupy. One of the biggest social changes in recent years has been in the dynamics of gender roles and expectations, both within the family and in the wider world. As family is the primary societal structure within which most children develop, its representation in texts can be a powerful tool for acculturation and, according to John Stephens, 'can never be said to exist without either a socializing or educational intention'.[5]

In his article 'Gender, Genre and Children's Literature' Stephens describes a set of 'longstanding schemata' for gender characteristics:[6]

Schema for masculinity	Schema for femininity
Strong	Beautiful (therefore, good)
Violent	Non-violent
Unemotional, hard, tough	Emotional, soft, yielding
Aggressive, authoritarian	Submissive, compliant

Transgressive	Obedient, pleasing
Competitive	Self-effacing, sharing
Rapacious	Caring
Protective	Vulnerable
'Hunter'; powerful	'Victim'; powerless
Player	Prize
Independent	Dependent
Active	Passive (active = evil)
Analytical	Synthesising
Thinks quantitatively	Thinks qualitatively
Rational (= culture, civilisation)	Intuitive (= nature, the primitive)

Stephens acknowledges that these descriptors of very 'traditional' markers for masculinity and femininity are 'still objects of conceptual struggle in contemporary societies'.[7] Indeed, the spatial organisation of his table with masculinity in the left-hand column and femininity in the right-hand column implies that the feminine descriptors merely shadow or reflect the masculine markers. Ursula Le Guin has argued elsewhere that such a layout denotes that 'the male is "normal" [...] and the female "other"', which reinforces the common culturally gendered assumption that masculinity is the legitimate pattern and femininity is transgressive.[8] Moreover, as Stephens points out, citing Helene Cixous, when the terms in each column function as binary opposites, the 'male' attributes are normally understood to be superior to those marked as 'female'.[9] Stephens suggests that readers can test, and confirm, this assumption if they 'will only interchange the headings and consider how gender-inappropriate the descriptors then become'.[10] The involvement of Wilson's child protagonists in this conceptual struggle become most evident when Stephens' exercise is applied to her characterisations; thus Tracy Beaker's outwardly *competitive*, *active* and occasionally *violent* behaviour and *aggressive* response to her circumstances (masculine schemata) stand in explicit contrast to her (later-to-become) friend Peter's *self-effacing*, *vulnerable*, *submissive*, '*victim*' position (feminine schemata). Such reversal of gender expectations is particularly prevalent in *The Story of Tracy Beaker*, as is clearly demonstrated in this night-time encounter on the stairs:

> But Tracy Beaker has a lot of bottle. I'm not scared of anybody. Not even
> ghosts. So I clasped my hand over my mouth to stop the scream and

pattered right on up the stairs to confront this puny little piece of ecto-
plasm. Only it wasn't a ghost after all. It was just snivelling drivelling
Peter Ingham, clutching some sheets.
[...]
'Goodness, you don't know anything, do you? How long have you
been in care?'
'Three months, one week, two days', said Peter.
'Is that all? I've been in and out of care all my life [...]. So why are
you here now then? Your mum and dad get fed up with you?'
'They died when I was little. So I lived with my nan. But then she
got old and then – then she died too', Peter mumbled. 'And I didn't have
anyone else so I had to come here. And I don't like it.'[11]

Tracy presents herself here as *strong, tough, independent* and fearless as
she confronts this potential ghost, while the adjectives she uses to
describe Peter – 'puny', 'little', 'snivelling', 'drivelling' – indicate his
vulnerable and *submissive* nature. Moreover Peter's *powerless* response to
ending up in care is implicitly contrasted to Tracy's *hard* and *unemo-*
tional question about his parents, as well as her *aggressive* boasting of
her own extensive experience of care. Ironically, the narrative goes
on to demonstrate that Tracy's self-constructed feisty response to her
circumstances is not as effective as Peter's submissive vulnerability in
achieving the outcome they both yearn for. In the finale, Tracy is continuing her campaign to be fostered by the reluctant Cam, while Peter
has already been chosen by Auntie Vi and Uncle Stanley, who 'want
to take me almost straight away'.[12] So while Tracy, a classic unreliable
narrator, persists in the 'masculine' denial of her emotional needs,
Peter's caring and compliant 'feminine' characteristics are shown to
be successful in obtaining a secure future. Thus Wilson's 'fearful boy'
occupies a crucial narrative position, challenging gender binarism and
simplistic reversals to indicate the malleable representation of gender
roles that became a feature of her writing.

Ideological constructs such as these in texts can, according to Peter
Hollindale, be interpreted in three main ways. First, the overt and
often didactic presentation of the writer's own 'explicit social, political or moral beliefs'; second, the 'passive' ideology which is rooted
in the writer's 'unexamined assumptions', and which may 'reflect the
writer's integration in a society which unthinkingly accepts them'.[13]
Finally, and importantly for Wilson's work, as the *Tracy Beaker* quotation above demonstrates, ideology is 'inseparable from language',
which is not conceptually limited merely to the author's choice of
words, but also interpreted through the strategies the reader brings to
the text.[14] Hollindale argues that children are not 'empty receptacles'

for ideological messages, but bring to their reading a mass of experiences, from life and literature, which inform their understanding of the messages encoded in the text. Thus while 'a large part of any book is written not by its author, but by the world its author lives in', it is the world inhabited by the child reader and 'the worlds they share' which are crucial in creating meaning.[15] Wilson is an author who, as her millions of fans, and the comments on her website attest, successfully fosters an intimate relationship with her readership; she appreciates that this sharing is crucial to her ideological impact and has also indicated in many media interviews her respect for the ability of young readers to create their own meaning from complex and sometimes controversial situations: 'I want to write to every age group, in a way that can prepare them for what happens in the real world, and raise the awareness levels of many life-changing situations. I want to be a friend, really.'[16] She says further, 'I think young people are far better [than adults] at dealing with these things and processing and understanding supposedly difficult or complex subjects'.[17] Such perceptiveness regarding her role and purpose as a writer extends to Wilson's awareness of the likely effect of her work:

> My job is not just to write about what I think will interest children, but to touch on tricky subjects they may have to confront in their lives. Over the years people have implied that I'm not responsible in the way I write, that I'm deliberately going round upsetting children, but my responsibility is to help to gently open their minds.[18]

Gender is now commonly understood to be a cultural rather than a biological concept, wherein masculine or feminine behaviours and identities are inscribed through a process of socialisation; as Simone de Beauvoir famously declared, 'One is not born, but rather becomes, a woman.'[19] It is therefore inevitably influenced by prevailing societal ideologies; the stability of gender is thus a fragile construct, since 'masculine' and 'feminine' characteristics, such as those listed by Stephens, are subjective terms, liable to change over time and to vary from one culture to another in line with the contemporary ideology of the society in question. Gender theory has been both developed and challenged in recent decades, most notably by the academic Judith Butler whose post-structuralist rejection of the binary oppositions 'male/female' is explored in her influential book *Gender Trouble* (1990). She states that 'There is no gender identity behind the expressions of gender, that identity is performatively constituted by the very "expressions" that are said to be its results.'[20] It is interesting to apply this definition of gender by function or 'performativeness' to Floss's two father figures in *Candyfloss*: Charlie, the chubby single parent ineffectually running a greasy-spoon cafe, is protected by his daughter, 'I couldn't spoil his fun', and is 'a big silly softie', crying at sentimental films, spending hours decorating his daughter's birthday cake, and buying her fancy and unsuitable clothes.[21] These 'feminine' markers position Charlie in stark contrast to Steve, Floss's macho stepfather, who 'worked out at the gym most mornings before work, showing off his big muscles', runs a posh company car and, when head-hunted for a high-powered job abroad, 'shrugged and smirked to show us he couldn't *help* being so brilliant and clever and in demand'.[22] Yet, while Steve is clearly the strong, competitive and powerful player of Stephens' schema for traditional masculinity, Charlie, it can be argued, is 'performatively constituting' a gender role for himself. Despite matching some of Stephens' feminine markers, such as '*emotional*' and '*caring*', Charlie is nevertheless '*transgressive*' in his rejection of the societal materialistic values embraced by Steve, and reiterated by Floss's friend Rhiannon, whose 'Dad earns fifty thousand a year [and is] always buying me stuff'.[23] This transgression is exemplified in Charlie's refusal to 'join the modern world and get a mobile and a computer'.[24] He is also '*independent*' in his determination to maintain his (albeit inadequate) business, refusing financial help from his ex-wife. Most crucially, as a positive, if flawed, father figure, he is '*protective*'. This last masculine marker is evident both in his emotional and physical care of Floss, whom he ultimately rescues single-handedly from a burning caravan, and in his courage when entering into a knife fight to protect his friend Saul.[25] Charlie both transcends and exists independently of the binary pattern, and his 'performed' gender role is validated by Floss who, while torn by her love for both parents, chooses to live with Charlie rather than her mother and the ultra-masculine Steve. Such flexible gender constructs occur frequently in Wilson's work, reinforcing Butler's hypothesis that

> Gender, understood as one way of culturally configuring a body, is open to a continual remaking. [...] Terms such as 'masculine' and 'feminine' are notoriously changeable; there are social histories for each term; their meanings change radically depending upon [...] cultural constraints on who is imagining whom, and for what purpose.[26]

In *Undoing Gender* (2004) Butler focuses on the question of 'what it might mean to undo restrictively normative conceptions of gendered life'.[27] This topic is extensively explored in Wilson's *Cookie*, which begins with the depiction of the protagonist's family as a traditional unit rigidly controlled by an aggressive authoritarian father who dominates his submissive, compliant wife and his shy, unconfident daughter. Beauty is a passive '*victim*' of her father's controlling personality and the gender-defined family roles are reinforced in the wider society outside the home: 'Dad had started off working on a building site at sixteen. He worked his way up until he ended up buying the building firm. Then he branched out, becoming a property developer, building lots and lots of Happy Homes.'[28] Mum, having formerly worked as 'just a receptionist at Happy Homes – and I wasn't even a *good* receptionist',[29] now occupies an equally subordinate domestic role, and the power structures within the family replicate the societal pattern, as Dad, on his return from a hard day at the office, makes perfectly clear: 'Dad shifted his knee, tipping her off his lap. "You go and make a start on tea, Dilly, I'm starving. Whack a steak under the grill. Even you can manage that."'[30] Dad's attitude to his wife as an inferior creature who, pet-like, can be 'tipped' off his lap, and then patronised for her apparent incompetence in performing 'even' traditional female tasks, is further reinforced when he destroys the cookies she has made for Beauty's birthday tea, clearly delineating the operation of gender roles in this particular 'happy home': 'Shove all that biscuit muck in the bin where it belongs. I don't want you to start all these damn cooking experiments, you're useless at it. Your job is to look beautiful, so brighten up and put a smile on your face, for pity's sake. Put some jewellery on'.[31] It is clear that Dad's enforced power dynamic has undermined Dilly to the extent that she has apparently become unable to 'perform' effectively, not only in the traditional wifely roles of cooking and housekeeping, but also within his own limited perception of appropriate femininity. However, this 'gendered life' changes dramatically when Beauty and Dilly leave home after the shocking death of Beauty's pet rabbit, deliberately released from its cage by Dad. The traumatic event forces Dilly out of her passivity and into an 'undoing' of her and Beauty's restricted lives. Butler points out that

> Sometimes a normative conception of gender can undo one's personhood, undermining the capacity to persevere in a livable life. Other times, the experience of a normative restriction becoming undone can undo a prior conception of who one is only to inaugurate a relatively newer one that has greater livability as its aim.[32]

While Butler herself expands on these themes in the light of the body, sexuality and sexual orientation, they can equally be applied to the psychological and social restrictions that underpin the 'normative' concepts of gender implicit in Stephens' schemata. After a series of misadventures, Beauty and Dilly manage to inaugurate a more 'livable life'; the undermining of 'personhood' they had experienced in the gender-restricted family unit is replaced by a newer awareness of their own possibilities. Beauty overcomes her shyness, makes friends at school and gains enough self-confidence to appear on TV. Dilly finds a job to support them both and then starts a successful business selling her home-made cookies. The change in their 'prior conceptions' enables them, when Dad finally tracks them down, to resist a return to the normative status quo ante.

> 'Hello, Gerry', said Mum calmly – although I could feel she was trembling.
> He stared at us, his face flooding purple. 'Right. Come on. Get yourselves out of this dump now.' […] 'I'm giving you one last chance, girl. Come back now and make the most of it – or I'll cut you off without a penny, you and the kid.'
> 'Gerry, I don't want your money', said Mum. 'That wasn't the reason I married you. I wanted you to look after me. But I'm not that stupid little girl any more.'[33]

While Wilson makes clear that her future is still uncertain, the potential for 'greater livability' has enabled Dilly to finally overcome fear, assert her economic and emotional independence and reject the infantilism imposed upon her by Gerry's narrow interpretation of gender roles. Beauty and Dilly are inspired in their determination to create a life in which they can maintain the changes in performative identity they have discovered. Dilly recreates herself as an independent businesswoman, rather than accept the offer of a cosy relationship with the warm-hearted Mike. And Beauty starts to rebuild the self-esteem her father had consistently undermined: 'This was the start of a whole new me. Cookie, cool and confident...'[34] Together they work to establish a different type of family unit that will sustain rather than undermine their progress towards that 'livable life'.

Family values: Women and work, fathers and feminism

> The important, and often neglected, part that can be played by the men and boys of the household is not forgotten. But the main weight of the shopping, cooking, making and mending, furnishing, minor household repairs, fuelling and heating, and above all, the budgeting and catering, is likely to fall on the housewife.
>
> (Ministry of Education pamphlet, 1949)

Wilson has discussed her own childhood family unit in two publicity interviews in the *Guardian*: *Jacqueline Wilson: My Family Values*[35] promoted a national exhibition[36] on her life and work, while *Question Time*[37] marked the publication of her autobiography *Jacky Daydream* (2007). Without straying too far into the murky waters of bio-criticism, it is nevertheless notable how familiar many of the personal situations she describes in these interviews, and in *Jacky Daydream*, would sound to her readers: a much-feared, domineering father; an unhappy parental marriage; a close and playful relationship between young mother and daughter; an isolated but creative child; and the use of storytelling as emotional outlet. More broadly, it is clear that many significant changes in the dynamics of family life and gender relations that have emerged in the late twentieth and early twenty-first centuries, and the resultant societal and familial effects which underpin Wilson's work, can most usefully be traced back to 1945, the year during which the cataclysmic Second World War ended, and in which Jacqueline Wilson was born.

During the war years women had been an essential component of the war effort, participating in the workforce as well as in the armed services, and maintaining the fabric of the country by working in factories, on the land and establishing voluntary services. Practical measures provided by the government had enabled such contribution; wartime nurseries reduced the burden of childcare, and domestic support, such as the British Restaurants, relieved women of many pre-war home-based responsibilities. This situation changed in 1945 as demobilisation was accompanied by a sharp reduction in the female workforce and the reassertion of men's economic interests; propaganda on the joys of motherhood and domesticity emerged once the wartime need for women's contribution to the workforce disappeared. In peacetime, the pre-war ideology of the family was revived; it was designed to act 'as a conservative force against the cultural degeneration linked to [...] modernism [and] women's rights', reinforcing the influential belief system based on the situation of the wife and mother being centred in the home.[38] The nuclear family model of wage-earning husband–father and home-based housewife–mother producing and caring for children was written into the administrative structure of the pro-natalist 1950s, a time when, as William Beveridge[39] put it, 'Mothers have vital work to do in ensuring the adequate continuance of the British race.'[40]

The traditional assumption of gender roles within families encoded in the pattern of 'ideal' family life promulgated during this period has proved remarkably durable, surviving the 'never-had-it-so-good' decade of the 1950s,[41] the cultural upheavals of the 1960s, second-wave feminism in the 1970s, the post-feminist world of the 1990s and remaining prevalent, albeit alongside competing discourses, in the twenty-first century. While female employment continued to rise during the post-war decades, and is now taken for granted, the twenty-first-century discourse on the desirability of mothers, particularly of babies or preschool children, undertaking work outside the home remains today as much a matter of unresolved debate as it was in the 1950s. Psychologist Oliver James's recent book *How Not to F*** Them Up* (2010), categorically stated that young children 'need to be in the presence of a responsive, loving adult at all times' and warned mothers who go out to work that 'day care is associated with more boastful, disobedient and aggressive children'.[42] Reviews of this book provoked a storm of debate on the website Mumsnet[43] between 'SAHMs' (Stay-at-Home-Mothers) and 'WMs' (Working-Mothers), with one contributor noting, 'Stay at home with the kids and you're inhibiting their confidence. Go to work and send them to daycare and you're breeding thugs. Damned if you do, damned if you don't springs to mind.'[44] Recent official studies have highlighted the economic and social developments that underlie such dilemmas: 'Over the past thirty-five years, the shift towards a post-industrial economy has combined with changes in family structures to challenge the assumption of a male breadwinner upon which the post-war welfare state was first founded.'[45] As a fiction writer, Wilson's contribution to this discourse reflects the reality of many women's lives, particularly those who do not have the luxury of economic choice. In virtually all of her novels, it is a given that 'bread-winning' is as much the role of women as of the men in the family; working to provide for their children, although frequently in poorly paid or menial jobs, Wilson mothers adopt the traditionally 'masculine' role of the provider, often in contrast to an economically unsuccessful or feckless male partner. Yet, their tendency still to assume primary responsibility for the traditionally 'female' domestic role in the household resonates with earlier patterns, including the 60-year-old government advice pamphlet quoted above. Marty's dad in *The Worst Thing about My Sister* (2012) gives up his high-street travel agency 'because the lease was too expensive and he didn't make enough money any more', and his attempts to run the business from home are a failure, so Mum supports the family by working as a school secretary as well as establishing a potentially successful dress-making business.[46] This benevolent but ineffectual dad 'has lots of naps now because he didn't have anything else to do', yet there is no suggestion that he will share the chores, despite the fact that mum 'gets grumpy all the time' in her struggle to meet the needs of both work and home:[47]

> My life is one *big* compromise. I have to cook and wash and clean and tidy for all you lot. I have to go out to work at the school, where all the parents ring me up making a fuss. When I eventually get to sew, I'm tired out and I've got a splitting headache.[48]

The charming and irresponsible actor father of *Clean Break* (2005) runs a market stall to supplement his income, but 'whenever Dad had an acting job he shut the stall up, and even when he wasn't working he couldn't always be bothered to trail down to the palace and sit inside his Fairyland'.[49] When Dad walks out on the family, Mum, Julie, already a full-time hairdresser, takes over responsibility for the stall in the hope that Frankie will return, as well as continues in her own job 'five days a week, sometimes six when they were short-staffed and working right through until ten on Thursdays, when it was late-night shopping'.[50] The effects on the family of her role as an unsupported single parent are made clear:

> 'Mum's no fun now', said Vita. 'She won't make me up like a grown-up lady or play Fairy Queens or do *anything* now, she just falls asleep.'
> 'Yes, I was telling her about this bad boy who pushed me and she didn't *listen*, her eyes kept closing', Maxie said indignantly.
> Gran was worried about her too. 'You're exhausting yourself, Julie. Never mind the blooming money. I wanted your deadbeat missing bloke to pay his debts. I didn't mean *you* should work yourself to death on his behalf.'[51]

Such issues of women's labour, both paid and unpaid, as well as essentialist attitudes to 'female' responsibilities, were addressed in the 'second-wave' feminism that emerged at the end of the 1960s, heralded in the UK by the 1970 Women's Liberation conference. This movement raised awareness of social challenges to traditional gender positions in the family by carrying the debate firmly into the political arena, and there is evidence of some success for its campaigns in the legislation enacted during this period.[52] Yet, not unusually, as Wilson's texts published two and three decades later demonstrate, attitudinal change has lagged behind legislation; while women, and mothers, were gaining rights in the workplace, men, and fathers, even sympathetic characters such as Marty's dad, were still to assume much, or any, responsibility for domestic work. Wilson's readers are encouraged to empathise with such gender imbalance, yet it is clear in her language that gender determinism is still internalised by women as well as men; it has become one of Hollindale's 'unexamined assumptions', 'just how the world is'.[53] Violet's mother in *Midnight* (2003), like Marty's mum, resents her domestic role, yet performs it diligently: "'It's my mum, she does all **her** housework and turns everything upside-down". [...] Mum did **her** housework *every* day and took it very seriously.'[54]

Of all the post-war social legislation, the effects of the 1969 Divorce Reform Act is most relevant to Wilson's oeuvre. It resulted in a huge rise in divorce rates, reaching a peak of 165,018 in 1993, two years after *The Story of Tracy Beaker* was published, and these have remained in six figures ever since. This increase challenged the norm of the traditional nuclear family, as has the more recent rise in the number of births outside marriage. The number of lone-parent families more than tripled and now stands at 3 million, 25 per cent of all families with children.[55] The ideological construct of the family has been slow to respond to these radical developments, and the dominant model of the nuclear family, operating as Beveridge had envisioned, persists in defiance of demographics, institutionalised by government, the professions and the media. The examination of a variety of non-traditional family patterns in Wilson's work constitutes an important challenge to such entrenched attitudes, with their embedded gender determinism. Her unflinching description of the effects of divorce, parental separation, single parenthood and abandonment in the lives of the characters examined here is a key theme in her writing and offers a specifically alternative position to current cultural and political expectations of the so-called 'normative' family.[56]

In accordance with her penchant for 'gritty realism', it is usually women who remain the primary carers in her works, although this is not always a given; the plot of *Candyfloss*, for example, is predicated on Floss's challenge to this assumption.[57] Nevertheless, the reality that only one in ten lone-parent families in the UK are headed by a father is reflected in the texts examined here.[58] The father figures in *Lola Rose*, *Clean Break*, *Candyfloss* and *Cookie* are all separated from their offspring for different reasons: Nikki in *Lola Rose* flees an increasingly violent relationship; Frankie in *Clean Break* leaves the family for another woman; Floss's mother in *Candyfloss* has a new partner; and the emotionally abusive father in *Cookie* finally oversteps the mark, driving his wife and child away. While each of these fathers strives in different ways, not always successfully, to maintain a relationship with their offspring, in her exploration of their family dynamics, Wilson offers a range of gender positions that both reflect and challenge societal assumptions.[59]

While the meaning and practices of fatherhood are clearly related to gender identity, the two contrasting types of fathers in these four texts – the fond failures of *Clean Break* and *Candyfloss* as opposed to the aggressive abusers of *Lola Rose* and *Cookie* – are depicted as multi-dimensional figures, whose interactions with their children can both reinforce, yet also reposition, accepted notions of 'masculinity' and 'femininity'. Despite the close attention Wilson pays to the mother–child dyad in much of her work, these texts demonstrate her awareness of the pivotal nurturant role of fathers or father-substitutes in the emotional lives of her protagonists, an importance validated by socio-psychological studies:'Fathers are no less important than mothers in a child's life.The closeness of fathers to their children influences the children's later psychological well-being [...]. If fathers are more closely involved children develop better friendships, more empathy, high self-esteem, better life satisfaction and higher educational achievement.'[60] This importance prevails regardless of the quality of fathering. Frankie in *Clean Break* is charming, affectionate, empathetic and adored by his children, including stepdaughter Em. 'He always said he loved me just as much asVita and Maxie. I hoped hoped hoped it was true, because I loved him more than anyone else in the whole world, even a tiny bit more than Mum.'[61] Yet he is also unreliable, self-centred and irresponsible; having promised Em after a family row that he will stay with the family 'for ever', he leaves overnight; later, excusing his failure to keep in touch, his solipsism is evident, '*I* felt dreadful [...] *I* just couldn't stand all the rows and the sadness and feeling that it was all my fault.'[62] Turning up at school unexpectedly, he takes the children on a surprise seaside trip, but the fun of their outing starts to pall for Em, as she realises that her playful father has not told her mother and grandmother that he has taken them. Her increasing anxiety on their behalf is belittled by Dad in a dialogue which reveals a typical scenario in the Wilson world of dysfunctional parent–child interaction: the loving but immature parent and the child forced against her will to adopt adult responsibilities in the relationship.[63]

'Don't worry Em, it's not twelve o'clock yet. We're not going to turn into pumpkins.'

'You did tell Mum and Gran you were taking us out, didn't you, Dad?'

'You're such an old fusspot, Em. You're my kids. I don't have to ask permission to take you for a fun time.'

I loved it that Dad included me as his kid. But the little worry inside me was getting bigger and bigger. 'But Dad, if you didn't tell them, won't they be wondering where we are?'

'Just leave it Em. Don't spoil things', said Dad.

I didn't want to spoil things. But I couldn't help thinking about Mum and Gran and how worried they would be.

'Tell you what Em', said Dad. 'We could all check into a little hotel […].'

'But we haven't got our pyjamas', I said anxiously. 'And we wouldn't be back in time for school.'

'Oh, for God's sake, don't be so boring. You sound more middle-aged than your grandmother', Dad snapped.[64]

Dad's apology when this conversation reduces Em to tears further demonstrates his self-centred immaturity and the injustice of the child–parent role reversal: 'Don't cry, Em. Please. Dry those tears. You're the brave little girl who looks after us all and never cries, right? Don't, darling, you're breaking my heart.'[65]

Having experienced a physically abusive father previously, Em's attachment to Frankie is the more profound, and these emotional needs are not mitigated by her growing awareness of his inadequacies. By the end of the book she has accepted that 'I didn't know whether I could believe in my dad or not.'[66] Physically as well as emotionally, he is transformed in her eyes from the 'special, so perfect' prince, to 'just this pale thin man with short spiky hair and a grubby denim jacket, telling me a whole lot of stories'.[67] In Wilson's fairy-tale conclusion, Dad returns to the family exactly a year after he left, in time for Christmas. The story has come full circle with matching opening and concluding lines, from the initial 'I thought it was going to be the best Christmas ever,' to the final 'Maybe it was going to be the best Christmas ever.'[68] Yet, notwithstanding his children's rapturous welcome, Em's cautious use of 'maybe' in the final sentence qualifies the optimism, references the growth of her more mature understanding and offers the implied reader alternative interpretations of this conventionally happy ending.

Fathers as economic failures are both a standard feature in Wilson's work[69] and an indication of her challenge to the prevailing hegemony. Her protagonists, like Em, tend to remain emotionally linked to the paternal figure despite, and sometimes because of, increasing perception of his inadequacies. So Floss, whose father runs a failing chips-with-everything café and acknowledges that 'I'm not much cop at *anything*', declares that 'I loved my dad even more because he wasn't tall and fit and handsome and clever.'[70] Such emotional truisms are notably evident in the 'fearful boys' whose need for stable father figures is linked to their yearning for role models as well as emotional security. As usual, Wilson is in touch with the zeitgeist here; research by charitable organisations such as Families Need Fathers has reinforced sociological studies and is now exploited by politicians of all persuasions in the face of changing social and economic patterns. The high-profile report *Doing Family: Encouraging Active Fatherhood* (2013), for instance, published by David Lammy, MP, is informed by 'that hole in my life' caused by his own father's desertion, and Wilson's perceptive depiction of such emotional 'holes' in her protagonists emphasises the critical need for fathers to provide nurturant care.[71]

In *Lola Rose*, in which Wilson delivers the triple whammy of an irresponsible, childlike mother, extreme domestic violence and maternal cancer, Kenny's devotion to his scary father survives his own terror, influences his view of adult relationships and colours his approach to masculinity, despite the fact that he himself fails to meet the patterns imposed upon him. Delighted to have a son, Jay is nevertheless cruelly blind to the failure of his attempts to inculcate his own version of maleness; 'Dad had always marched [Kenny] to the barber's for a number one haircut [and] went on about him being a real tough nut', and refuses to acknowledge that 'our Kenny was the wimpiest kid on the whole estate'.[72] Bullied by the other children at nursery, Kenny is far from the 'regular little bruiser' of his father's masculine illusions, yet internalises (and, presumably, may go on to replicate) Dad's familial behaviour as a justified norm:[73]

'Dad isn't part of our family now, Kendall', I [Lola Rose] whispered.
'Why not?' Kendall sounded astonished.
'You know why!' I hissed. 'Because Dad's horrible and keeps hitting Mum. He hit me too. It still hurts whenever I move my jaw.'
'He doesn't hit me', said Kendall.
'Don't you feel sorry he hits Mum?'
'But she deserves it', said Kendall.
'How *dare* you say such a wicked, stupid thing!'
'But she *does* deserve it. Dad says so', Kendall said, starting to whimper.[74]

The hyperactive Maxie in *Clean Break* becomes similarly in thrall to a conventional vision of masculinity that is alien to his nature. Named after Max of *Where the Wild Things Are*,[75] Maxie is introduced as a sensitive and nervous boy who 'couldn't ever tame Wild Things [and] wouldn't be up to taming wild fluffy baby bunnies'.[76] In contrast to Jay, Maxie's feckless father Frankie is neither violent nor intimidating, and Maxie is initially more than happy to curl up with cuddly toys and wear his sister's pink jelly sandals to school, despite being teased for 'babyishness'. Yet the effect of the father's behaviour on the son's male identity is similar; when Frankie walks out, Maxie adopts obsessive behaviour patterns, fusses about his food and longs to become

'Maxie the Man'. But, exhorted by his father on a weekend outing to '"be a man"'. Maxie couldn't even manage to be a little boy. He whimpered like a baby.'[77]. Maxie later blames his father's desertion for his own gender-specific failings: 'I'll be a big brave boy if he comes back.'[78] Wilson assigns such 'fearful boys' the crucial narrative role of foregrounding the psychological damage done by such inadequate fathering, a key ideological message embedded in her characterisations of father–son interaction. While Wilson's narrative voice is almost invariably female,[79] in these texts the failure of the father to be an effective parent is the root cause of low self-esteem for both male and female protagonists; as Julia Kristeva observes, it is 'the bankruptcy of the *fathers*' that is the source of abjection.[80]

Wilson's contrasting models of positive father figures tend to challenge, rather than display traditional masculine markers; successful masculinity, in contradiction of Stephens's schemata, is embodied in '*caring*' and '*sharing*' rather than '*strength*', '*competitiveness*' or '*power*'. As with the non-competitive Charlie in *Candyfloss*, representation of good fathers is marked by the provision of emotional security, reliability and often humour, rather than material success. So in *Clean Break* Em envies Molly whose father can be trusted to keep his promises: 'he came back in *exactly* ten minutes, because I counted. [...] I wished wished I had a dad like that.'[81] Harpreet's father in *Lola Rose* 'could be horribly strict about bedtimes', but the worst thing Harpreet can remember about him is being shouted at when she ran into the road.[82] And *Cookie*'s Beauty is amazed when Rhona makes fun of her play-acting father, reflecting on the contrast to her own situation: 'I wonder what *my* dad would do if I called him stupid.'[83] Mike, Beauty's substitute-father, may be, like Charlie, 'quite old and quite fat', but as well as providing a positive paternal role model, his character interrogates received gender assumptions in his application of the traditionally 'feminine' skills of cooking, cleaning and homemaking to his bed-and-breakfast business.[84]

Wilson further addresses masculinity and the hegemony of male power in her depiction of relationships between the fathers and their female partners; she represents these as a 'crisis in hegemonic masculinity' by placing the transgressive men inside the domestic household.[85] Yet even here Wilson's subtle depictions avoid polarised gender binarism. Nikki, Julie and Dilly may initially be the stereotypically passive 'victims' of their own powerlessness in relationships with the male partners on whom they depend and who, additionally, dominate them physically (Jay), emotionally (Frankie) and economically (Gerry). Each, however, ultimately develops a new regime of power ('biopower' in Foucaultian terminology) that enables them to take control of their lives, and of those around them, often in most unlikely ways.[86] After years of physical abuse, Nikki, in contradiction of her previous history, decides to leave Jay when he hits Lola Rose for the first time: 'Now he's started on you he won't stop. I'm not having that.'[87] Dilly walks away from the domineering Gerry whose psychological abuse of his 'useless ageing dumb blonde' wife has included derision of her appearance, intelligence, earning potential and practical abilities.[88] Dilly ultimately finds agency in turning her talent for baking cookies into a highly successful business, envisaging 'Bunny Cookies in every up-market food emporium – Fortnum and Mason, Harrods, Selfridges...'[89] This transference of a 'female' skill into an enterprise to rival that of her husband's building firm is a nicely ironic twist on Wilson's part. And while Julie accepts Frankie's fairy-tale return to the family, she is now realistic about his failings, having learnt to 'toughen up a bit', and recognising that, 'we can't just wave a magic wand and pretend all this year hasn't happened'.[90]

The reader and the writer: Role models and realism

My role as a writer is to hold out a metaphorical hand to these children and to reflect the difficulties they face in an imaginative way. Sometimes it's best to work by imagination, and leave out the gory details – I'd hate to think I'd given kids nightmares.

(Jacqueline Wilson, 2008)

The texts discussed here assume a ten-plus female implied reader[91] and Wilson has a profound understanding of how gender conditioning on the cusp of adolescence may affect this demographic. The worries of the central characters about attractiveness, preoccupation with body shape, and use of food as emotional crutch are linked to the parent–child and, in these texts, specifically to the father–daughter relationship. Peer pressure is acknowledged, but while all the protagonists yearn for friendship, this is shown to be fostered by 'non-girly' activities; Floss's house-decorating with the quiet, unassuming Susan in *Candyfloss* is far more enriching than outings to the mall with boy-band-and-make-up-obsessed Rhiannon. It is, however, in the home that gender concerns are polarised and internalised. The universal soubriquet of 'princess' is used by each of the fathers, affectionately by ineffectual Charlie and Frankie, and with undertones of menace by abusive Jay and Gerry. This subject position is accepted without question by all the daughters, whose failure to measure up to the required model of femininity conflicts with their desire for paternal acceptance. The unfortunately christened Beauty, fat, plain and bespectacled, is bullied at school and at home for her failure to achieve a feminine ideal: '"Good God, you're a right sight!" said Dad! "You look uglier than ever! Don't you *want* to look pretty?"'[92] Beauty, not at all a 'feisty' heroine, is introverted and insecure, 'fearful' of her bullying father, and concurs with this judgement: 'My hair drooped, my face twisted like a gargoyle, and my body blew up like a balloon. Dad was right. I did look a sight.'[93] Mother Dilly's attempts to restore her confidence fail and it is only with support from the kindly father-substitute Mike that she begins to rebuild self-esteem.

Lola Rose and Em, while more determined, are, again in contradiction of Wilsonian stereotype, not so much feisty as forced into responsibilities that are developmentally inappropriate. Em's unwilling adoption of adult concerns when dealing with an immature father figure is matched by Lola Rose's reluctant acceptance of parental obligations in support of an irresponsible mother: 'She tries to turn *me* into the mum. I hated it that I had to be the one to be sensible.'[94] Reader engagement with the protagonists is balanced by Wilson with role models who offer an alternative construction of femininity. Splendid Aunty Barbara, the deus ex machina of *Lola Rose*, is large, competent and independent as a counterpoint to the fragile, emotionally needy Nikki. She demonstrates that it is possible to be fond of fashion, dress beautifully and still have the martial art skills that enable her to demolish the threat of Jay's return to the family. Foregrounding a vision of gender in which female autonomy and strength of character inhabit a femininity that empowers rather than diminishes its subject, Barbara, who 'used to be scared to say boo to a goose', is a marker for ideological positioning in the text.[95] No easy solutions are offered, but Wilson's characters (and, by implication, her readers), whether feisty or fearful, are enabled to explore coping strategies that will ameliorate their problems, acquiring confidence in their potential to move beyond deterministic gender boundaries.

In the post-Harry Potter world of children's literature, dominated by fantasy and dystopic fiction, Wilson's work sits firmly in a tradition of realism that harks back to the earliest didactic Puritan writings for children. Sheila Egoff defines the characteristics of modern realistic novels as follows: they are emotionally explosive; have protagonists with deep and subtle temperaments who deal with change; and, after sharp and bitter experiences, the protagonists become the determining influence in their own lives; all these descriptors are clearly evident in the texts discussed here.[96] Wilson does not prescribe a non-gendered politically correct world of unlikely equality where all men iron and all women engage in lucrative careers; her work aligns with Stephens' description of realism as a genre that 'typically illuminates life as it is [...]; it reflects society, and in doing so can offer its audience new experiences and help children mature intellectually and emotionally by enabling them to experiment with subject positions [...] at one remove from consensus reality.'[97]

Wilson's high profile in this genre began with *The Story of Tracy Beaker* in 1991, at which time many goals of the second-wave feminists appeared to have been achieved and the deradicalisation of the late 1980s had led to the popularity of 'post-feminism' as a concept. This ill-defined term is variously used to describe a backlash against second-wave feminism, a challenge to essentialist views of femininity (which has resonances in Butler's gender theories), a belief that feminism is no longer relevant because male/female equality has been achieved, a reconstruction of 'women's liberation' as the cause of many problems facing women in the new millennium or a recurring historical trend that appears whenever women have made substantial strides towards equal rights.[98] Wilson has engaged in these societal debates both at the basic level of story as well as in overall narrative discourse by promulgating positive (and feminist) role models for her readers. Lissa Paul devised a famous list of questions to apply to feminist readings of texts: 'Whose story is this?; who speaks?; who acts?; who is acted upon?' and so on.[99] Using these it is evident that Wilson's work is gynocentric; both the narrative voice and the main characters are female, and, as Roberta Trites observes, 'voice often serves as a metaphor for female agency'.[100] Wilson gives expression to the marginalised; struggling against circumstances in which they are apparently powerless, her heroines exercise power by telling their stories in their own voice.

Trites points out, however, that 'ultimately the effect of feminism on children's literature is to [...] speak to readers of both genders'.[101] And although the covers of the texts analysed here attest to their overwhelmingly female readership, in providing evidence of powerful survival in adversity through a variety of family units, Wilson's books have important messages for boys as well as girls, informing current discourses on gender by offering positions that transcend the masculine–feminine polarities described by Stephens.[102] The fathers and the 'fearful' boys (as well as the 'feisty' girls) are crucial narrative operators, who, whatever the quality of their masculinity, play an active role in determining the outcome of the story. Along with the female characters, they engage in transformed representations of gender relations and the recuperation of negative stereotypes of both sexes.

While Wilson's popularity and prodigious rate of production[103] have been factors in her influence on children's literature, it is her materiality and ability to speak directly to the reader that has been crucial in highlighting social realism as a viable genre, while the empathetic understanding of her audience ensures her predominance over lesser 'issue' writers. The realistic settings enable Wilson to interrogate and illuminate contemporary discourse on gender and the family; she variously echoes, affirms and challenges twenty-first-century gender debates, sharing rather than imposing ideological meaning for the world that both she and her readers inhabit, with 'an actuality which the young reader believes in'.[104] The wide readership ensures that her works are an important contribution to this current discourse; in today's media-dominated society, children are aware of such debates, and exploring these social conundrums through story can offer enlightenment and comfort, allowing readers to 'cognitively map' their social world, even if the circumstances depicted are outside their personal experience.[105] She is able to 'gently open [readers'] minds', so that they appreciate issues of gender and familial power structures, and, if they are affected directly, to offer that valuable 'metaphorical hand'. Mallan avers that 'an enculturating function of children's literature is to propose ways of being in the world that are both desirable from a societal point of view and rewarding for the individual'.[106] In growing up with and through her characters, Wilson's readers are likely to benefit from such enculturation and be empowered by the diversity of perspectives offered to them. She has demonstrated par excellence that popular realist literature can, in Myers' words, 'shape the psychic and moral consciousness of young readers'.[107] In thus achieving her aims as a writer, as well as meeting the needs of her audience, Jacqueline Wilson addresses fundamental aspects of gender construction while offering both entertainment and challenge to young readers in their search for identity.

Notes

1 Pre-publication description of Opal Plumstead, protagonist of Wilson's 100th book, on the Jacqueline Wilson website. Opal Plumstead, JacquelineWilson.co.uk, http://www.jacquelinewilson.co.uk/library. php? b=73 [accessed 3 June 2014].

2 Mitzi Myers, 'Missed Opportunities and Critical Malpractice: New Historicism and Children's Literature'. *Children's Literature Association Quarterly* 13:1 (1988), pp. 41–43, p. 42.

3 Margaret Meek, 'Symbolic Outlining: The Academic Study of Children's Literature'. *Signal* 53 (1987), pp. 97–115, p. 100.

4 Peter Hollindale, 'Ideology and the Children's Book'. *Signal* 55 (1988), pp. 3–22, p. 17.

5 John Stephens, *Language and Ideology in Children's Fiction* (London: Longman, 1992), p. 218.

6 John Stephens, 'Gender, Genre and Children's Literature'. *Signal* 79 (1996), pp. 17–30, pp. 18–19.

7 Ibid., p. 18.

8 Ursula K. Le Guin, *Earthsea Revisioned* (Cambridge: Green Bay, 1993), p. 24.

9 Helene Cixous, 'Castration or Decapitation?' *Signs: Journal of Women in Culture and Society* 7:1 (1981), pp. 41–55, p. 44.

10 John Stephens, 'Gender, Genre and Children's Literature', p. 19.

11 Jacqueline Wilson, *The Story of Tracy Beaker* (London: Doubleday, 1991), pp. 54–55.

12 Ibid., p. 155.

13 Peter Hollindale, 'Ideology and the Children's Book', p. 10/12/13.

14 Ibid., p. 15.

15 Ibid.

16 Jacqueline Wilson, in Amol Rajan and Imogen McSmith, 'Children Being Robbed of their Innocence, Says Former Laureate', *Independent* 3 March 2008, p. 4.

17 Jacqueline Wilson, in Who Cares? Trust, 'Jacqueline Wilson'. *Who Cares? Trust*, http://www.thewhocarestrust.org.uk/pages/jacqueline-wilson. html (n.d.) [accessed 16 December 2013].

18 Jacqueline Wilson, in Eleanor Morgan, 'This Much I Know: Jacqueline Wilson', *Observer* 26 February 2012, p. 10.

19 Simone de Beauvoir, *The Second Sex* (London: Jonathan Cape, 1953), p. 281.

20 Judith Butler, *Gender Trouble: Feminism and the Subversion of Identity* (London: Routledge, 1990), p. 25.

21 Jacqueline Wilson, *Candyfloss* (London: Doubleday, 2006), p. 43, p. 64.

22 Ibid., p. 34, p. 69.

23 Ibid., p. 213.

24 Ibid., p. 9.

25 Ibid., p. 293.

26 Judith Butler, *Undoing Gender* (Abingdon: Routledge, 2004), pp. 9–10.

27 Ibid., p. 1.

28 Jacqueline Wilson, *Cookie* (London: Doubleday, 2008), p. 17.

29 Ibid., p. 64.

30 Ibid., p. 21.

31 Ibid., p. 157.

32 Judith Butler, *Undoing Gender*, p. 1.

33 Jacqueline Wilson, *Cookie*, p. 262, p. 265.

34 Ibid., p. 278.

35 Juliet Rix, 'Jacqueline Wilson: My Family Values', *Guardian* 10 March 2012, p. 8.

36 At Seven Stories, the National Centre for Children's Books. *Daydreams and Diaries: the Story of Jacqueline Wilson* ran here for a year until October 2012, and then toured the country.
37 Hannah Pool, 'Question Time', *Guardian* 15 March 2007, p. 25.
38 Kimberley Reynolds, 'Sociology, Politics, the Family: Children and Families in Anglo-American Children's Fiction, 1920–60' in Kimberley Reynolds (ed.), *Modern Children's Literature: An Introduction* (Basingstoke: Palgrave Macmillan, 2005), pp. 23–41, p. 27.
39 Architect of the post-war establishment of the Welfare State.
40 William Beveridge, in John Stevenson, *British Society 1914–45* (London: Allen Lane, 1984), p. 177.
41 'Let's be frank about it; most of our people have never had it so good. Go around the country and you will see a state of prosperity such as we have never had in my lifetime.' (Prime Minister Harold Macmillan, *Political Speech, 20.7.1957*)
42 Patrick Sawer, 'Naughty Children? Blame Mothers, Says Oliver James', *Telegraph* 22 May 2010, http://www.telegraph.co.uk/women/mother-tongue/7752644/Naughty-children-Blame-mothers-says-Oliver-James.html [accessed 6 December 2013].
43 Mumsnet is currently the most influential online parental contact network.
44 Mumsnet Forum Post (22 May 2010), www.mumsnet.com/LutyensCBA [accessed 6 December 2013].
45 Julie MacLeavy, 'A "new politics" of Austerity, Workfare and Gender? The UK Coalition Government's Welfare Reform Proposals'. *Cambridge Journal of Regions, Economy and Society* 4:1 (November 2011), pp. 289–302, p. 356.
46 Jacqueline Wilson, *The Worst Thing About My Sister* (London: Doubleday, 2012), p. 14.
47 Ibid., p. 18.
48 Ibid., p. 106.
49 Jacqueline Wilson, *Clean Break* (London: Doubleday 2005), p. 95.
50 Ibid., p. 95.
51 Ibid., p. 200.
52 For example: the 1967 Abortion Act decriminalised abortion; the 1970 Equal Pay Act changed the legal position of women in the workplace; contraception became available in the NHS in 1974; the 1975 Sex Discrimination Act extended legal protection beyond employment to the provision of goods, services and housing; the Equal Opportunities Commission was established to fight cases of gender discrimination; the 1975 Employment Protection Act made it illegal to force pregnant women to leave work.
53 Peter Hollindale, 'Ideology and the Children's Book', p. 12.
54 Jacqueline Wilson, *Midnight* (London: Random House, 2003), p. 127. Note the adjectival use of the female pronoun rather than the definite article in this quotation. No bold in original text.

55 Source: ONS, Census 2011 & Labour Force Survey 2012: Social Trends Archive.

56 It was, for example, allegedly as a response to politician Ann Widdecombe's criticism of the acclaimed *The Illustrated Mum* (on the basis that the two sisters have different fathers) that Wilson decided to write *The Diamond Girls*, depicting a family with five siblings who have five different fathers. Achokablog, 'Tory Slates Illustrated Mum'. *Achuka* (1 January 2004), http://www.achuka.co.uk/achockablog/archives/2004/01/tory-slates-ill. html [Accessed 18 December 2013].

57 Jacqueline Wilson, 'I Was a Girl for Gritty Realism', *Guardian* 24 February 2007, p. 3.

58 Although this does translate to over 400,000 families – 13.5 per cent of all single-parent families. (Source: ONS, UK Fatherhood Statistics 2012).

59 Again, a realistic pattern according to a recent study; one in ten fathers do not live with their children and 13 per cent of fathers never see the children they do not live with. (Source: Economic & Social Research Council, *Fathers, Work and Families in 21st Century Britain: Beyond the Breadwinner Model?* 2013).

60 Judy Dunn and Richard Layard, *A Good Childhood: Searching for Values in a Competitive Age* (London: Penguin, 2009), p. 18.

61 Jacqueline Wilson, *Clean Break*, p. 4.

62 Ibid., p. 288 (My emphasis).

63 Helen Limon discusses how this dynamic is deployed in *The Illustrated Mum* in Chapter 5 of this volume.

64 Ibid., pp. 135–136.

65 Ibid., p. 137.

66 Ibid., p. 296.

67 Ibid., p. 10, p. 290.

68 Ibid., p. 1, p. 302.

69 Gerry, the highly successful businessman father in *Cookie* (2008), is a notable exception.

70 Jacqueline Wilson, *Candyfloss*, p. 219, p. 75.

71 Self-published submission to the Labour Policy Review.

72 Jacqueline Wilson, *Lola Rose* (London: Doubleday, 2003), p. 188, p. 15.

73 Ibid., p. 15.

74 Ibid., p. 49.

75 Maurice Sendak's famous picture book – a typical Wilson metafictive device.

76 Jacqueline Wilson, *Clean Break*, p. 3.

77 Ibid., p. 73.

78 Ibid., p. 168.

79 Her stories for younger readers occasionally utilise a male narrative voice.

80 Julia Kristeva, *Powers of Horror: An Essay on Abjection* (New York: Columbia University Press, 1982), p. 172. My emphasis.

81 Ibid., p. 270.

82 Jacqueline Wilson, *Lola Rose*, p. 120.

83 Jacqueline Wilson, *Cookie*, p. 81.

84 Ibid., p. 222.

85 Beverley Pennell, 'Redeeming Masculinity at the End of the Second Millennium: Narrative Reconfigurations of Masculinity in Children's Fiction' in John Stephens (ed.), *Ways of Being Male: Representing Masculinities in Children's Literature and Film* (London: Routledge, 2002), p. 57.

86 Literally, 'control over bodies': philosopher and social theorist Michel Foucault's term for managing groups of people.

87 Jacqueline Wilson, *Lola Rose*, p. 30.

88 Jacqueline Wilson, *Cookie*, p. 256.

89 Ibid., p. 303.

90 Jacqueline Wilson, *Clean Break*, p. 295.

91 Reading and interest ages recommended on www.booktrust.org.uk. However, as reader comments on her website demonstrate, Wilson is also read and enjoyed by many younger and older readers.

92 Jacqueline Wilson, *Cookie*, pp. 96–97.

93 Ibid., p. 97.

94 Jacqueline Wilson, *Lola Rose*. pp. 21–22.

95 Ibid., p. 251.

96 Sheila A. Egoff, *Thursday's Child: Trends and Patterns in Contemporary Children's Literature* (Chicago: American Library Association, 1981), p. 31, p. 53.

97 John Stephens, *Language and Ideology in Children's Fiction*, p. 242.

98 Most famously explored in Susan Faludi's book *Backlash: The Undeclared War Against American Women* (New York: Doubleday, 1991). See also Elizabeth Wilson, *Only Halfway to Paradise: Women in Postwar Britain: 1945–1968* (London: Tavistock Publications, 1980).

99 Lissa Paul, *Reading Otherways* (Stroud: Thimble Press, 1998), p. 20.

100 Roberta Trites, *Waking Sleeping Beauty: Feminist Voices in Children's Novels* (Iowa City: University of Iowa Press, 1997), p. 6.

101 Ibid., p. 9.

102 Pink predominates in Nick Sharratt's cover illustrations for *Lola Rose*, *Clean Break*, *Candyfloss*, *Cookie* and *The Worst Thing About My Sister*; an artistic decision that is as likely to be influenced by marketing factors as by ideology.

103 A minimum of two books per year since 2000.

104 Peter Hollindale, 'Ideology and the Children's Book', p. 15.

105 Frederic Jameson, 'Cognitive Mapping' in Carey Nelson and Lawrence Grossberg (eds.), *Marxism and the Interpretation of Culture* (Chicago: University of Illinois Press, 1988), pp. 347–357.

106 Kerry Mallan, *Gender Dilemmas in Children's Fiction* (Basingstoke: Palgrave Macmillan, 2009), p. 197.

107 Mitzi Myers, 'Missed Opportunities and Critical Malpractice', p. 42.

5

The Illuminated Mums: Child/ Primary Carer Relationships in the Fiction of Jacqueline Wilson

Helen Limon

In an article published in the *Observer* magazine in March 2014, timed to coincide with a national exhibition about her work and life, Jacqueline Wilson describes her childhood with parents who 'weren't cruel, but it wasn't a cosy, happy family' as being a 'wonderful environment for the writer who wants to write the sort of books I do'.[1] From her account, Wilson's post-war childhood was unhappy in an apparently conventional way. However, she is particularly well known for her portrayals of unconventional families, and the books she has written validate the experiences of children from many different backgrounds including those from 'functional' nuclear families, like her own, and those from a kaleidoscope of non-traditional 'dysfunctional' families. While her books draw on a range of relationships between children and their parents, Wilson is most attentive to the relationships between children and their, often single, mothers, and while she is careful not to put forward the view that non-traditional means incomplete, many of Wilson's juvenile characters struggle with their desire to make good the gaps in their experience of nurturant primary care by their birth mothers. Taking in the span of her work, it is clear that mothers and mothering is a focus for Wilson and it is the subject of this chapter. Wilson, a mother herself, is respected for her capacity to portray incomplete mothering with compassion and to illuminate the difficulties these child characters experience with their maturation because of this. What is notable in Wilson's writing is that her novels allow birth mothers to fail and demonstrate that when this failure is irrevocable, the children are able to find good enough primary care elsewhere: despite the poor start experienced by these children, her stories are optimistic in as much as, in extremis, the children, and the mothers, do find nurturant care from the wider community, including schools, other parents, other children and from the local authorities.

In this chapter I offer the view that in two key texts, *The Illustrated Mum* (1999)[2] and *Dustbin Baby* (2001)[3], Wilson's children experience forms of 'distributed' mothering. They show that struggle and ambivalence is a normal characteristic of child–primary carer relationships and for the most part well within the capacities of the child and the adult to manage. They show the experience of child–carer relationships as transformative – a practice that requires hard work and dedication – rather than the automatic outcome of being or having a mother, and that incomplete mothering need not prevent the child from being able to mother at least well enough in the future. Through these texts young readers are encouraged to understand that not everyone is able to provide nurturant care for a child, but that when (birth) mothering fails, there are often others who are willing and able to intervene: protecting children is the responsibility of wider social groups than those bound by blood. There is a communal, collective responsibility to ensure that children are cared for and an understanding that failure of mothering is damaging.

Writing in the 1950s, paediatrician and psychoanalyst Donald Winnicott encouraged women not to attempt to be 'ideal' mothers, attempting to anticipate and meet their children's every need. Instead he valued the 'good-enough' mother which he characterised as one who, by using her imagination and common sense, maintains a safe, playful and creative holding environment in which the child comes to understand itself and others as autonomous beings. For Winnicott, good-enough mothering in early childhood gives the child a stock of psychic well-being that will be drawn on all through its life.[4] By this he means that the experience of good-enough mothering makes children less vulnerable to psychic distress and gives them embedded resources to deal with painful experiences, including the fear and guilt associated with separation, later in their lives.

The notion that good-enough mothering ensures a 'stock of psychic well-being' is a feature also found in more recent writing about baby care such as in the work of Sue Gerhardt, who argues that there is a direct link between what she regards as a dysfunctional capitalist society and the quality of care experienced by generations of children during their early years. She suggests that the powerful and negative consequences of incomplete mothering have significant and enduring consequences for society, and that it is 'important to understand these connections between our infancies and the kind of world we create'.[5] Gerhardt sees poor care in childhood as the *cause* of a greedy and selfish society, while Winnicott draws a direct line between incomplete mothering and delinquency (what he called the anti-social tendency).[6] Winnicott argues that if antisocial behaviour is not transformed by the completion of emotional development through some sort of suitable 'home substitute', 'they [the young person] will force us [meaning society] later to provide stability in the shape of an approved school, or, in the last resort, four walls in the shape of a prison cell'.[7] Some of the issues of delinquency are explored by Wilson. For example, in *Dustbin Baby* and *Bad Girls* (1996) with its shoplifting protagonist Tayna who appears in both texts, the idea of incomplete mothering leading to criminality is offered and the necessity for society to provide 'home substitutes' is played out with understanding and compassion.

Wilson is also striking for her portrayal of families who do not fit the model of the 'good' middle-class family: Sue Diamond in *Diamond Girls* (2007), for example, relies on benefits and feeds her children junk food, and the mother in *Lily Alone* (2011) is a teenage single parent who leaves her children in order to go out clubbing. Contemporary political and social comment such as the work of Owen Jones suggests that such families are an enduring subject of unpleasant populist cari-cature. He argues that the personification of the 'Chav' mother as one who sees pregnancy as a career option and 'pasty-faced, lard-gutted slappers who'll drop their knickers at the blink of an eye' vilifies the sort of vulnerable working-class mothers that Wilson portrays in a way that would be completely unacceptable were they from another social or cultural group.[8]

Winnicott and Gerhardt represent dominant theories about motherhood by concentrating on mothering by women, specifi-cally birth mothers, but as Elizabeth Thiel explores in her work on 'transnormative' families, children's literature has long portrayed nur-turant primary care by those other than birth mothers or even human females.[9] Nancy Chodorow, whose *The Reproduction of Mothering* (1978) added a political and feminist rationale to this premise, called for a completely new approach to thinking about what mother-ing is, who does it and whether changing mothering was central to changing culture.[10] It was she who initially sought to replace the term 'mother' with 'primary carer'. *The Reproduction of Mothering* argues that mothering by women, associated as it is with intense and exclusive nurturing, is problematically constructed. In it Chodorow questions why this model of mothering as a psychological role requir-ing specific relational capacities associated with women has been reproduced over generations. She concludes that people create and recreate aspects of their earliest relationships and therefore 'people's experience of their early relationship to their mothers provides a foundation for expectations of women as mothers'.[11]

The profoundly damaging and avoidable consequences of what for some women are unrealistic expectations of their capacities to mother well enough is explored in the work of psychiatrist Estella Welldon. In *Mother, Madonna, Whore: The Idealization and Denigration of Motherhood* (1988) Welldon argues that the reproduction of mothering can encompass the reproduction of perverse mothering with the adult woman turning her infantile fear into violence against someone weaker such as the woman's own child.[12] With great compassion Welldon calls for social policy that neither idealises nor denigrates motherhood but instead locates it at the centre of human difficulty. Wilson's work encompasses both the self-destructive and the violent mother. For example, her portrayal of the seemingly perfect, 'fairy story' mother of Dixie's friend Mary in *Diamond Girls* illuminates the effect of post-natal depression on a woman who despite having many of the socio-economic benefits that the Diamond family lack is abusive to her daughter.

In *Dustbin Baby*, a newborn baby girl is found abandoned in a dustbin behind a pizza restaurant, on the first of April. 'Dustbin Baby', as she is called in the press, is rescued by a 17-year-old boy, Frankie, and handed over to social workers who name her April. The book begins with April being fostered by a single woman, Marion, who is a retired teacher. Marion is not April's first foster mother and as a consequence of her fragmented history, April lacks a sense of who she is in the world. She dreams of finding her birth mother, believing that this will provide her with a sense of identity and stabilise her life. In this book, formal surrogate arrangements – Winnicott's 'suitable home substitute' – are put in place by official institutions because the child's mother has decided not to look after her, and so, in Winnicott's terms she has had her mothering 'interrupted' and has suffered a failure in her environment. The fact that she needs to have her biological mother replaced means that this novel belongs to the significant category of Wilson's stories that feature abandoned children who have been deprived of a stable home life. In this text the child protagonist, April, struggles with her sense of self and expresses concern that she is not quite 'real': 'I'm like an actress. I've had to play lots and lots of parts. Sometimes I'm not sure if there's any real me left. No, the real me is *this* me, funny little April Showers, fourteen years old. Today' (p. 10). While she is no longer an infant, this text illuminates Winnicott's contention that the sense of personal existence derives from caring and that 'if maternal care is not good enough, then the infant does not really come into existence, since there is no continuity of being'.[13] As Bruno Bettelheim explains, stories about abandonment arouse strong emotional responses in children because there 'is no greater fear in life than we will be deserted, left all alone'.[14] In these stories fear of desertion is closely linked to ambivalence because the longing for the one who has abandoned them is matched by the hurt and anger felt about being rejected. There is often, however, a particular kind of anxiety about ambivalent feelings towards a second or surrogate primary carer; having been rejected by the first carer the possibility of rejection is very real. Until she encounters Marion, and only after Marion's retirement from teaching, April has been 'rejected' by a series of surrogates starting with her abandonment by her birth mother. While the circumstances of the rejections, which include suicide, are different these surrogates have all failed to provide the continuity of care the child needs to develop a robust sense of identity. As well as difficulty in accepting and trusting a surrogate carer, this story addresses an often unexpressed anxiety that the children at the centre of the narrative may share their birth mothers' failings. Such fears are well founded: as Chodorow explains, the skills and attributes of mothering/primary caring tend to be reproduced unless effective interventions interrupt cycles of failed relationships.

Replacement primary carers arising from abandonment or other kinds of failed mothering occur frequently in children's literature, from traditional tales to recent novels such as the ones discussed in this chapter.[15] Such texts encourage readers to explore feelings and issues of abandonment and the development of a sense of identity They also introduce a diverse range of alternative primary carers, all of whom provide the kind of safe and stable holding environments that Winnicott described as being the role of both the mother and the therapist in meeting neglected developmental needs. Focusing for the moment on progression and regression, however, it is notable that in *Dustbin Baby* it is April's reflective journey through her childhood (a kind of regression into a psychic space) that allows her to move forward. Real and psychic transitional environments (what Winnicott called the 'place where the secret is') provides April with the support she needs to manage her transition to autonomy and so helps bring into being the moment when adolescent ambivalence is transformed into a new, mature and mutually more satisfying relationship between mother/primary carer and child.[16]

That April believes her current relationship to be dysfunctional is made clear at the start of the book when, on her 14th birthday, she is disappointed at receiving a gift of earrings rather than the hoped-for mobile phone. Marion's hostility towards phones as 'an absolutely outrageous invention' and her apparent lack of understanding about April's desire to have what her friends have, and not feel left out, provokes an outburst of anger: 'Doesn't she want me to keep in touch with everyone? Maybe she wants me all to herself. Well, I don't want her.' (p. 16) Failures in April's infancy are still unresolved, so on this day another failure (the earrings) triggers feelings of not existing. Resentfully April truants from school and makes a tour of all the foster homes she has lived in. April's primary care has been undertaken by a number of women, and April believes that if she revisits these people and places from her past she will also somehow locate herself in the present. April is in search of what might be described in Winnicott's terms as her 'True Self' or the source of what is 'authentic in a person', and she believes that this can be given to her only by her mother.[17] Her truanting is a necessary regression for her return to a past or infant state which allows a release from an arrested state of development. In running away, she is rejecting Marion, who she cannot call 'mum' and who gets things like birthday presents and packed lunches 'wrong'. April feels guilty about her hostile feelings towards Marion, but justifies these on the grounds that Marion is not her *real* mother. This suggests that April idealises mothering, believing that her *real* mother would be more responsive to her wishes and not provoke negative emotions.

April believes that only her birth mother can truly identify her: 'I think about me. I don't know how to be me when I'm by myself. I don't know who I am. There's only one person who can tell me and she's got no way of getting in touch.'(p. 17) Although April formulates this thought, it is in fact Marion who insists that April should be given access to her personal file, on the grounds that it is her basic moral right to learn about her past. (40) April's 'mothering' has not been good enough in Winnicott's terms because it has not yet given April a sense of where the boundaries between 'me and not me' lie. By giving her the file, Marion does what she can to give April a sense of her identity, but April feels herself to be like a cut-out doll, staying the same basic shape but being coloured in differently with each change of home. The analogy suggests that April's sense that her nurturant care has been incomplete is preventing her from feeling coherent and real. This block is dismantled in the course of the novel, for gradually it becomes clear that she *has* been cared for in as much as her cognitive and emotional growth has been supported by loving engagement with imperfect others (though not in all cases successfully), and she *does* have the capacity to move forward as a mature and coherent young woman.

With the help of the information in the file, April goes in search of the people who have done the 'colouring in' over the years to retrieve or reclaim a dimension she believes has been missing. When she arrives at the first home, however, her first foster mother, Pat, does not remember April until she is reminded that April was the 'dustbin baby' who cried a lot. This signals the extent of Pat's mothering and, unsatisfied with this encounter, April moves on. After her time with Pat, April was adopted by a married couple. Their relationship is not happy, 'there were lots of lumps in our relationship', and April signals her adoptive mother's unease with her physicality: 'She never hugged me tight or whirled me around or lumped me about on her hip. She'd sit me on her lap occasionally when I cried but she was as tense as a spring underneath her soft slippery skirt, and I soon slid off of my own accord' (p. 59). When her adoptive father leaves, her mother's confidence slips further. 'She said she was a useless mother [...] and I'd be better off without her too' (p. 65). Her failure to fulfil the mothering ideal is shown by Wilson to be self-destructive; in as much as not living up to it causes her to end her mothering role by ending her life. While April wanted to have 'Mummy' all to herself, she now suspects that she was only adopted to help Mummy to keep 'Daddy'; when that failed and 'Mummy' committed suicide April was returned to care. In this text good-enough primary care appears to be unable to encompass a competing sexual relationship which takes attention from the child.

Revisiting the children's home where she was placed next, April is happy to see that Gina — a former resident who led April into criminal activity — is now one of the counsellors. Gina has evidently been helped by the provision of a suitable home-substitute, just as Winnicott suggested is possible through the provision of appropriate institutions which provide a 'strong stable environment with personal care and love and gradually increasing doses of freedom'.[18] Seeing Gina with her own baby, April's conscience begins to prick her and she considers phoning Marion, who she knows will be worried. She unconsciously associates Gina's attentive and loving mothering with Marion's care for her. However, she does not call, rationalising this again as Marion's fault for not buying her the mobile phone she wanted for her birthday. April feels entitled to punish Marion for failing to 'mother' her on her terms and in an idealised way.

April recalls that it was at her next home, Fairleigh, that she met Marion, who was her history teacher. Deciding not to revisit Fairleigh, April describes the school as a place where she 'felt as if someone had stuck a pair of strong spectacles on my nose. I could see straight at last.' The decision not to return seems to be informed by her largely comforting and vivid memories of the transformative experience it offered. Instead of a physical return, she reflects on her education and her full and stable life with Marion. While not yet ready to acknowledge her as 'mum', she does acknowledge that Marion's attentive concern for her makes her 'almost as good as a real mother' (p. 141). She thinks about her birth mother and what she might be doing now. She considers the difference between Marion, who has fulfilled the role of primary carer, 'a mum', who she knows cares about her and who she misses, and her vision of her 'real mum', who left her in the bin. April questions her assumptions about the relative significance of these two women and her investment in an idealised mother she thought she must find in order to feel secure in herself. The text encourages readers to realise along with April that Marion's imperfections and her ambivalent feelings towards her are a normal part of good-enough mothering and not a 'problem to be solved'. By moving beyond her romantic notion of mothering, April is able to experience the benefits of the good-enough mothering Marion has provided. The acknowledgement of ambivalence as normal indicates maturation in the child and a transformation in the child–carer relationship.

There is only one place left for April to visit on her journey of self-discovery; she makes her way back to the pizza restaurant where she was found and there discovers a message written on the bin with a phone number. The number belongs to Frankie, the boy who first found her and who is now married with children of his own. At his urging she calls Marion, realising that both Frankie and Marion are, in their own ways, truly attentive to her, truly care about her and that they are 'family'. This gives her a secure enough identity to be confident to accept that her birth mother has not been the 'real' mother of her imagination. She is able to project herself into the future and see herself as a good caring person who will be able to mother differently. Her mothering will be reproduced, but it will be the good-enough mothering which she has received from Marion that she passes on, rather than the incomplete mothering she experienced from her birth mother or the ideal mothering which she has been unfairly measuring Marion against. This is the sense of self she has been searching for: she has stopped treading water looking for her 'real' mum and now she has the new beginning, the normality, she craved.

Learning to value and accept her mothering relationship with Marion stabilises April. Significantly, Marion is not presented in terms of a sentimental ideal: she makes mistakes that April exaggerates. More importantly, however, she gets the right things right and, in accepting her own ambivalence and Marion's good-enough mothering, April has found a person who enables her to locate and identify herself in relation to others. April has been fearful that her abandonment has defined her life, forever depriving her of an authentic identity, 'normality' and the ability to mother. In this optimistic text, Wilson stresses the agency of the child and the manageability of ambivalence so that April's search ends when she realises she *is* being mothered, and the fact that it is by a surrogate rather than her biological mother does not negate the fact that she is loved, and that she has the capacity and the desire to love back. The dominant message in *Dustbin Baby* is that sometimes children have to be helped to recognise when good-enough mothering is taking place and to feel confident in the relationship. With its richly drawn and compassionate portrayal of April's life it also functions to assist readers towards this realisation. Beneath the surface of the story is a very conventional belief that unlike the failed mothers represented by Pat and 'Mummy', good-enough mothers do not divide their attention between a child and a partner but concentrate on the needs of the child. It is not insignificant that Marion is a single woman.

Dustbin Baby, which shows surrogate primary care being undertaken by women who are not the child's birth mother, demonstrates to young readers that it is possible to recover from abandonment and interrupted mothering and that ambivalence need not be fearful or damaging. April experiences the feeling of being 'unreal'. As Freud observed, most children go through a stage of rejecting their parents and this text shows that this is normal and that most people come through this phase with their relationship changed but still intact. But, they also show that taking on the role of primary carer is demanding and that growing up is partly facilitated by recognising this and being less absorbed with the self and learning to empathise with others starting with the primary carer.

While *Dustbin Baby* was concerned with abandonment, ambivalence and the reproduction of mothering over generations, in *The Illustrated Mum* the nurturant care the two young sisters provide gives rise to fears about the loss of childhood and consequent conflicted feelings about their new role. In this text, the girls who intermittently have to care for their bipolar mother are young, and consequently the challenges of their episodes of caring work differently for them and their mother:

> 'You've been drinking', Star said coldly, though Marigold's voice wasn't really slurred. 'Dol, you should go to bed.'
>   Marigold giggled. 'It's like you're the mummy, Star. Should I go to bed too?' (p. 45)

Marigold, the illustrated mother of the title, is having her birthday celebrated by her two daughters, Star and Dolphin. They are trying hard to accommodate her mercurial moods and spontaneous urges for yet another tattoo but, despite their best efforts, the morning ends in disharmony. Marigold gets her new tattoo and stays out all night celebrating at the pub. The two girls comfort one another and protect themselves from unwelcome external interference by preparing to disguise their distress. Nevertheless, they are fearful of being taken into care because of Marigold's stories about her own childhood. While they wait they talk about their mother; while the younger Dolphin remembers the fun her mother's behaviour can generate, her older sister has darker memories.

> We ate Cornettos and Mars and Soleros and Magnums, one after another, and then when they all started to melt Star mixed them all up in washing up bowl and said it was ice-cream soup.
>   'We lived on stale bread and carrots all the rest of that week because she'd spent all the Giro', said Star. (p. 39)

Star equates mothering with the provision of good, nourishing food rather than childish treats like ice-cream. The role of food as a typical marker of the 'good' family in children's literature is explored by Ann Alston and Wilson uses it in this text and others such as, for example, Marion's provision of breakfast in bed for April's birthday, the home-cooked meals of the 'good' family in *Bad Girls* and the randomly timed take-away meals eaten by the children in *Diamond Girls*.[19] Star is impatient with Marigold, whose brain she knows is 'wired a different way from other people's' (p. 40). Marigold will not seek help and Star, who believes this unwillingness to get treatment means she does not love them, is struggling to cope with caring for both her mother and her sister. She works hard at school because she sees this as the way to escape her material situation, which she recognises as both inadequate and the best her mother will ever be able to provide. For the younger Dolphin, the need for connection to her mother is more pressing than autonomy. She mourns the loss of toys and teddies forgotten, repossessed and abandoned because of the family's nomadic existence. These elusive transitional objects 'scooped up in a rubbish cart and spewed out on some awful rubbish dump' symbolise the fragility of her hold on Marigold and her mothering (p. 84). However, on occasion, Dolphin is able to confide in her mother, who comforts and reassures her: 'She pulled me on her lap and rocked me as if I was a big towel baby' (p. 44).

On a walk initiated by Dolphin to distract her mother from using a new credit card, Marigold asks for reassurance about her mothering and gets it from Dolphin. Her favourite fairy story, in a book Marigold assumes she stole from the library, is *Hansel and Gretel*, about children lost together in the woods. The work of Bettelheim suggests this is a text Marigold may have been particularly drawn to in her own childhood because it reflects her psychic pain. Marigold promises Dolphin that despite the bad things she has done she will never leave them. In an episode that illustrates what Bettelheim describes as the immature oral fixation at the centre of *Hansel and Gretel*, Mother and daughter make a house together from the pieces of cake Marigold has brought to feed the ducks. Marigold confides in Dolphin about her own lack of mothering.

'I *had* a mother, She just didn't want me. I didn't care though. Know what I really did want?' Marigold looked at me, her green eyes very bright. 'A sister. I was desperate for a sister. That's why I'm so glad you and Star have each other.'
'And we've got you too. You're like our big sister', I said. (p. 57)

Marigold desires to provide something her own mothering lacked, but instead of offering the nurturant care and attentive love she has missed and establishing herself as a mother, able to provide a stable family environment and caring behaviour, she transfers her role to that of a sister and so requires her daughter to care for her. This text works as a fictional illustration for children of Chodorow's theory that without the intervention of other sources of good mothering, interrupted, failed mothering will be replicated over generations of daughters.

Despite the symbolic house-building and assurances that she will not leave them, Marigold is spinning away from her daughters, and Dolphin, who is bullied at school, looks for a place of refuge. She finds it in the school library with its 'giant teddy bear', librarian, and a new friend, the gentle Oliver, who has mother troubles of his own (p. 67). The reappearance of Star's father, Mickey, in Marigold's life precipitates a crisis. Mickey is much more interested in parenting Star than partnering Marigold, and he makes it clear that he is not going to resume their relationship. Seeing this as a chance for escape, Star plans to take Dolphin to Brighton with her to be with her father, leaving Marigold behind.

Star's ambivalence towards her mother causes her pain and confusion as her fears of being unable to 'escape' from Marigold are matched by her feelings of love and responsibility towards both her mother and her sister. With her father's prompting, Star openly questions Marigold's ability to care for her and her sister and expresses her unwillingness to continue to care for Dolphin herself: 'Why should I always have to look after you?' (p. 120). Because the roles of mother and sister are conflated, this is more traumatic for Star and positions her as being able to meet either her own or Marigold's needs, but not both. Her dilemma becomes more acute when Dolphin will not leave her mother and is angry with Star for abandoning them. Star is now 'torn in two' – precisely the way Parker describes the sensation of ongoing maternal ambivalence – and she chooses to meet her own needs for support.[20] Although at one level this signals a failure of care for Marigold and Dolphin, by deciding to care for herself she sets in motion changes that eventually benefit all the members of her family and restore Dolphin and Star to their proper condition as children. The transformation is not easy or immediate, however, and Star's abnegation briefly transfers the responsibility of carer to Dolphin. After an exhausting day of searching for Star, Marigold begins to collapse; to keep her going until they can reach home, Dolphin decides to play the game of mothering that Marigold likes: '"Yes, I'm the mum and you're my little girl Marigold. Dear, dear, you've got yourself in such a silly state, darling. Let mummy wipe your nose again", I said. "Now come along with me, there's a good girl. I'll tell you a story as we go, right, precious?"' (p. 114). In this situation, playing mother is not just a game. With Dolphin's assumption of authority over their journey home, there is a definite change in the relationship between them: Dolphin's enactment of mothering calms Marigold. But while this mothering is comforting, it is neither sustainable nor transformational; mother and child are incapable of restoring their equilibrium.

Star's absence precipitates a breakdown in Marigold which Dolphin realises she is not able to manage by herself. Despite knowing Marigold's fear of hospitals, Dolphin calls an ambulance and Marigold is taken into hospital. After Marigold is admitted to hospital Dolphin is, as she feared, left alone. It is her friend, Oliver – another child carer – who helps her now. They track down Dolphin's father who begins the official process of having her looked after, conveying that this is a right children can expect to demand from those linked to them by blood ties; however, the rights and responsibilities of blood ties in relation to care are shown to be far from simple or automatic. Dolphin's father, who has other children and who is apparently much less self-interested in his unofficial daughter than is Star's father, manages her care in collaboration with the social services. Dolphin goes to a foster home while Marigold is being treated. Counting Star, Dolphin's foster mother is Dolphin's third experience of being looked after but her first experience of the kind of stable home life and caring behaviour that Winnicott would regard as good enough.

In contrast to Marigold's childhood experience and Dolphin's fears, she finds her foster mother, Aunty Jane, to be a kindly woman whose house is filled with good food, plentiful hot water and nurturing symbolised by the presence of happy babies who Dolphin is able to help care for, so showing her strongly developed nurturing capacity. This reinforces the idea that figures other than the birth mother – and especially the state – can provide mothering. Being fostered is pleasant and reassuring for Dolphin, and when Star arrives to join her she guards the relationship jealously: 'What makes you think you've got the right to barge in here? This is *my* foster home, not yours. I had to get it all sorted out because you left me' (p. 217). Dolphin seems to be expressing a desire to punish Star for letting her down similar to that which April expressed toward Marion in *Dustbin Baby*, but she is also acting out normal sibling rivalry indicating that they are now both children rather than mother and daughter.

The emotional and physical cost of mothering/primary caring has been well recognised by therapists such as Winnicott, who describes the job of parenting into adolescence as 'the long tussle which you will need to survive', and theorists such as Chodorow and Welldon, who see the dilemmas and consequent unhappiness of mothering being passed on from one generation of women to the next.[21] This 'passing on' is explored towards the end of *The Illustrated Mum* when Marigold reveals her own problematic and incomplete mothering and her desire for a different, sisterly rather than motherly, relationship with her own children. One of the interesting things that Wilson shows in these two texts is that 'good-enough' mothering as the *only* good mothering suggests that the idea of a 'perfect' mother is actively harmful – April is measuring Marion against a perceived ideal which is unattainable, and Marigold is measuring herself against a similar ideal which – because it is completely unattainable – discourages her from trying to address the genuine problems with her mothering, since she assumes she would have to become a completely different person.

The relationship between failed mothering/primary caring and the mental illness of the mother/carer was a feature of *Dustbin Baby*, which showed depression leading to the suicide of April's first adoptive carer. Jacqueline Wilson presents this woman's depression as a process of withdrawal – a kind of abandonment – which plays out in her growing inability to keep April safe and which positions the child as an overwhelming burden. The notion of children as burdens is not new; for instance, it occurs in many fairy tales, most clearly in a story such as *Hansel and Gretel*. The theme of longed-for-yet-burdensome children – another source of a carer's ambivalence – is explored in the work of teacher Carolyn Steedman, whose *The Tidy House* (1982) exposes mythologies about working-class mothering through an analysis of the creative writing of young girls as they explore their notions of what mothering means and the conflicted emotions they anticipate they will experience when they come to mother.[22]

Analysing the children's response to Carl, the fictional child they created and imagined raising, Steedman asserts, 'They understood the desire for babies, their pretty talk, their funny ways, but they knew at the same time their mother's deep ambivalence about their presence. The irritation of Carl's presence was a representation of the difficulties they knew they presented to their own mothers.'[23] Steedman's research clearly shows that even at a young age children are aware that a portrayal of primary care which ignores the emotional burdens it can bring only represents the sentimental ideal – love of babies' pretty talk and funny ways. The rest of this chapter explores how far this understanding can be drawn upon when roles are reversed and children find themselves in the position of caring for parents. Although there are benefits from assuming a caring role, the importance of ensuring that this is a temporary reversal of roles is underlined in Wilson's books through the responses of other characters to what they see as the inappropriate burden that caring places on a child.

While there are many stories in which children 'have prematurely exposed themselves to experiences for which they are not ready' this tends to be portrayed as a consequence of leaving home rather than as a consequence of remaining within the family.[24] The view that childhood is a distinct phase with its own needs, and that children as carers miss out on important aspects of childhood, is enshrined in legislation such as the Children's Act (1989) and the UN Convention on the Rights of the Child (1990). But alongside a disquiet which drives the growth of support services for young carers, there is also an acknowledgement, echoed in this text, that caring has the potential to bring out desirable qualities in young people. Findings in two reports by the Joseph Rowntree Foundation stress that 'Young carers matured quickly and gained practical skills that aided independence' and that 'the positive impacts [of caring] included maturity, responsibility, life skills, and a close and loving relationship with parents'.[25] Described in this way, the benefits of the caring undertaken by these young people include many of the outcomes of Winnicott's good-enough mothering. However, Winnicott was very clear that in taking on responsibility too soon the child, specifically the unhappy adolescent who becomes the 'establishment', loses 'all the imaginative activity and striving of immaturity'.[26] Wilson's portrayal of Dolphin conforms to this assessment. When her mother is in hospital and after she has settled in her foster home with kindly Aunty Jane and her family of babies, Dolphin is given a star at school (her first) for her piece of imaginative writing, signifying that her ability to relinquish a caring role has given her access to a more productive imaginative space.

The Illustrated Mum explores what may happen when gaps in nurturing are too big, and illustrates the diversity and distribution of sources which may fill those gaps and through which healing may come. It also portrays fractured and unreliable nurturing, when mothering becomes a game of pass the parcel between people who are unable to mother adequately over an extended period. In this way Wilson's text suggests that children should not be expected to take on caring responsibilities which are beyond their capacity or inappropriate for their age. *The Illustrated Mum* also helps readers understand the need for the kind of support provided by professionals such as D. W. Winnicott and Welldon, who helped not just children but those mothers who struggled with mental health issues associated with the work involved in caring for children.[27] Additionally, it reassures children that they are not expected permanently to take on the role of carer and that others, including the state, have a responsibility to look after vulnerable people like Star, Dolphin and Marigold.

As the book comes to a close, Marigold has a moment of insight into her own mothering and there is recognition that chimes with Chodorow's theories about the way mothering is reproduced, '…in the end I blurted out all sorts of ugly things about my mother and all she's done to me and how I hated her. Then I realised, I'm the same. I've done some of the same stuff to you two. You must both hate me' (p. 222). But they do not hate her. They have experienced ambivalent feelings both in caring for Marigold and being looked after by her. Their hate has been matched by love, and managing this ambivalence has brought positive changes to all their lives. Their sense of self-hood through connection to others undergoes huge transformations in the course of the novel. In being able to care for Marigold well enough and for long enough, they have found care in a greatly expanded network of others including their fathers, school, friends and social welfare organisations. Between them a diverse group of 'imperfect others', including Marigold, will keep attentive love present and visible in their lives. The cycle of incomplete mothering has been interrupted.

As these examples show, Wilson explores issues around child–primary carer relationships for child readers in ways that make many of the same points about ambivalence, gender roles and social attitudes explored by the theorists who have studied such relationships from the perspective of adult carers. There is a considerable body of work for adults about mothering and caring for children which ranges from serious academic studies to popular manuals. By contrast, children's primary source of information about relationships is stories. Wilson has done a valuable job in showing both that biological connection does not guarantee that someone will make a good primary carer and that there are many possible sources of nurturant care. The books discussed here are just two of a number of the many works by Wilson that have provided reassuring messages to children about who and how they may be cared for. They also show that the ideal of perfect mothering is both unattainable and harmful to those doing the mothering. They are equally representative of another important message frequently found in Wilson's writing for children: that carer–child relationships are not always perfect and that both child and carers will feel a mixture of emotions about caring and being cared for. The depictions of the child–carer relationship in these two texts are just some of the many ways Wilson's books may help child readers to think about their rights and needs in relation to their care and to understand the sometimes volatile relationship between those who are primary carers and those who are being cared for.

Notes

1 Rachel Cooke, 'The Story of Jacqueline Wilson', *The Observer Magazine* 23 March 2014, p. 14.

2 Jacqueline Wilson, *The Illustrated Mum* (London: Corgi Yearling, 2007).

3 Jacqueline Wilson, *Dustbin Baby* (London: Corgi, 2002).

4 Carol Mavor, *Reading Boyishly* (Durham, London: Duke University Press, 2007), p. 62.

5 Sue Gerhardt, *The Selfish Society: How We All Forgot to Love One Another and Made Money Instead* (London: Simon and Schuster, 2010), p. 7.

6 Donald Winnicott, 'The Anti-Social Tendency' in *Collected Papers: Through Paediatrics to Psych-analysis* (London: Tavistock, 1958), pp. 306–315.

7 Donald Winnicott, *The Child, the Family and the Outside World* (London: Penguin, 1991), p. 231.

8 Owen Jones, *Chavs: The Demonization of the Working Class* (London: Verson, 2011).

9 Elizabeth Thiel, *The Fantasy of Family: Nineteenth Century Children's Literature and the Myth of the Domestic Ideal* (Oxford: Routledge, 2007).

10 Nancy J. Chodorow, *Reproduction of Mothering*, 2nd edn. (Berkley: California Press, 1999).

11 Ibid., p. 57.

12 Estella Welldon, *Mother, Madonna, Whore: The Idealization and Denigration of Motherhood* (New York: The Guilford Press, 1992).

13 Donald Winnicott, 'The Theory of the Parent-Infant Relationship'. *International Journal of Psycho-analysis* 41 (1960), pp. 585–595, p. 594.

14 Bruno Bettelheim, *The Uses of Enchantment* (London: Penguin Books, 1976), p. 145.

15 See Margaret Rustin and Michael Rustin, *Narratives of Love and Loss: Studies in Modern Children's Fiction* (London: Verso, 1987).

16 Donald Winnicott, *The Child, the Family and the Outside World*, p. 77.

17 Adam Phillips, *Winnicott* (London: Penguin, [1988] 2007), p. 10.

18 Donald Winnicott, *The Child, the Family and the Outside World*, p. 230.

19 Ann Alston, *The Family in English Children's Literature* (Oxford: Routledge, 2008).

20 Rozsika Parker, *Torn in Two* (London: Virago, 1995).

21 Donald Winnicott, *Playing and Reality* (London: Routledge, [1971] 2005), p. 193.

22 Carolyn Steedman, *The Tidy House* (London: Virago, 1982).

23 Ibid., p. 23.

24 Bruno Bettelheim, *The Uses of Enchantment*, p. 168.

25 Chris Dearden and Saul Becker, *Young Carers in the UK: The 2004 Report* (London: Carers UK, 2004), p. 5.

26 Donald Winnicott, *Playing and Reality*, p. 197.

27 See for instance Donald Winnicott, 'What Irks?' in *Winnicott on the Child*, (Cambridge, MA: Perseus Publishing, 2002), pp. 139–154.

6

The Irrepressible, Unreliable, Lying Tracy Beaker: From Page to Screen

Helen Day

The Story of Tracy Beaker (1991) is a book about lies and truthfulness, and features a protagonist who is obsessed with telling her own story, on her own terms; a story that features all manner of lies and deception. This chapter will use a combination of approaches to unreliability combined with psychological and linguistics theories of lying to explore what such narrative strategies reveal about Wilson's characterisation of Tracy Beaker. As a point of comparison, at the end of the chapter, *The Story of Tracy Beaker* will be contrasted with episodes from the first TV adaptation in order to demonstrate how effective the use of an unreliable narrator can be in communicating the confessional story of a child in care.

The Story of Tracy Beaker features what I term a 'lying narrator'. This is my own term and is used to define a narrator who not only lies but also, significantly, admits to lying (which is something an unreliable narrator seldom does). To complicate matters further, *The Story of Tracy Beaker* is a fictional autobiography in the form of Tracy's 'Book about Me', the book given to all the children in the care home. Beginning with headings, such as 'Name', 'Birthday', 'Appearance', 'Favourite Things' and so on, the bulk belongs to 'My Own Story'. As in all autobiographies and diaries, the author (Tracy) does have a narratee in mind. Barbara Wall defines a narratee as 'the more or less shadowy being within the story whom, it can always be shown, the narrator addresses' but this is, to my mind, an over-simplification.[1] It is not always easy to discern exactly who this 'person to whom the narrative is addressed' is; indeed, Tracy does not seem sure herself. On the one hand, her narratee could be a sympathetic other to whom Tracy can confess, perhaps someone who she can persuade more easily than other characters within her story. On the other hand, her book is partly intended to persuade potential adoptive parents of her

119

merits. Clearly any such book is also partly private, a place to express herself freely, although, as will be discussed later, Tracy does not always admit her feelings or her lies to herself. This self is thus exposed both consciously, when Tracy admits to lying, and unconsciously through narrative unreliability. Because of the nature of fictional first-person confessional narratives, theories of unreliability, and of how lying might work within texts, are particularly useful for understanding how such texts function.

In the course of this chapter I will also be distinguishing between the child reader and the critical reader of *The Story of Tracy Beaker*. As this is a book for children, within the 8–12 category, the implication might be that the ideal reader is a child of a similar age to Tracy: 'I am 10 years 2 months old.'[2] A child reader generally (although not always) has less worldly experience and less readerly experience; in other words a child reader will probably have less experience of the reasons why children, and indeed adults, might lie, both to themselves and to other people, and might equally be less attuned to narrative unreliability and its techniques. The critical reader, on the other hand, is addressed in this chapter as one who has more worldly and readerly experience and will, by the end of this chapter, be able to adopt and apply a range of reading strategies developed from theories of unreliability and lying.

Introduced first by Wayne C. Booth in *The Rhetoric of Fiction* (1961), the term 'unreliable narration' describes the discourse of an untrustworthy narrator who misrepresents or misevaluates characters or events. Until fairly recently, Booth's well-known formulation – 'I have called a narrator *reliable* when he speaks for or acts in accordance with the norms of the work (which is to say the implied author's norms), *unreliable* when he does not' – remained unchallenged.[3] According to Booth, the distinction between reliable and unreliable narrators is based on 'the degree and kind of distance' that separates a given narrator from the implied author of a work. However, as Ansgar Nünning points out, Booth himself admitted that his own definition was inadequate, leading to Yacobi's conclusion that the problem of reliability in narrative is 'as complex and (unfortunately) as ill-defined as it is important'.[4]

Current narrative theories of unreliability tend to be segregated into cognitive and rhetorical approaches.[5] One major bone of contention between them is whether unreliability remains a product of the distance between the narrator and the implied author of a work, identified primarily in textual strategies (Booth and more recent rhetorical narratologists such as James Phelan and Mary Martin), or located in the interaction between text and reader with readers making use of their real-world knowledge (cognitive narratologists). This later approach does involve, to a certain extent, diagnosing characters, a strategy which literary critics are often warned to avoid. However, when it comes to understanding how lying functions within a text, a critical reader does need to know how lying functions in 'the real world', if only to understand how a child reader might recognise lying and how they might evaluate a character who lies. The recent 'narrative turn' encompasses more and more disciplines as narrative theory travels between the humanities and other research domains including medicine, psychology and, in particular, the cognitive sciences.[6]

Theorists like Nünning have attempted to synthesise the rhetorical and cognitive approaches, positing a tripartite system consisting of an authorial agency, textual phenomena and reader-response.[7] Nünning's work has influenced my own approach, which attempts to combine cognitive, rhetorical and stylistics approaches to unreliability and additionally considers linguistic and psychological definitions of lying by relating them to unreliable first-person narration. This combination of approaches can be extremely fruitful when analysing texts like *The Story of Tracy Beaker* as it takes into account Wilson's agency in constructing Tracy as an unreliable and lying narrator, identifies and evaluates textual cues of unreliability, considers the context of a first-person confessional narrative and brings in the different types of reader who may or may not recognise and respond to Tracy's unreliability in specific ways.

The first strand that will be considered is the cognitive approach to unreliability. This relies on the reader's worldly experience and perceptions, which is why it matters so much how old and how 'experienced' the reader of *The Story of Tracy Beaker* is. In the cognitive view, the reader must draw upon a number of frames of reference (referential frames) which might include literary conventions (including whether or not a reader has previously come across unreliable narration); criteria of verisimilitude; culturally agreed-upon moral and ethical standards; and, perhaps most importantly for *Tracy Beaker* and for my research, psychological theories of personality and behaviour, including lying. Wilson's ideal reader is perhaps one who understands how and why Tracy's behaviour deviates from 'normal' childhood behaviour and, especially, how and why she lies. As Piaget's research on lying shows, however, children develop their moral judgement over time, so the response of an eight-year-old to Tracy's lies might be very different from that of a 12-year-old and both will probably differ in some respects to that of an adult. Adults may also be less likely to empathise with some of Tracy's more antisocial lies, whilst being more sympathetic to her bravado ones, so it is helpful to the critical reader to be able to distinguish between different types of lie.

Xu et al. identify two types of lies that are of importance during a child's socialisation: the prosocial and antisocial lie.[8] Rather simplistically, they call antisocial lies those that are typically told to benefit oneself at the expense of others. These are usually discouraged by children's caregivers from an early age. The prosocial lies are defined as those that are told with an intention to help, not harm another individual. Their discussion of prosocial lies identifies them as taking place in a politeness situation, for example, faking liking an undesirable gift in front of the gift giver.[9] Such prosocial lies are morally sanctioned and are frequent in everyday practice. Although Tracy (interestingly) does not actually use prosocial lies herself, she has highly developed emotional intelligence and recognises the lies that adults tell to handle children like her in care. She understands that when Jenny the care worker calls her into the kitchen to give her a hand in getting lunch ready, this is a 'ploy' used 'to distract you'. Sometimes it works with 'the thicker kids' she brags, 'but it usually has no effect on me whatsoever' (p. 33). Wilson is perhaps drawing the child reader's attention to different types of lies and the reasons one might tell them. Whilst many people would argue that prosocial lies are acceptable, if not essential, to ensure smooth social relations, others – especially those like Tracy, who are bright enough to recognise when such lies are being used – find them manipulative. While not prosocial lies per se, Tracy recognises the techniques and deceptive behaviour that others use to manage social relations, accusing Louise of putting on 'this sweet little baby act when there are grown-ups about' (p. 76). Her admission that 'our little Louise can be even worse than me when she wants' is an acknowledgement that her own behaviour is often designed with the intent to influence adults (p. 76).

Tracy is, however, a far more prolific user of antisocial lies, lies told in order to try to get herself out of trouble. She confesses easily to her 'tendency to tell a few fibs now and again', what her foster Aunt Peggy used to call 'Telling Fairy Stories' (p. 25). For example Tracy tells Aunt Peggy that her mum turned up and took her to town and bought her a huge bottle of scent, 'just like the bottle Uncle Sid gave you for your birthday' (p. 25). Whilst playing Murderers she says, her own bottle tipped over: 'It's gone all over me as I expect you've noticed, but it's my scent not yours. I don't know what's happened to yours. I think one of the other kids took it' (p. 26). It is left to the child reader to work out what really happened: that Tracy stole and broke

Aunt Peggy's perfume and has constructed an elaborate lie to explain how she happened to be covered in its scent. In case the child reader needs a little more prompting, Tracy appeals directly to her: 'You know the sort of thing. I'd make it dead convincing but Aunt Peggy wouldn't even listen properly' (p. 26). This clearly identifies the narratee as a child who, like Tracy, sometimes tells lies to avoid punishment. The frequency of Tracy's 'fibs', however, suggests that they are verging on what Ford terms 'pseudologia fantastica' (pathological lying) and that they therefore have a more complex role in the formation and maintenance of her identity.[10]

Xu et al. create a simple binary opposition between the prosocial and antisocial lie and offer no real analysis of the psychology behind such lies or the complexities of individual instances of lying. What this binary opposition does not cover, for example, is the lie that is told to benefit oneself but is *not* at the expense of others. Xu et al. seem to infer that their term 'Antisocial lie' also covers the 'Self-Protective' lie, which they define as a lie told to avoid negative consequences.[11] This might, for example, be a lie told to protect oneself from physical or emotional harm. However, I find the idea of a self-protective lie as a more distinct category (rather than a subset of an antisocial lie) as it could then be extended to cover lies told in an attempt to make oneself more likeable to another or a lie told to oneself or others to make one feel better about oneself or a situation. The self-protective lie is a lie that many child readers would recognise so that, even if they could not fully comprehend its function and forms, there will be some understanding of Tracy's unreliability. Defining and recognising such lies is therefore useful for the critical reader of unreliable narration, in children's literature especially.

Tracy tells many self-protective lies. From the first paragraph Tracy lies to her narratee. She declares that she had to share her birthday, and thus her cake, and its associated wish, with 'that dopey Peter Ingram' (p. 7). But, she is quick to qualify, 'wishing is for babies anyway. They don't come true' (p. 7). This is what Dorothy Rowe calls a 'bravado lie', a lie aimed at 'bolstering the sense of being a person when it is under attack', such as 'it didn't hurt' or 'I wasn't frightened'.[12]

Tracy pretends that she does not care that she was denied a whole wish. In fact, she claims throughout her story that she does not care about many things that obviously affect her deeply. When her first foster placement fails, she tells us that she did not like Aunt Peggy and Uncle Sid or the other kids so she 'didn't care when they got rid of me' (p. 16). The phrase 'got rid of me' as if she was rubbish clearly points to the fact that she *does* care.

Tracy is desperate to be fostered and even tries to persuade her social worker Elaine to foster her. She does this by attempting to manipulate Elaine, using an honest appraisal of her own behavioural problems and acknowledging that foster parents get paid. 'I bet they'd give you lots extra [money] because I'm difficult, and I've got behavioural problems and all that', she pleads (p. 29). When Elaine tells her it is 'just not on', Tracy immediately denies she was serious, claiming, 'I was only joking.' Because she has exposed her real feelings she has to rebuild her sense of self and does this by attacking Elaine: 'Yuck. I can't stand the thought of living with you. You're stupid and boring and you're fat and wobbly' (p. 29). The reader knows this is Elaine's weakness when she immediately sucks in her stomach, a testament to Tracy's emotional intelligence.

There is pathos here since a 'joke' is supposed to be funny. The situation of a ten-year-old child pleading to be fostered by her social worker is anything but funny. Tracy's response is especially revealing to the narratee as it is an excellent example of where she lies to the narratee but qualifies this with statements that allow the emotionally experienced reader to understand what is really going on. 'I told her I wasn't a bit angry' (lie), 'though I shouted as I said it' (qualification: since shouting is an expression of anger). 'I didn't care a bit' (lie), 'though I had these silly watery eyes' (qualification: since crying is an expression of being upset and of caring) (all 29). This is an example of what Rowe calls 'psychic numbing', a way of lying to yourself and telling yourself that you do not feel the emotions you see as a weakness.[13]

While a child reader might be able to recognise that Tracy's feelings towards adults, and in particular towards the mother who has left her in care, are complex and even contradictory, the critical reader who makes use of developmental theories of lying can carefully unpack the evidence.

Tracy often presents a picture of her mother as a superhero, who will rescue her: 'If she found out how many times that Aunt Peggy smacked me then wow, ker-pow, splat, bang, I bet my mum would really let her have it' (p. 51). 'She comes for me lots of times', Tracy tells Justine, 'she's going to come and take me away for good, we're going to Hollywood together' (p. 136). More subtle is where she reveals, sometimes without meaning to, that her mother not only keeps leaving her but manipulates her into believing it is her fault:

> It's no use looking sad or sulky if you want people to like you. Mum always tells me to give her a big smile. Even when she's saying goodbye

to me. You can't look gloomy or it just upsets people and they don't
want any more to do with you. (p. 68)

Through such emotional blackmail Tracy has learnt that the more
upset or insecure she feels, the more she must pretend otherwise.
Ford argues that latency-age children (those beginning school and
thus establishing interpersonal relationships beyond the family) begin
to experience conflicts between the values and truths taught in the
home and those of others outside the home. They also learn that
intimate details of the family must be kept secret, thus learning how
to deceive. As a consequence, he argues, such children learn mental
'double-book-keeping' activities in order to keep family secrets.[14]
When Justine reveals the shaky ground upon which Tracy has built her
sense of herself as a beloved child of a glamorous rather flighty mother
by verbalising Tracy's innermost fears, her response is to hit Justine and
keep on hitting her until she is removed to the Quiet Room:

> 'Louise told me about your mum. She's nothing. And she's never coming
> for you. She hasn't been near you since you were little. I bet she's forgot-
> ten all about you. Or she's had heaps of other kids and doesn't want to
> think about that boring ugly Tracy ever again.' So I hit her. (p. 136)

It is in this room that Cam, the visiting writer, finds her and asks
Tracy whether she really believes the lies she tells about her mum.
She finally admits, 'Sometimes I know I'm sort of making it up'
(p. 139). Throughout her 'Own Story', Tracy attempts to both
construct an ideal reader who believes her lies and is therefore on
her side throughout and simultaneously one who understands why
she lies and makes allowances for her. Indeed one of the reasons
why Tracy likes Cam so much is that the writer sees through her
attempts at bravado. Rather than accusing Tracy of lying Cam asks,
with genuine interest, 'Do you believe it, Tracy?' (p. 139).

Before exploring the rhetorical approaches in detail, it is worth
reconsidering, in a little more detail, the fact that this is a first-person
confessional narrative. The folklorist Sweetser suggests that whether
a statement is considered a lie depends on the motivations of the liar
and these, in turn, will depend on the context in which such a statement is made.[15] The prototypical setting of lying is informational
where the primary purpose of discourse is to relay information. In a
politeness setting, the primary purpose of discourse is to establish and
maintain positive social relations. A first-person confessional addressed
to a child audience, I would argue, requires an alternative setting. In

a (fictional) confessional situation where a first-person narrator 'confesses' to a narratee we have both:

- a *politeness* setting in that the narrator is trying to get the implied reader on side, which requires the establishment and maintenance of positive social relations, and also
- an *informational* setting in that one of the main purposes is to inform the narratee/implied reader about what has happened.

Unreliability may occur when the reader expects such a confession to conform to either a politeness or informational setting but the narrator has another goal in mind. This goal, I believe, is *persuasive*. A setting that contains elements from both the informative and politeness contexts might be what I am calling a rhetorical – or even more precisely, a *confessional* – setting, in other words a setting where the narrator is trying to persuade the narratee/implied reader about their intentions or motivations. In such a setting the veracity of the first-person narrator is key. William Riggan argues that this identifiable narrator is often 'metaphorically grabbing us on the arm, gesturing to us, or addressing us individually or collectively from time to time' and so 'imparts a tangible reality to the narrative situation and a substantial veracity to the account we are reading or "hearing"'.[16] Whether in her desire to be understood or even greater desire to be fostered, Tracy clearly has a vested interest in getting her potential readers on side. Wilson too is, I feel, urging her child readers to sympathise, if not empathise, with her protagonist, evidenced by Tracy's acknowledgement of her lies, her loyalty to her mother and her desperate attempts to be fostered.

From the first few pages where Tracy tells us this is 'my private book' (p. 8) we feel privy to an intimate relationship with Tracy. Her first prototypical lie, 'My hair is fair and very long and curly', is also the first time she confesses a lie, 'I am telling fibs. It's dark and difficult and it sticks up in all the wrong places' (p. 9). We feel somehow proud that we are the one being told the truth to and this bonds us to Tracy. Even though she lies to us many times, we also feel, at the same time, that we are her confidantes. Inexperienced child readers often fail to understand that first-person narration is itself also potentially unreliable, in that the narrator, with her human limitations of perception and memory and evaluation, may have missed, forgotten or misconstrued incidents, words and motives.

Theories of rhetorical unreliability are useful for the critical reader as they draw out some of the consequences for the actual reader, of such unreliability. The adjectives in James Phelan's notion of 'bonding' versus 'estranging' refer to 'the *consequences of the unreliability for the relations between the narrator and the authorial audience*'.[17] In bonding unreliability there is a sense that the authorial audience endorses the feelings or actions of the narrator and thus feels bonded to her in some way. This can happen in *Tracy Beaker* when a child reader especially empathises with her feelings about having to share or about lying to get out of trouble or being found out in a lie. This is related to what Suzanne Keen calls 'broadcast strategic empathy', which 'calls upon every reader to feel for a character or members of a group, by emphasizing common vulnerabilities and hopes through universalizing representations'.[18] A reader does not have to be a child in care to empathise and bond with Tracy. However, such children may well feel a much closer bond as they also recognise on a deeper level the emotions behind some of her lies. They may empathise with the actual narrative situation if it is linked to a memory of a comparable personal experience.

On the other hand, a reader, perhaps an adult reader, might find it difficult to adopt Tracy's perspective, particularly if she has strong ideas about lying (and especially a child lying to an adult, lying *to her*). This would not really be an example of Phelan's estranging unreliability however, since Wilson clearly intends the reader to empathise or at least understand and sympathise with Tracy. A resisting reader who reads against the grain by rejecting the idea that children lie for all kinds of reasons has misunderstood the purpose of a confessional narrative where a narrator reveals her intimate thoughts and feelings in a way that simply would not happen outside such a setting (think of the purpose of diaries and psychotherapy).

In real life Sissela Bok argues that when lied to, since we have no way to judge which lies are the trivial ones, and since we have no confidence that liars will restrict themselves to just such trivial lies, the perspective of the deceived leads us to be wary of *all* deception.[19] While I am not sure that this is true for everyone, in first-person confessional fiction it is certainly not necessarily the case. Even though Tracy admits she is a liar, as critical readers we seek the 'emotional truth' of Tracy as this enables us to recognise what and who she really cares about. In contrast, some child readers fail to recognise when she is lying at all.

While the cognitive approach to unreliability draws on real-world experience and, in this case, a recognition of lies and how they function, the rhetorical approach pioneered by theorists like Phelan and Martin, as we have already seen, focuses on the communicative strategies between the narrator and what they term the 'authorial audience'.[20] Such strategies are extremely useful in the case of a first-person confessional by a narrator who is unreliable and who is addressing different narratees within a novel which, as children's literature, has both child and adult readers (some of whom are critical).

Phelan and Martin's rhetorical model of unreliability states that narrators perform three functions which result in different kinds of unreliability. Narrators, they argue, *report* on characters, facts and events (axis of facts/events), *evaluate* or regard the characters, facts and events (axis of ethics/evaluation) and *interpret* or read the characters, facts or events (axis of knowledge/perception).[21] Narrators can therefore be unreliable along each axis either by falling short or by distorting. Consequently, Phelan and Martin distinguish six main types of unreliability:

- Underreporting and misreporting (e.g. not telling you everything/ not reporting correctly)
- Underregarding and misregarding/misevaluating (e.g. not seeing the whole picture clearly/not perceiving something wrong as wrong)
- Underreading and misreading (e.g. not working out exactly what something means/reading something or someone's actions inaccurately).[22]

The critical reader should never forget that Tracy, however precocious, is still a ten-year-old child. Both her age and the fact that her sense of self has been damaged by being put into care have an impact on her reading of situations. When it comes to her mother Tracy nearly always 'misreads' in her attempts to convince herself of her mother's love. When Tracy is filling in the section on 'My Family' in her book she reports that when she was little she lived with her mum and they got on great until 'she got this Monster Gorilla Boyfriend' (p. 15). This is what she tells her narratee:

> I hated him and he hated me back and beat me up and so I had to be taken into care. No wonder my mum sent him packing.
> **My own family live at** … I'm not sure exactly where my mum lives now because she has to keep moving about because she gets fed up living in one place for so long. (p. 15, emphases in the original)

This is a prime example of Tracy's incongruous reasoning. It is a combination of her own misreading of the situation and subsequent attempt to construct a narrative where her mum acts on her behalf. If her mother did indeed send Monster Gorilla packing after he beat Tracy up, why did she need to be put into care? And why does she still not know where her mother is? While many readers may miss the contradiction relating to her mother's boyfriend, they might be more likely to recognise that Tracy is trying to hide the fact that her mother obviously has not tried very hard to keep in touch. The reason Tracy offers for this seems to have come from her mother: 'she has to keep moving about because she gets fed up living in one place for long' (p. 15). The reader, an adult reader especially, might imagine a woman saying this to her child because she cannot bring herself to tell the truth – that she cannot or does not want to cope with her daughter.

A clear example of 'misreporting' is that, when Justine 'tells' that Tracy has broken her Mickey Mouse clock, Tracy informs the reader that she escapes the house and has a great time wandering around town: 'First I went to McDonalds […] and then I want to the pictures […] and then I went off with this crowd of friends to an amusement arcade […]' (p. 40). The reader might or might not realise that this is a series of what Anna Freud terms 'fantasy lies' where a child talks about wishes as if they were true.[23] The reader does know that Tracy is obsessed with having friends and having a proper home but the lies get less and less credible (and the run-on sentence, complete with 'and thens' is stylistically distinct) until the story cannot be sustained:

> And this girl there, we made friends and she asked me if I'd like to stay the night […] in fact she said I could stay there permanently […] so I said …
> I said: 'No thanks, I'd sooner go back to my crummy children's home.' (p. 41)

In case the sarcasm is not enough to alert some readers, Tracy then admits that she didn't do any of these things as she tells fibs sometimes as 'it makes things more interesting' (p. 42).

Phelan and Martin's categories, however, are not necessarily always useful in determining and analysing the type of lies told by children (which is why their approach is best when combined with a cognitive analysis). For example, Tracy actually reveals a huge amount about herself through the fairy story she tells, despite the fact that it begins with 'once upon a time':

> If you're very good and very beautiful with long golden curls then, after sweeping up a few cinders […] this prince comes along and you live happily ever after. […] But if you're bad and ugly then you've got no chance whatsoever. You get given a silly name like *Rumplestiltskin* and nobody ever invites you to their party … you stamp your feet in a rage […] and you get locked up in a tower and they throw away the key. (p. 24)

From this the reader can deduce that Tracy feels bad, ugly, lonely and forgotten with 'no chance whatsoever'. Long golden curls are a preoccupation of Tracy's and this fairy story has to be placed in the context of other information. The only present we know her mum did give her was a doll with 'long golden curls' who used to tell her that her mum was 'coming back really soon' (p. 38). Readers (both child and critical) are expected to work hard to remember such details and use them to build up a picture about Tracy's feelings and motivations.

Despite being extremely fruitful and enabling the critical reader to produce careful and psychologically sound interpretations of *The Story of Tracy Beaker*, what neither the cognitive or rhetorical approaches make absolutely clear is how precisely readers recognise an unreliable narrator. Stylistics, with its emphasis on speech acts, schema and linguistic indicators of deviation can help the critical reader identify clues about the narrator's credibility. The third strand of my approach (cognitive–rhetorical–stylistic) thus involves making use of stylistics. Because Tracy is a child who Wilson has given very realistic speech and thought patterns, analysing typographical emphases (italics, repetition and so on) can be illuminating. Typographical emphasis is used to make inferences about Tracy's responses to help the reader work out what she is lying about and thus what her real feelings might be or to offer an alternative perspective on events that Tracy might be misevaluating.

Tracy states throughout her story that she never cries. In the early instance where Elaine refuses to consider fostering her, Tracy admits to getting 'silly watery eyes' but states that she does not '*ever* cry' and that when people think she does, it is her 'hay fever' (p. 29). At this point a child reader might believe her (although most adults would probably recognise this attempt at bravado for what it is). In the phrase 'I don't *ever* cry' italics are used as an indicator of lying since the word '*ever*' is superfluous if the statement itself is true. Emphases such as these are an indication of where Tracy is intent on convincing the reader.

Information about Tracy's crying comes to the reader intermittently, which enables the observant reader to build up evidence over time. Awake at midnight, Tracy attempts to convince the reader and herself that her tears are slavers: the word 'yes' is evidence that she has only then decided what lie to tell: 'Imagine a Mars Bar as big as this bed […] I'm slavering at the thought. Yes, that's what those little marks are on the page. Slavers. I don't cry. I don't *ever* cry' (p. 37). Later in the night she slips up, stating that 'crying makes me hungry' but then qualifying it with 'Not that I've been crying now. I don't *ever* cry' (p. 52). By this point enough of a pattern has emerged that most child readers will pick up on the fact that she is, and therefore, already has been, crying. What also makes this interesting is the fact that many readers would not even suspect she was crying without her repetitious denials.

Stylistics also enables us to notice other repetitious phrases or 'tells'. For example Tracy uses hyperbole in an attempt to convince as when she tells us she has 'heaps and heaps' of best friends (p. 11) and repetition of the rebuttal in 'I didn't didn't didn't break Justine's rotten clock' (p. 44).

Capital letters are used as another form of emphasis, such as where she tells the reader that she got turfed out of her foster home 'THROUGH NO FAULT OF MY OWN' (p. 16). From this a worldly experienced reader would understand how unfair she thinks this is, whilst at the same time recognising that this may have been, in some way, her fault. In the book Tracy is so upset by what happens that, although she tells the reader that she was so mad she smashed by her bike, she doesn't 'want to write about it' (p. 16) and we have to wait until halfway through the book to get the real story. Julie, her foster mum, gets pregnant and Elaine tells her that Tracy does not always get on with little children, citing the example of when she shut a baby in a cupboard and the ghost game that got out of hand. 'Oh that!' Tracy replies, 'All those little kids *loved* that', another use of italic emphasis which reveals that underneath Tracy knows that she went too far (p. 49).

In adult unreliable narration it often takes many chapters, sometimes an entire book for the reader to recognise that the narrator was lying to her or deceiving herself. Because this is a book for 8–12-year-olds, Wilson has chosen to make it easier for the reader to work out the truth by providing necessary evidence, generally (although not always) within a few pages. On page 31, for example, is a paragraph printed in a handwriting font which has been written by one of the other characters: 'If [Tracy] is so super-intelligent, how come she wets her bed like a baby'. Tracy immediately tells us to 'ignore the stupid scribble' as 'it's all lies anyway' (p. 31). Yet a few pages on (p. 35), in the middle of the night, she admits to sharing a secret with Louise (in order to show that they are the 'bestest friends') about her 'nighttime problem' (p. 35). The fact that this problem involves wetting the bed is not stated but can be worked out, as can the fact that Louise has obviously told Justine, Tracy's worst enemy, and that she is the one who has written in Tracy's book. The fact that Tracy is awake at midnight implies that she has wet the bed, but also that she is upset about Louise's betrayal. Unreliable narration in 8–12 fiction is very unusual, and the reading process that *The Story of Tracy Beaker* invites is thus far more complex than many children's books and is, I believe, a stunning example of unreliable narration.

To consolidate how effective Wilson's text is, it is worth comparing it with the TV series. This will demonstrate how, while *The Story of Tracy Beaker* rewards active and careful readers and can support a range of interpretive strategies to create a complicated and credible character of a child in care, the TV programme renders its viewers much more passive and such strategies unnecessary. While there are some scenes which have a more powerful effect when seen, and the TV series certainly makes clever use of Sharratt's illustrations and flashbacks, the case study of the story of the Mickey Mouse Clock that ends this chapter reveals just what is lost by transferring the story into screen.

There are many differences between the book and TV adaptation. Series One of the TV series *The Story of Tracy Beaker* has 26 episodes and reaches far beyond the plot of the first book. For this chapter I will focus on two episodes, Episode One 'Tracy Returns to the Dumping Ground' and Episode Four 'Cam's First Visit' since these cover most of the events in the book.[24] The pace is much faster on TV, meaning that many more scenes and plots are required to make an entire series. There is an ensemble cast and the director has chosen to show what happens to many of the main characters when Tracy is not in shot. This proliferation of characters has proved successful for its longevity, not least because the character Tracy Beaker has not returned to the renamed *The Dumping Ground* (2013), series. While it *is* possible to focalise a TV series more from one character's point of view, as in the more young adult *My Mad Fat Diary* (2013), here, although Tracy is the star, the other children have their own storylines too. There is dialogue instead of internal monologues and reported speech so the viewer often finds it easier and quicker to make up her mind about the veracity of events.

Both the book and the TV series make use of Nick Sharratt's illustrations but, interestingly, it is the TV series that makes more use of them, using extended mini cartoons to fill in the gaps left by the lack of Tracy's internal monologue and choosing to make it absolutely clear to the viewer when Tracy is fantasising or lying.

Like all Jacqueline Wilson books, *The Story of Tracy Beaker* is illustrated by Nick Sharratt throughout. Unlike some books where the illustration carries the primary meaning or even a different meaning to the text, Wilson's text and Sharratt's illustrations are largely 'symmetrical'.[25] There are occasionally examples where the illustration does more than the text or helps clarify interpretations, requiring some interpretive work on the part of the reader. For example, while the reader might have worked out that Tracy's nightmare where her previous foster parents refuse to let her on stepping stones and push her into a pool is partly related to her guilt over breaking Justine's clock, the illustration makes this clearer. The pond is depicted as a giant clock with children and foster parents bearing sticks on the 12 stones around the edge while Tracy is shown as the hands of the clock in the middle, complete with Mickey Mouse ears (p. 57). However, for the most part, the illustrations depict Tracy's fantasies, such as her imaginary trip to town (p. 41) or her wish that her mum would spank Aunt Peggy (p. 51): they do not generally reveal anything that the text does not. In other words, the illustrations do not often provide evidence about whether Tracy is lying or not.

This is rather different in the TV episodes where Nick Sharratt's mini cartoons have a distinctive role. Because there is no narrator, complete with internal monologue, they do the work of differentiating Tracy's wishes, desires and dreams from the main action. In Episode One Tracy tells Justine and Louise that Ted and Julie only wanted her as a slave so she asked to be brought back to the home. Against a cartoon showing Julie crying, Tracy narrates that 'there were tears, sobbing, the works' and that they even tried to bribe her, shown by Tracy surfing a wave of tears on a surfboard covered in presents. The end of the wish-fantasy is shown by wavy lines across the screen cutting to Julie and Ted telling Tracy that they can't foster her anymore. This makes it absolutely clear to the viewer, immediately, that Tracy was lying to the other girls.

As Ford argues, an important component of deceit depends not only on the words used but also 'on control of one's nonverbal communications, including facial expressions and body movements'.[26] Non-verbal communication is extremely difficult to discern in written fiction, especially first-person confessionals. Sharratt's illustrations do some work in this regard: for example, Tracy's annoyance that Cam is not paying her exclusive attention is shown by Tracy's frowning eyebrows and firmly crossed arms (p. 115). The typographical emphases discussed earlier also provide an equivalence of tone of voice.

On screen Tracy's facial expressions and body language, as well as the tone and volume of her voice are all used to communicate emotion to the viewer. Virtually the first shot in Episode One shows Tracy, her head filling up most of the screen, face scrunched and red with anger, stamping her feet and yelling at her foster parents for returning her to the Dumping Ground. This exaggerated portrayal of anger and frustration makes it easy for a young viewer to discern how Tracy feels (even if they do not really understand why).

It is perhaps this paucity of understanding that reveals what is lost in the screen version. Right from this first episode Tracy is defined by other characters as 'a big fat liar'. After Tracy tries to convince Justine that her mum is a famous actress, Louise accuses her of always telling lies, especially about her 'precious mother' (a foreshadowing that colours anything Tracy subsequently says about her mother). What we get here is immediate gratification and the resolution of what, in the book, is revealed slowly and carefully to a reader who is expected to build up evidence and come to their own conclusions. The same is true of the question of whether or not Tracy cries although, to be fair, it is very hard to disguise tears on screen. While *readers* may take a while to realise that Tracy really is crying when she claims she doesn't *ever* cry, at the end of Episode One Tracy is shown standing at the window watching Justine and her dad in the garden, wiping away tears while insisting that 'Tracy Beaker never cries.' This first, important, TV episode seems less concerned about deeper aspects of Tracy's identity such as when and why she lies and her desperate desire to be fostered, and more about establishing an instantly recognisable character (a loud-mouthed, entertaining yet sympathetic troublemaker) who can then be placed in any number of subsequent scenarios in the Dumping Ground.

The attempts of the TV series to fill in some of the gaps in the book (such as why Tracy ended up in care) raises the question of whether it is more effective to show a scene or leave it up to a reader's imagination. Visuals can sometimes have a huge emotional impact on the viewer and can convey motivations and emotions, even trauma, very effectively. In 'Episode 4: Cam's First Visit' for example, a Sharratt cartoon is used to show yet another of Tracy's fantasies about her and her mum. This time she and her mum go to the fair, staying on the big wheel for 'what felt like days'. Tracy is shown with a massive smile on her face being cuddled by her mum. However, the voiceover 'Me and my mum, we went everywhere together' is used to cut from the bright cartoon to a scene in dark muted colours showing Tracy's mum kissing her goodbye before being dragged off by a man, leaving Tracy alone in a room. The juxtaposition is powerful, showing the real distance between Tracy's desires and what actually happened, something we do not get evidence of in the book.

One of the most effective scenes in this series is also in Episode Four, where Tracy is humiliated by her attempts to get visiting writer Cam to notice her. A comparison with the same scene in the book reveals how sometimes visuals can have a more visceral effect. Tracy, as we have seen, is perhaps overly concerned with impression management.

Self-presentation is the goal-orientated conscious or unconscious process in which one attempts to influence the perception of her image.
Although one motive for self-presentation is expressive, for Tracy it is
more instrumental. Her goal is to present herself in a special way so
that Cam will pick her out for a special feature. Underneath is also the
desire to be fostered and, as we have already established, she sees every
available adult as a potential foster parent. Instead of increasing her
self-esteem, however, her strategy backfires and she is left humiliated.

In the book the *reader* is told of Tracy's failure before the details
emerge: 'I don't want to write down what happened' (p. 64). Tracy
tries to make herself look pretty by putting her hair in plaits (like baby
Camilla's, which everyone cooed over) and borrowing Adele's make-
up. She wears a mohair sweater with her name on the front and an
old skirt with ink stains down the side. The Nick Sharratt illustrations
show that Tracy's attempts are not successful as the make-up is exces-
sive and clownish and the clothes do not fit or match (illustration 65).
Plastering a huge smile on her face she bursts into the sitting room,
only to be met by smirks and 'the wrong sort of smiles' (p. 69). When
Justine starts reading aloud from her book Tracy loses it and ends up
in the Quiet room: 'I yelled some very rude words at [Cam]', letting
rip 'like a right raving loony' (p. 82). Although Tracy's reluctance to
tell her narratee what has happened is evidence of just what an impact
this event has had on her, it does not have anywhere near the emotional resonance of the same scene on TV (p. 64).

The *viewer* sees Tracy sitting in front of a mirror with lipstick in her
hand but we don't get to see the finished result until we see her burst
into the living room. This big 'reveal' is perhaps more effective than
in the book where we can anticipate what is going to happen more
easily from the illustrations. Seeing Tracy's bright blue eyeshadow,
huge red lips and red circles on her cheeks and hearing the jeers from
the children is so much more poignant. As Justine steals her book
and reveals to everyone that Tracy has cut a picture from a magazine,
pretending it is her mum (something the reader might suspect in the
book but which is never clarified), Tracy flies at her, teeth bared, pain
and anger all over her face. As Tracy takes her frustration out on Cam
who comes to see her in the Quiet room, I found my own face gri-
macing with pain as I heard her voice break and saw just how much
she wanted to be liked. The combination of the aural and visual makes
it easier for the viewer to mirror Tracy's pain.

Despite these instances, where the TV series clearly evokes strong
immediate emotions from the viewer, it is the reader who is offered
a sustained, intellectual and emotionally complex journey. My final

comparison between the book and TV series returns to the case of Justine's Mickey Mouse Clock. It highlights the differences between the reader and the viewer's roles, revealing the subtlety and cleverness of the book, the interpretive work the reader has to do and the rewards for doing so.

In Episode One the *viewer* actually sees Tracy snooping in Justine's room. We see her pick up Justine's clock and a close-up of her fingers spinning the hands, cutting back to reveal her eyes as they widen with shock and surprise before showing the broken hands of the clock. There is thus absolutely no ambiguity about whether Tracy did break the clock, and also no sense that she might have done it on purpose as there is in the book. Seeing the actual episode also means there is no conflict between story and discourse, as there is in the book, where Tracy returns to the incident, its rationale and impact, again and again.

In the book Tracy's denial that she broke the clock is her largest antisocial lie and it structures both the plot and, in some way, most of her relationships. The first mention of the clock is in the section **'If I was … older, I would …'** where Tracy claims she would have her own 'huge bedroom with all her own things' especially 'a Mickey Mouse alarm clock like Justine's' (p. 22). At this point this lacks any special significance beyond her desire for her own belongings. Justine then steals Tracy's book and writes in it that Tracy wets her bed like a baby, which leads to Tracy imagining how she might punish Justine: 'Any ideas ticking away inside my head?' (p. 35). The words 'Tick, Tick, Tick' give her an idea ('*I* know … Justine Littlewood. Oh you're going to get it') but what she does is not revealed at this point (pp. 36–37).

We find out that Tracy is being punished for her revenge attack on Justine before we know what she has done. Tracy tries to hide that she regrets her actions, 'acting as if' she could not care less when Jenny has a real go at her although Jenny is not taken in, 'I think you really do care, Tracy … Deep down I think you're really really sorry' (p. 37). The phrase '[Justine] sneaked on me' could be considered a confession, as does the fact that she runs off to hide (p. 40).

Tracy lies to the reader by omission: 'Clocks break all the time' (p. 40). In his developmental model of lying Piaget determines three stages of moral understanding. In the first stage 'a lie is wrong because it is an object of punishment'.[27] If the punishment aspect is removed and the lie remains undiscovered, it is not considered by the child as a lie. At around ten years old, the lie becomes something that is wrong in itself. Tracy still feels that, as Jenny has 'no proof whatsoever' that she broke the clock, she should be believed. She also questions whether anyone can categorically state that she broke the clock since she herself does not 'one hundred per cent *know* that [she] broke it' (p. 44). She confesses that she did pick up the clock to look at it and that when she twiddled the knobs both the hand and the little Mickey fell off 'with his paws in the air, dead' (p. 44). But, she rationalises, 'it might have been about to take its last gasp anyway' (p. 44).

Interestingly, in Episode One, Tracy is invited into Elaine's office where she shouts that she 'never broke her stupid clock' leading Elaine to reply, with a knowing look on her face: 'Ah, so you know it's about a clock.' This idea of an adult catching out the children in their lies and tricks runs throughout the show. In many ways the TV series is more didactic than the book as it shows that adults always find out or know when a child is lying. As with many films and TV shows, there seems to be a greater concern about what a child may take away from watching 'unacceptable' behaviour.

In order to work out how Tracy feels in the book, the reader has to be able to imagine how she might feel in the same position or to have some understanding of guilt and its associative behaviour. Following the breaking of the clock Tracy has the nightmare where Aunt Peggy smacks her into a pond and Julie and Ted turn their backs on her. She even wets the bed. The Mickey Mouse Clock was given to Justine by her dad who, unlike Tracy's mum, does visit her. The reader is invited to infer that there is a direct link between the clock and loving parents and that not only is Tracy jealous of Justine's relationship with her dad but that she sees their relationship as rubbing her nose in it, exposing the fact that Tracy's mum does not visit: 'Well, she's always going on about [the clock] because she's got this boring thing about her dad. She makes out he's so flipping special when he hardly ever comes to see her. The only thing he's ever given her is that stupid tinny old alarm clock' (p. 44). We also find out later that it was as a direct result of this clock that she lost Louise as a friend to Justine. Tracy was so jealous and nasty to Justine when she first brought it home that Louise turns on her and changes allegiance.

Tracy does apologise to Justine but manages to do this without confessing, something which most children do and would recognise: 'I'm sorry about what happened to your alarm clock', whilst informing us (in a moment of direct appeal to her narratee) 'I'd be a fool to admit it, wouldn't I?' (p. 58).

However, this isn't the end of the storyline. When Cam visits she shows the children her Mickey Mouse pen causing Justine to blurt out that 'some *pig*' broke her Mickey Mouse clock deliberately. The use of italics in Tracy's response 'I glared back, making out I couldn't care less. And I *couldn't*' reveals her continued guilt (p. 78).

The book ends with Tracy visiting Cam and, for once, being given what she wants – attention, a birthday cake to celebrate her Unbirthday and Cam's Mickey Mouse pen. Back at the home Tracy finds Justine sitting at the window waiting for a dad who has not turned up. Tracy then surprises even herself with a kind and empathetic act, appealing again to her narratee to recognise her sacrifice: 'I thought I was going to give [Justine] a Smartie. But you'll never guess what I did. I gave her my Mickey Mouse Pen' (p. 157).

Bok argues that different evaluations are given to the effects of deception, depending on whether the point of view is that of the liar or the one being lied to. She goes on to say that those who have been lied to are usually 'resentful, disappointed and suspicious'.[28] The viewer of the TV show never really feels lied to, partly because there is not an intimate sense of Tracy engaging with her directly but also because her lies are revealed so quickly that there is no time to explore how we might feel about them or take them personally. Some readers of unreliable narration (often those not familiar with its discourses), however, do feel 'wronged', and believe that the narrator's manipulation of them has made them 'unable to act [or respond] as they would have wanted to act [or respond] had they known all along' (Bok p. 20). There are also readers, often, in the case of *Tracy Beaker*, those who are too young, who significantly 'underread,' in Abbott's terms.[29] They may end the book baffled or annoyed or may stop reading before the end. Alternatively they may latch onto parts of the story that make sense and ignore those that are more confusing. My eight-year-old nephew when asked whether he thought Tracy was crying, after reading one of the sections where she claims that she never *ever* cries, answered 'No'.

Most readers however, especially those who recognise the unreliability and understand that it is their job to detect the clues and build up evidence, enjoy the experience of taking on the role of a first-person lying narrator and having to work for their gratification. The child reader can also, through reading *The Story of Tracy Beaker*, develop both their reading strategies and their understanding of the motivations for lying. They can experience both empathy and sympathy.

Bok argues that 'lying requires a *reason*, whilst truth-telling does not'.[30] It seems obvious but if a narrator is lying, they must have a reason and thus the reader will be interested in and drawn into their motivations. My argument is that lying in fiction is *always purposive* for a lie to have narrative purpose it needs to be recognised at some point. There needs to be what I call a 'lie-off', the payoff where the lie is exposed, although whether this is to the narratee or another character depends on other aspects of the narrative.

This lie-off might or might not be in the form of an easily identifiable and interpretable statement or visual evidence as in the TV series. In unreliable narration, the reader must usually piece together 'the truth' by examining the cues and clues of unreliability rather than relying on such revealing evidence. In *The Story of Tracy Beaker* this truth is complex and sometimes hard to accept (not all children get fostered by loving parents). While the TV viewer is entertained and moved, it is the reader who is compensated for their extratextual work by a sense of mastery over the text, readerly pleasure and an increase in human understanding.

Notes

1 Barbara Wall, *The Narrator's Voice: The Dilemma of Children's Fiction* (London: Macmillan, 1991), p. 4.
2 Jacqueline Wilson, *The Story of Tracy Beaker and The Bed and Breakfast Star* (London: Corgi Yearling, 1997), p. 7. All further references in this chapter are from this edition.
3 Wayne C. Booth, *The Rhetorics of Fiction* 2nd edn. (Chicago: The University of Chicago Press, 1983), pp. 158–159.
4 Yacobi, cited in Ansgar F. Nünning, 'Reconceptualizing Unreliable Narration: Synthesizing Cognitive and Rhetorical Approaches' in James Phelan and Peter J. Rabinowitz (eds.), *A Companion to Narrative Theory* (Oxford: Blackwell, 2008), pp. 89–107, p. 89.
5 Elke D'hoker and Gunther Martens (eds.), *Narrative Unreliability in the Twentieth-Century First-Person Novel* (Berlin: Walter de Gruyter, 2008).
6 David Herman et al., 'Narrative Turn in the Humanities', *Routledge Encyclopedia of Narrative Theory* (New York: Routledge, 2008), pp. 377–382, p. 380.
7 Ansgar F. Nünning, 'Reconceptualizing Unreliable Narration'.
8 Xu et al., 'Lying and Truth-telling in Children: From Concept to Action'. *Child Development* 81:2 (March/April 2010), 581–596.
9 Ibid., p. 581
10 Charles V. Ford, *Lies! Lies! Lies! The Psychology of Deceit* (Washington, DC: American Psychiatric Publishing, 1996), p. 61.
11 Xu et al., 'Lying and Truth-telling in Children', p. 583.
12 Dorothy Rowe, *Why We Lie* (London: Fourth Estate, 2011), p. 73.
13 Ibid., p. 280.
14 Charles V. Ford, *Lies! Lies! Lies! The Psychology of Deceit*, p. 76.
15 Kang Lee and Hollie J. Ross, 'The Concept of Lying in Adolescents and Young Adults: Testing Sweetser's Folkloristic Model'. *Merrill-Palmer Quarterly* 43:2 (1997), 255–270.

16 William Riggan, *Picaros, Madmen, Naifs and Clowns: The Unreliable First-Person Narrator* (Norman: University of Oklahoma Press, 1981), p. 19.

17 James Phelan, 'Estranging Unreliability, Bonding Unreliability, and the Ethics of *Lolita*', in Elke D'hoker and Gunther Martens (eds.), *Narrative Unreliability in the Twentieth-Century First-Person Novel* (Berlin: Walter de Gruyter, 2008), pp. 7–28, p. 11. Emphases in the original.

18 Suzanne Keen, 'A Theory of Narrative Empathy'. *Narrative* 14:3 (October 2006), 207–236, 215.

19 Sissela Bok, *Lying: Moral Choice in Public and Private Life* (New York: Vintage, 1989), pp. 20–21.

20 James Phelan, 'Estranging Unreliability, Bonding Unreliability, and the Ethics of *Lolita*', p.11.

21 James Phelan and Mary Patricia Martin, 'The Lessons of "Weymouth": Homodiegesis, Unreliability, Ethics and *The Remains of the Day*', in David Herman (ed.), *Narratologies* (Ohio: Ohio State University Press, 1999), pp. 88–109, p. 95.

22 Ibid. Explanations in brackets are mine.

23 Anna Freud, cited in Charles V. Ford, *Lies! Lies! Lies! The Psychology of Deceit*, p. 72.

24 'Episode One: Tracy Returns', *The Story of Tracy Beaker: The Best of Me: Series One*. Right Entertainment, 2005. DVD. Written by Elly Brewer. 'Episode Four: Cam's First Visit', *The Story of Tracy Beaker: Series One*. Written by Elly Brewer. http://www.youtube.com/watch?v=F8xj9rehR3Q [accessed 01 December 2013].

25 Joanna Golden, *The Narrative Symbol in Childhood Literature* (Berlin: Moulton de Gruyter, 1990), p. 105.

26 Charles V. Ford, *Lies! Lies! Lies! The Psychology of Deceit*, p.74.

27 Jean Piaget, *The Moral Judgment of the Child* (London: Routledge, 1968), p. 168.

28 Sissela Bok, *Lying: Moral Choice in Public and Private Life*, p. 20.

29 H. Porter Abbott, *The Cambridge Introduction to Narrative* (Cambridge: Cambridge University Press, 2008), p. 86.

30 Sissela Bok, *Lying: Moral Choice in Public and Private Life*, p. 22.

7

'I'm Not Used to Writing about Me. It's Always Us': 'Double Acts' in Jacqueline Wilson's Metafictional Novels

Clémentine Beauvais

Jacqueline Wilson's rich representations of the experiences of childhood and adolescence in contemporary society are frequently accompanied by a reflection on the role of reading and writing in these experiences. Diaries, letters, autofiction, even self-representation – her work is peppered with *mises en abyme* of the literary endeavour, generally focused on what could be called discovery-writing the self. Wilson's writerly protagonists are exclusively female, from Tracy Beaker in 1991 to Rosalind Hartlepool in 2012 – inscribing the works that feature them firmly within the genre of 'Stories for girls about girls who write stories', as Ruth Berman puts it.[1] They write with apparent spontaneity, and a seemingly self-centred desire to process their experiences. However, their enterprises are often also self-consciously directed towards intradiegetic readers, and their development as writers is rarely far from their minds. Wilson's representation of young girls writing thus often deviates from the genre of the secret diary, introducing subtle but serious thinking about the act of writing not just for self-discovery but also for an audience and as a semi-professional activity. As such, her writerly heroines are closer to Jo March than to Georgia Nicholson, and her metafictional novels qualify as examples of *Künstlerroman* – tales of artistic maturation – perhaps more than as *Bildungsroman*.

Prominent examples of these heroines (aside from the celebrated Tracy Beaker, discussed in Helen Day's chapter for this volume) include Ruby and Garnet in *Double Act* (1996), Charlie in *The Lottie Project* (1998) and Rosalind in *Four Children and It* (2012). Charlie's school project, the fictional diary of Victorian chambermaid Lottie, is presented in parallel to her own diary. The twins Ruby and Garnet's story is being written as it unfolds, first in a big red book marked 'Accounts', before it later splits into two notebooks. Rosalind, finally, is the young fictional writer of *Four Children and It*, having received, at the end of the story, an empty notebook to begin writing up the adventures of the four children. In all three books, the literary *mise en abyme* is explicit, and the novels wilfully metafictional: the story is being written or has been written by one or more characters, and they engage explicitly in reflection about the act of writing, anticipating on their imagined readers' reactions.[2]

There is much to be said about the treatment of literary creation in these three different novels; about the ways in which the heroines see themselves as present or future writers, about why they write, about their attitudes towards reading, writing and being read to, and the mutual exchanges between their 'real' lives and their writing. Following Colabucci and Parsons's meticulous theorisation of child writers in children's literature, most aspects of this common figure are present in the books studied: namely, the fact that writing 'benefits' the characters in the following ways: '(1) helps them cope with life experience, (2) serves to document their experience, (3) builds relationships, (4) validates their identity'.[3] These aspects will all be tackled in this chapter. However, what interests me particularly in these metafictional representations of budding writers is what apparently always accompanies them: *doubleness*.

Indeed, in these novels, the figure of the young female writer is markedly accompanied by the shadow presence of another self, very much like her own, conjured up or controlled by the act of writing. The irruption of this malleable 'double' in the fictional lives of the writerly heroines gives rise to complex narratives; narratives which map not just the development of one teenager into a writer, but also her grappling with her tendency to *divide* into simpler categories both the world and herself. While their engagement in writing provides these heroines with some degree of control over their lives, it also artificially stabilises their selves into two halves, each of which apparently whole, but both in essence illusory.

Part of the heroines' journeys, therefore, entails overcoming this illusion through an increasingly mature engagement with writing, and through a better understanding of their lives and acknowledgement of their complexity and *uniqueness*. It is only when they successfully accept themselves as incomplete, unpredictable beings, but also as meaning-makers, that they mature both as writers and as individuals. This entails seeking the readerly approval of others, specifically adult figures. They are then reconciled with their developing selves in all their subtleties, shed the dualistic comfort of their early writerly representations of themselves, and envisage their professional futures as storytellers reaching out to an audience. Their real audience, meanwhile, is invited to consider themselves as equally capable of abandoning comfortable but immature dreams of ideal selves and to consider themselves as singular beings, powerful and creative.

Writing the *other* to stabilise the self

A quick overview of the three novels discussed should highlight what I mean by the concept of the writerly 'double'. In *The Lottie Project*, young Charlie, who lives with her single mother, responds originally to a school project on the Victorians by writing the fictional diary of a nursery maid called Lottie. Meanwhile, the reader has access to Charlie's own life narrative. It soon becomes clear that Lottie's 'adventures' are a Victorian translation of Charlie's daily life. Lottie's parallel life, and her painful treatment by her employers, puts into perspective Charlie's difficulties.

Four Children and It is a contemporary rewriting of E. Nesbit's classic, *Five Children and It*, which the young heroine Rosalind is reading in the story. Accompanied by her brother Robbie, her unbearable stepsister Smash and their little half-sister Maudie, Rosalind unearths the Psammead from a sandpit, and each child is allowed to live, for a day, their dearest wish. Though Rosalind has the benefit of foresight – having read the book, she knows that the Psammead's wish-fulfilment is temporary – she plays along with the fantasy. Throughout, Rosalind's implicit point of intertextual reference is her ideal double Anthea, her 'equivalent' in *Five Children and It*. However, she is also cursed by her 'evil double', Smash, who criticises her reading choices and mocks her writing – but is also turned by Rosalind, as we shall see, into a convenient literary antagonist.

Finally, *Double Act* is the sophisticated coming-of-age tale of two twins, Ruby and Garnet, who begin to write down 'their' story, first as co-writers. Though Ruby and Garnet, at first, are presented as similar in all respects, the illustrations subtly belie that fact: uncommonly for a book by Jacqueline Wilson, the pictures are drawn by two illustrators (Nick Sharratt and Sue Heap) who each draw one twin. The difference is slight, but noticeable: though Heap is careful to imitate Sharratt's style, her Garnet is more cross-hatched than his characteristically neat Ruby. Within the text, font changes further indicate switches from Ruby to Garnet. Italicised Garnet is the more thoughtful, and meeker, writer and twin; Ruby, the dominant and bold one. Life separates them, not just as individuals but as writers; the bittersweet ending sees Garnet departing to a boarding school, and Ruby beginning a new notebook. The novel subtly reflects on the twins' act of *writing together* in parallel with that of living 'one life' despite two distinct personalities.

These young writers and their 'doubles' present interesting points of contact and differences. I have identified different types of 'doubles' in those metafictional novels: the complementary double of *Double Act*, the parallel double of *The Lottie Project*, and the antagonistic, mimetic and aspirational doubles of *Four Children and It*. They share one central characteristic: they are *illusory*. And the main function of the illusion is to stabilise the writerly heroine's sense of self by expelling complex and undesirable traits into an appropriate *other*. In all cases, the presence of this 'double' in the writing project is ambiguous. Writing the self seems to *require* a simultaneous writing of the other; there can be no self-portrayal without expelling, in character form, some aspects of the self into an *other*.

Ruby and Garnet are first introduced to the reader in Ruby's voice. 'We're twins. I'm Ruby. She's Garnet. We're identical. There's very few people who can tell us apart. Well, until we start talking.'[4] It is no coincidence that the distinction between the two 'identical' selves only begins with language. The twins may indeed be 'identical' physically (though, as mentioned, Sharratt's and Heap's styles are faintly different), but they are certainly not identical on a verbal level: their voices diverge. Garnet, singled out as the 'non-dominant' twin, 'can't get a word in edgeways' (p. 2). When she does, it is to contradict her sister. However, Ruby does not, at first, accept Garnet's divergent voice. The beginning of the novel is particularly dominated by Ruby's voice. Not content with writing about herself, Ruby also writes about Garnet, and therefore *writes her off* as an active narrative voice, despite her claim that the Accounts book is shared. Faced with Ruby's prolific writing about both twins, Garnet engages in discreet but firm contradictions of her sister's words:

> We're going to be famous too someday, you bet. So I've started writing our life-story already. It's funny, Garnet is usually the one who writes stuff. Her writing's neater than mine. So often I get her to do my school-work. She doesn't mind.
> *Yes I do.*

I was rifling through one of the boxes of books upstairs and right at the bottom there was this lovely fat red book. Ruby red, with a leather spine [...] So I'm scribbling away.

I'm not.

Yes you are. I keep letting you have a turn. And I'm not just writing about me, I'm writing about us. Giving an account of ourselves. (9–10)

The contrast between Ruby's imperious voice (which effectively absorbs her sister's experiences into her own) and Garnet's barely audible corrections is humorous but profound. The italicised interstices of the dialogic text hint at a subversive strand, coming from Garnet, which grows throughout the novel and finally leads to her breakaway from the duo. Ruby, however, perceives their duo as perfectly balanced; she constructs Garnet as her *complementary double*. Her sincere conviction that Garnet is actually writing (when she clearly is not), and her recurrent use of 'us', 'we' and 'ourselves', signal her inability to detect in her sister's denegation any potential menace to their harmony. She is also unable to detect her sister's greater talent at writing – she puts it down to penmanship. This oversight causes tremendous drama at the end of the novel, since Garnet's superior writing wins her a scholarship at an expensive boarding school; a scholarship Ruby never doubted they would either both get or just herself.

Ruby is clearly, at the beginning of the story, an assured and stable individual, because she treats her sister – and *writes her* – as a non-threatening, but polarised *other*, entirely part of herself but also complementary in its difference: an ideal double. In an imperialistic fashion, she needs Garnet to be both different and compliant. To confirm the existence of the twinship, Garnet is 'allowed' to write a few words here and there, and to express discontent; but her comments are immediately absorbed into the 'whole' that their dialogue forms, further strengthening Ruby's position. Garnet repeatedly begins her interventions with 'yes, but' (pp. 15, 16, 51, 56, 64, 65); but Ruby either ignores or contradicts her sister's rectifications, which become incorporated within Ruby's hegemonic discourse. Garnet is seemingly the *lacking* self, who needs Ruby's dominant discourse to continue to exist. She is also instrumentalised as a writer of some aspects of their lives, temporarily 'hired' by Ruby to narrate moments which Ruby does not want to narrate; for instance, their mother's death, or saying goodbye to their grandmother. '*Ruby doesn't want to write it. She always leaves the worst bit to me. I don't want to write it either,*' says Garnet (p. 45), but still writes it against her declared will. Ruby thus writes her sister as an illusion of ideal otherness, both necessary to her world and completely subservient to her will. She will, of course, experience a painful return to reality.

Charlie's writing in *The Lottie Project* is underscored by the same desire to write both herself and an *other*, and to make that other a stabilising force. Her 'expelled' double is entirely controlled by herself, contrary to Ruby relative to Garnet. Lottie is Charlie's creation, a 'parallel' other, so to speak: her chapters alternate with Charlie's, are titled similarly and tackle similar themes ('Family', 'Home', 'Food', etc). Despite Lottie's different nature, there are numerous similarities between the Charlie/Lottie duo and the Ruby/Garnet twinship, specifically their polarised personalities. Charlie's tempestuous, outspoken and vivacious character contrasts with Lottie's meek, serious and bookish attitude. But Charlie is generous in her imaginings of Lottie: she makes her a star pupil, grants her higher skills of resilience and forgiveness, and arguably a more mature character – the latter partly due to the fact that Lottie, because of her situation as a Victorian child of the working class, has to work to survive. Charlie's double appears, in many ways, to be a fantasised self; but it is also clearly, in part, a *lesson* to herself. While Charlie's life is objectively difficult – she lives, in typical Wilsonesque fashion, with her single mother, and little money – Lottie's life puts Charlie's into perspective: she has to leave her family to work ceaselessly. While Charlie's encounters with the intellectual upper class (in the form of her classmate Jamie) merely cause temporary annoyance, Lottie's rich employers exploit her. Lottie's tale exacerbates the unpleasant aspects of Charlie's daily life, and by doing so, minimises them. By writing Lottie's existence, Charlie partly *unwrites* the most disturbing aspects of her own.

She does so almost instinctively: there is an 'automatic writing' aspect to Charlie's compulsive narration of Lottie's parallel 'life'. Charlie marvels at how much the character of Lottie seems to be taking over; her ink-and-paper twin appears to be dictating her life to the young writer:

> It was weird. I read stuff in books and then started writing and it was as if this other girl entirely was scribbling it all down. The servant girl. Lottie the nursery maid. She'd started to feel real, like I'd known her all my life. I knew her better than I even knew Lisa or Angela. I just picked up a pencil and all *her* thoughts came rushing out on the paper.[5]

Note the objectifying 'this other girl', 'the servant girl', the italicised *her*, which place Lottie at a safe distance from Charlie. Charlie is here hiding from herself – but not from the reader – that this interposed otherness eases her own relationship to *herself*. It is no mystery, no 'weirdness', that Charlie 'knows' Lottie so well; Lottie is, after all, Charlie, in a comfortably estranged form. Just like Garnet for Ruby, Lottie is for Charlie the narcissistic escapist fantasy of a familiar but different *double*, who becomes the pacifying receptacle for her fears and desires, organising and managing them in an orderly, writerly form.

This escapist fantasy is a Victorian fantasy, an interestingly recurrent motif in Wilson's writing. *The Lottie Project* is one of several novels which either fully or partly take place in the Victorian or Edwardian eras. The celebrated *Hetty Feather* series (2010–2012) springs immediately to mind, but *Four Children and It* is also 'haunted' by its Edwardian literary double. Underscored by a tension between contemporary and Edwardian times, *Four Children and It* makes the first-person narrator, Rosalind, a prophetic voice able to navigate the two. An avid reader and very much a 'historical fantasiser', Rosalind is animated by a nostalgia of the Edwardian age, based on the children's novels she reads. Meanwhile, Smash, her evil stepsister, dwells very much in the present and is unable to grasp the charm of either literature or bygone eras. The novel opens with an argument between Rosalind and Smash, which revolves around diverging perceptions of classic literature for children:

> '*Five Children and It*', Smash read in a silly voice. 'Well, that's a stupid title for a start. [...] Why are they wearing these weird clothes?' [...]
> 'It was written more than a hundred years ago', I said. 'So the children are dressed in Edwardian clothes, pinafores and knickerbockers.'
> 'Knickerbockers to you too', said Smash. 'I hate historical books.' [6]

This exchange (arguably audacious for a contemporary children's book) may well reflect, for the young reader, actual conversations. It appears clear, at this stage, that the reader should align themselves with Rosalind – it is of course possible that the young reader of *Four Children and It* may be already familiar with *Five Children and It*, and that they should therefore empathise with Rosalind. However, should the reader secretly side with Smash, they will, perhaps to their own surprise, discover that the novel grows increasingly ambiguous about its support for the Edwardian age and its reflection in classic children's books. Smash's disgust for books and for the Edwardian age remains constant throughout the novel. As shall be developed later, it is actually Rosalind who will change her mind about the latter, after experiencing it 'for real'.

But Rosalind's initial position is one of superiority. Being endowed with the knowledge that the novel affords, she is able to identify the Psammead when it appears to the children (p. 32), and to predict that its wish-granting abilities are limited to one day. She is the only one enthralled, at first, by the intrusion of literature in her life. The Psammead fuels her nostalgic longing by noting how much times have changed since the Edwardian era: 'Dear goodness, names have become very short and brutal in this new age' (p. 31), he says, indirectly flattering Rosalind to the detriment of Smash. He also articulates Rosalind's lament about her difficult family situation: 'Family life seems particularly complicated nowadays' (p. 32), idealistically suggesting that family life used to be much simpler. Turning to Rosalind, he finally says about the five children of E. Nesbit's novel, 'I remember, I was particularly fond of the eldest girl, Anthea. You remind me of her a little' (p. 33), which '[delights]' Rosalind and makes her 'blush'. The Psammead, in other words, clearly starts out (even before he begins to grant them any wishes) as Rosalind's personal wish fulfilment – and strengthens her belief in another, past, ideal world, in which another, better *self* could exist.

Rosalind, contrary to Charlie and to Ruby and Garnet, has several 'doubles', and none of them are being 'written', so to speak, as the story unfolds, since Rosalind only 'writes' the novel a posteriori. But the different doubles that she garners also serve to compartmentalise, and thus stabilise, her sense of self, shaken by her parents' divorce. Smash is, in fairy-tale fashion, presented outright as the evil stepsister; this archetypal characterisation lasts for the first half of the novel. Rosalind writes into her the horror of her father's second marriage and amorousness with Alice, his new wife and mother of Smash and Maudie. Smash, the tomboyish bully, condenses Rosalind's jealousy towards the beautiful and sensual Alice (Alice's 'light' side, meanwhile, appears displaced onto the 'cute' little Maudie). By making Smash the embodiment of the pains of her parents' divorce, Rosalind creates an inherently *stable* antagonistic duo. She and Smash are polarised others, leading to incessant conflict, but also paradoxically 'safe' in their incompatibility; as long as Smash is horrible and stupid, Rosalind's father and brother will still favour her, and she will remain validated as the intelligent and kind Cinderella figure.

But Rosalind also has two other doubles onto which to write other aspects of herself. They are *indulgent* doubles; one which I would call mimetic, the other aspirational. Her 'mimetic' double is Anthea, Rosalind's 'equivalent' in *Five Children and It*. Anthea is not mentioned often in the novel, but, as the Psammead's words reveal, Rosalind clearly identifies most strongly with this character. When they finally meet (the Psammead having magicked the four children away into the world of *Five Children and It*), Anthea and Rosalind get on immediately.

'So you really wished to meet *us*?' says Anthea, to which Rosalind replies, 'Yes, I always thought we might – we might be friends', again 'blushing and feeling a fool' (p. 153). Her thought is met with enthusiasm by Anthea. Anthea is the ideal friend for Rosalind. They share their love for books in a long conversation (pp. 153–154) which reads as a complete reversal of Rosalind's initial row with Smash. 'It's so *lovely* to meet girls who like my sort of books!' (p. 153), says Rosalind. And when Smash mocks her again for thinking of exploring the town out of historical interest, Anthea supports Rosalind: '*I* like to get good marks too. I *love* history – and English' (p. 166).

Anthea is an ideal other because she *is* Rosalind under the exotic guise of an Edwardian-era child. She is a 'mimetic' double, giving Rosalind the illusion that a perfect soul mate would be one very similar to herself; not one in which to expel the negative aspects of her life, like Smash, but a mirror image wherein to see herself and her thoughts reflected and valued. Again, Anthea as Rosalind's double reinforces and validates Rosalind's sense of self. And the relevance of this particular doubleness goes further than character level. Rosalind's discovery of her ideal literary double mirrors the young, bookish, shy reader's similar discoveries of ideal literary doubles – not least in Jacqueline Wilson's numerous books – and represents the fantasy of meeting them 'for real'. On an extradiegetic level, this doubleness has the added advantage of validating Rosalind's *character* as the rightful successor to Anthea, and *Four Children and It* as the rightful successor to *Five Children and It*. By building a web of similarities between Rosalind and Anthea, *Four Children and It* seeks to claim its own place in the literary canon of 'classic' children's books; an intertextual and metafictional self-assuredness which is not uncommon in parodies, continuations or pastiches of classic texts.

Rosalind's third 'double' is aspirational: it is the Rosalind she becomes for one day in Smash's wish, which wills them all to be 'rich and famous'. At first, Rosalind does not know what she is 'rich and famous' for, but she is suddenly told that she is a successful children's writer, about to do a book signing at Harrods. For the first time she gets a glance of her 'double': 'It was a postcard of *me*, sitting at a desk with one hand cupped under my chin, gazing dreamily into the distance. Underneath the photo there was a little caption: *Rosalind Hartlepool, children's writer*' (p. 87). Note the italicised '*me*', which expresses Rosalind's surprise, but also subtly estranges this word from the rest of the sentence – the same typographical strategy, we may recall, as in *The Lottie Project* and *Double Act*. Rosalind soon discovers that her 'latest book' is *Four Children and It*; again, she says, 'It really was *my* book' (p. 92), the italics hinting again at her incredulousness, which reappear later on, when describing one of her fans: 'She was shy of *me*!' (p. 93). Rosalind Hartlepool, '*child wonder writer*' (p. 93), as she is labelled, is not her; it is *her in italics*, nothing else than another double, an aspirational *döppelganger*. This Rosalind of the Psammead's creation validates, by making them public and publicly praised, Rosalind's secret writing ambitions. This episode also sows the seeds of the literary *mise en abyme* which grows increasingly important throughout the book, and will culminate in a metafictional 'loop' when Rosalind, at the end, begins to write their story – finishing the novel, therefore, with the sentence that began it.

It is clear from these analyses that the multiple 'doubles', which people the (intradiegetically) real and imagined lives of the writerly heroines, have the main function of stabilising, reinforcing and validating, but also of *simplifying*, the young girls' senses of self. By creating a sophisticated gallery of contrary, aspirational, mimetic or complementary doubles, they write their ideal 'others' so as to emphasise to themselves the complete and satisfying nature of their own experiences. They expel the undesirable complexities of their existences into these doubles, which are therefore, at all times, a creation, an illusion.

When the illusion collapses

But what is the nature of this illusion? Strikingly, none of the writerly heroines fully *believes* in the 'reality' of her double(s). Instead, they argue that they 'seem' or 'feel' real. Thus, in *The Lottie Project*, Charlie, overwhelmed by her own writing skills, mentions that Lottie has 'started to feel real' (p. 51). Rosalind's narcissistic wonder at her 'writing success' is tempered by awareness of its illusory nature; she acknowledges that she 'knew it was only happening because of the Psammead, but it seemed real all the same' (p. 93). Conversely, when Ruby lets Garnet write about their mother's (real) death, she says, 'All right. But tell it quickly. The bit about Mum. Tell it as if it was a story and not real so that it won't hurt so much' (p. 18). Garnet, accordingly, creates another 'double' of their double act: speaking in the third-person voice, and beginning with 'Once upon a time', she tells the 'story' of their parents' marriage, the twins' birth and their mother's death. But Ruby cannot help interfering; she clearly cannot fully play along with the 'fictionality' of Garnet's tale. Charlie, Rosalind, Ruby and Garnet are not stupid; they know that these 'doubles' they create for themselves are illusory. They do not ever *mistake* them for reality.

Instead, they happily live on *alongside* their doubles and the stabilising *copies of reality* within which they evolve.

Contemporary French philosopher Clément Rosset provides, in *Le réel et son double* ('The real and its double', 1984[7]) a relevant theorisation of the nature of illusion. Rosset argues that illusion is commonly misunderstood as a denial of reality. Instead, he thinks, illusion signals the refusal of reality *in its unicity* (and therefore its determinacy), and the consequent escape into a 'copy' of reality: a double. There is an 'oracular' dimension to our existences: we confusedly believe that they should develop in a meaningful and orderly form. But our experience of reality is dissatisfactory and unsettling: even though there is nothing inherently *strange* to our lives solidifying in a certain way, we *perceive* it as strange, as *fake*, because we do not accept that it is quite literally all there is to it, in its messiness and disorderliness. We continue to act *as if* there was another life, one which *feels* real, in spite of – but not in ignorance of – reality. In so doing, we *act* the life we are actually living, and 'feel as real' the illusory double of that life. Rosset takes the example, in Proust's *In Search of Lost Time*, of Charles Swann's 'illusion' concerning his lover Odette de Crécy. Swann has been told by many people that Odette is a courtesan; he uncontroversially *knows* it. And she indeed costs him money; he *pays* her monthly to be his lover. This makes him, by all definitions of the term, her client, and makes her a courtesan. But Swann's relation to this problem is paradoxical – and, according to Rosset, typical of illusion. He acknowledges that they are both indeed *acting as if* they were a courtesan and her client; in appearance there is nothing to suggest that they are not. But he does not question it further than that; as Rosset puts it, 'it is less an erroneous perception than a *useless* perception': Swann is able to see that they are in a mercantile relationship, while continuing to 'feel' that they are not.[8] This leads to a stabilising *doubling* of the real – an illusion – but not a denial of reality. Swann's feeling is that the life he is actually living is a fake; a performance of reality, a deceptive world of appearances. Meanwhile, the life he is *not living* (where he and Odette are not in a mercantile relationship) is *felt* to be the 'real' one. The rejection of his existence in its unicity leads to a doubling of the real.

Examples of such 'illusional' behaviour in the three novels have already been pinpointed: there are moments when obstacles and problems, or the illusory nature of one's life, are clearly acknowledged, but then tidied away, so to speak, and not properly taken into account. Ruby's acknowledgement of her sister's resistance to acting in a film, Rosalind's acknowledgement that her day of writing success is entirely controlled by the Psammead and Charlie's acknowledgement that Lottie is not a 'real' person do not seem to lead to any modification in their behaviours. They continue to use these doubles as a means of balancing, managing and orchestrating their lives by splitting them into twos, acting *as if* they had not noticed their actual unicity.

But, as Rosset theorises, there are moments when the illusion collapses; when life in its unicity, determinacy and rigidity 'reappears', and reveals the illusory nature of the double. This is the typical moment of the *catastrophe* in classical tragedies, especially when it signifies the fulfilment of an oracle. Oedipus is stunned to realise that his life went *exactly* as predicted – he married his mother and killed his father. The unicity of this life suddenly reappears – a life from which he never escaped. He may *feel* cheated, but there is nothing deceptive about his fate; it was never anything else. Rosset's sophisticated theorisation applies, of course, to everyday life; we find ourselves, at certain times, stunned to realise that our life *is* what it is, and *just* what it is, having taken all the space, so to speak, of the 'something' it was supposed to be instead. These are moments when we suddenly see how well we managed to perceive, but then set aside, the illusory nature of the desires, beliefs and embellishments we had clothed this existence with. These moments, Rosset articulates, are of an oracular nature: 'The expected event comes to coincide with itself, whereby comes the surprise: because we were expecting something different, although connected, the same thing but not exactly in the same way.'[9]

Such moments (which are, of course, of high didactic power) occur in all three books. Ruby and Garnet's 'catastrophe' happens when Garnet learns that she has obtained a scholarship to go to Marnock Heights, a selective boarding school. It was Ruby's idea to ask for this scholarship. Although it was always stated that there was only *one* grant, Ruby remained convinced that each of the twins would get one, despite Garnet's rational worries:

> *I don't see the point, as there's two of us and only one scholarship.*
> We'll wangle two, somehow. Once Miss Jeffreys gets to know us. She likes us already. (p. 133)
> *Ruby ... what if you get accepted for the scholarship and I don't?*
> We're both going to get a scholarship.
> *But what if we don't? Would you go to Marnock Heights without me?*
> I keep telling and telling you, we're going together. (p. 139)

Ruby's illusional behaviour is extremely clear, and amusingly similar to Rosset's theorisation. Ruby *knows* that there is just *one* scholarship (in Rosset's terms, she acknowledges the unicity of this 'reality'), but she continues to act *as if*, 'somehow', they could give the twins two scholarships. Tragically for Ruby, having used Garnet as a complementary double for years for self-stabilisation and validation, she does not realise that Garnet has been, all this time, an individual in her own right, and a writer in development. The letter which carries Miss Jeffreys's message (very akin to the messenger's fateful letter in *Oedipus-Rex*), has the effect of *stunning* both Ruby and Garnet. It leads them to disbelief in the face of reality, a textbook illustration of Rosset's conceptualisation: when the world appears in its unicity, one first feels cheated and *duped*, even though it was always clear that reality would be like this – in this case, just one scholarship. Ruby becomes, appropriately, 'silent' as a writer: Garnet takes over the narrative.

> *We couldn't believe it. We thought Miss Jeffreys had got us mixed up.*
> *'She means me', said Ruby. 'She must mean me.'*
> *'Yes, it can't be me', I said. 'Ruby will have got the scholarship.'* (p. 142)

The impression that reality is not what it should be for Ruby and Garnet is ironic; the reader receptive to Wilson's careful foreshadowing has had plenty of time to understand that Garnet was always the better writer and the more studious twin.

Ruby's discovery of her twin's independent existence – of her twin's *unicity* – leads to a symbolic change in her behaviour: she chooses to *reject* her double, and exacerbate her own uniqueness. She stops writing in the Accounts book, picking, instead, another notebook of her own, which will be 'all about Me' (p. 160). She cuts her hair entirely, so that she cannot be mistaken for Garnet anymore. Thus she briefly plunges into another illusion – another 'double' life whereby she acknowledges her twin, but acts as if she did not. Only at the very end are they are reconciled. Ruby sticks into her notebook Garnet's first postcard, symbolically acknowledging her twin's independent life and independent writing. Finally reconciled with life *as it is*, namely, not as an interdependent pair of twins but as two different individuals with different aspirations, Ruby is able to end the tale with a lucid and tender statement: 'We're still Ruby and Garnet, even though you're there and I'm here. We're going to be Ruby and Garnet forever' (p. 188).

Rosalind's multiple illusions collapse at different moments of the text; her various 'doubles' rise and fall with the plot. Her 'aspirational' double, the writer, is easily discarded once the day ends. Not so for the other two, which 'collapse' during a central event in the text: Rosalind's loss of her Edwardian fantasies. After her indulgent day with Anthea and her siblings, Rosalind accidentally wishes to stay in the Edwardian era 'forever'. Anthea is whisked away, alongside all her family, and Rosalind is left alone in the suddenly much less quaint 'reality' of the Edwardian age. Taken to the orphanage and the workhouse, she experiences the pain and cold of a 'real' Edwardian childhood. Thankfully for her, Smash manages to wish her back into the twenty-first century. This is a turning point in the story, where Rosalind's mimetic double – Anthea – has lost much of her appeal, and her antagonistic double – Smash – suddenly upgrades from evil stepsister to prince(ss) charming: 'Oh, Smash!' exclaims Rosalind, 'I just can't believe this. You risked everything to rescue me. You're a true *heroine*' (p. 188). Note, again, the casual but meaningful 'I just can't believe this': Rosalind's refusal, up to now, to register awareness of Smash's grit and bravery leads to her being temporarily *incredulous* when it is evidenced. Smash suddenly appears as the complex, courageous and interesting character she actually always was – but she was, until then, 'dressed up' by Rosalind as her archetypal nemesis. Rosalind, seeing the world as it always was (without an ideal friend from another age, and with a stepsister whose differences will have to be tolerated), accepts and embraces it. The second half of the novel is, accordingly, much less conflictual than the first, allowing both girls to develop together. This also has the effect of reconciling the potentially two different types of readers of *Four Children and It*: the studious and bookish young reader, potentially already familiar with Nesbit's text, for whom Rosalind was a literary 'double'; and the less willing reader, not disposed to fantasise about classical children's texts, for whom Smash might have secretly been a 'double' since the beginning – a fantasy now made acceptable.

In *The Lottie Project*, the illusion not so much collapses as gives way to Charlie's 'real' life when tragedy strikes. Charlie is indeed faced with an event that topples her world: her mother, Jo, begins to flirt with a man, Mark. Charlie, in her usual dramatic way, tells Mark's five-year-old son Robbie that his father does not love him anymore now that he is with her mother. The same night, Robbie runs away, and is not found until the morning. He has caught pneumonia, and must stay in hospital for several days. Robbie's disappearance and illness are mirrored, in Lottie's diary, by an equivalent event: the kidnapping and illness of Freddie, the baby Lottie is looking after. But at this stage Lottie's life is barely a vignette in the margins of Charlie's. Only a few pages are devoted to telling this story, while Charlie's 'space' amplifies; and the resolution of Freddie's predicament occurs very swiftly, while Robbie's is long drawn. As Charlie is pressed by 'real' events to envisage the changes triggered by her mother's new relationship, Lottie's function as double is compressed. There is little Charlie can do to avoid facing reality, which is quite literally a wake-up call – she is woken up in the night by Mark's phone call saying that Robbie has vanished. Charlie holds herself responsible for Robbie's running away from home; she realises that she has exaggerated the tragic nature of Jo and Mark's relationship, both to herself and to others, and that she has failed to take into account Robbie's higher sensitivity and gullibility. This throws light upon her own tendency to *tell herself tales* of her own life in a hyperbolic form, heightening tensions, drama and difficulties; this tendency, that has led her to create Lottie as a narcissistic 'stabiliser', is suddenly revealed as treacherous and threatening.

Writing for others: The reader as ultimate double

All four heroines eventually 'vanquish' their double: they learn to accept the complexities and the idiosyncrasies of their own personalities, and the illusory nature of the various 'doubles' which artificially stabilised their senses of self. Importantly, they do so through fiction – or rather, autofiction – and this writing *will be read*. This is an essential aspect of the texts: the endpoint of the writing, whether or not the heroines realise it, is its being shared with others. This sharing occurs, generally, *post-illusion* – when the heroines are already partly or fully 'liberated' from the haunting presence of their double, and are now ready to reach out to a reader or a listener.

The Lottie Project provides a particularly touching image of this newly shared experience. Throughout the whole novel, Charlie's writing endeavour has been kept secret; she knows that Miss Beckworth never asked for a fictional diary. When Jamie first attempts to read her 'project', Charlie hits him. In response to his (understandable) indignation, she says,

> 'Just stop messing about with my private stuff, right?'
> 'It's just your Victorian project, for goodness' sake. And you're doing it all wrong, not a bit the way Miss Beckworth said.'
> 'I'm doing it *my* way', I said. (p. 54)

Charlie, when writing Lottie's diary, is thus dimly aware that it will have to be read, but she chooses not to think about it: 'I couldn't stand the thought of Miss Beckworth speckling it with her red biro. It was private' (p. 51). She comforts herself, temporarily, by saying that there is still a long time until she has to submit it (Ibid). When she finally does, she is resigned to getting a bad mark for it; she knows it is an atypical piece of work. But to her surprise, Miss Beckworth gives it the second-best mark, and lauds it publicly: 'Jamie's brilliant project tells us almost all there is to know about Victorian times. But there's one other project here that tells us what it *feels* like to be a Victorian' (p. 189). Charlie's project has succeeded *as a piece of writing*, not just as a school project.

Miss Beckworth then asks Charlie to read some extracts from Lottie's diary to the rest of the class, and Charlie movingly discovers the pleasures of reaching out to others through writing: 'Everyone got a bit shuffly and sighing to start with – but by the time I'd got to the bottom of the first page *they were riveted!*' (Ibid). It is difficult not to read in these evocative lines a personal account of Wilson's own experience as a reader of her own work to children, just like Rosalind's fantasised 'Child Writer Wonder' double could be read as Wilson's recollection of an author event with emotional fans. This biographical reading, however speculative, throws light upon the interesting transition between writing the self and its double for *oneself*, and writing for someone *else*; between diary and novel, between secret aspirations and public ambition. Above all, it marks the end of the writerly heroine as sole 'self-reader', and the advent of a new *other*, a new 'double', a much more gratifying and 'real' double: the reader.

Readers in Rosalind's fantasy are the captivated, tearful fans of a world-famous author. In Charlie's life, they are, more prosaically, her classmates; but the scene is arguably more eloquent, and rings truer, than Rosalind's wishful enjoyment of a star-status signing at Harrods. Rosalind's eventual conversion into a 'real' writer, it is implicit in the text, comes with *work*; she has to go back to the *beginning* of the story and work her way through it with a pencil on a notebook. Wilson's rendering of the writer's life in these texts is thus interestingly multifaceted, its gratifications and difficulties scattered over different episodes: the book signing, the book-writing process and the school visit. All of these episodes, however, are subsumed by exhilarating encounters with *readers*.

Ruby's 'catastrophe', as detailed earlier, comes from Miss Jeffreys's appreciation of Garnet's writing as better than Ruby's. Miss Jeffreys's judgement reads like an evaluation of the twins' Accounts book: '[Ruby's] written work is lively if a little slapdash ... If she could only apply herself more vigorously then I'm sure she could reach a far higher standard. ... [Garnet's] essay was outstanding – extremely sensitive and mature' (pp. 140–141). This is Ruby and Garnet's first encounter with a 'real' reader: someone who takes the time to assess and appreciate their prose. Garnet is rewarded for her work, studious-ness and sensitivity, while Ruby is shown, for the first time in her life, that her sister's heretofore derided qualities made her, in this situation, the 'better' twin. Miss Jeffreys appears to be a clairvoyant reader, in the sense that she has exactly and lucidly decoded the illusional and oppressive reliance of Ruby on Garnet, and Garnet's dependence on Ruby, simply through their writing; just like the reader of the novel has done up until then. And by publicly revealing this imbalanced relationship, she has transformed their lives.

Rosalind's maturation into a writer is expanded into the paratext of *Four Children and It*, where she is represented in the endpapers as an authority figure giving eight 'Writing tips', some of which enhance the idea that writing is a long process which requires concentration, daily writing, reading and 'thinking hard'. She is now reaching out directly to the would-be writers among the readers, and her autho-rial status is heightened by the fact that it parades off as non-fictional. Two pages later, Jacqueline Wilson herself intervenes, encouraging readers to read E. Nesbit's works, and sharing her own experience as a published writer. Quite clearly, in *Four Children and It*, it is not enough to *write*: being a *published writer* is the central aspiration. The insistence on the professionalisation of this activity (contrary to Ruby, Garnet and Charlie, for whom writing 'to be published' is not an explicit concern) highlights a desire to get the writing child to reach out to a wide audience in an organised way, and makes a statement as to the possibility of 'upgrading' from diary-writing to successful novel-writing. A *wishful* statement, perhaps – but an inspirational one nonetheless. As Julia Eccleshare analyses, Wilson's depiction of writers and of the writerly life in her books – from *The Story of Tracy Beaker* to *Clean Break*[10] – wilfully encourages aspiring writers, and does not shy away from representations of stardom: 'Wilson shows children as readers and writers and the writers that inspire them as highly suc-cessful. It is an upwards spiral of success; both sides are achievers with all the signifiers that entails in a modern world.'[11]

These aspirational narratives, which all end with recognition of the heroines' writing skills *by others*, are characterised by a 'centrifugal' force: a movement away from the narcissistic centre of the young heroines' lives, and towards the outside world, and the unknowable other. Their 'doubles', which pulled them back towards themselves and allowed for complacent or therapeutic simplifications of their daily experiences, have collapsed; and now their writing energy can concentrate on addressing others. The reader emerges as the new ideal double: someone who will read, react, respond to the text in gratifying and unpredictable ways; someone upon whom they will have gained some form of power thanks to their writing skills. In two of these novels the first reader is an adult character in a position of authority; this is, as Colabucci and Parsons note, a common motif in narratives of child writers. Miss Jeffreys's and Miss Beckworth's 'validation' of the heroines' efforts are not without didacticism. Nonetheless, the reader as the ultimate *other* to conquer remains the horizon towards which these three narratives tend. By metonymy, characters which are readers *in the text* refer to the actual readers *of the text*; as we have seen, Miss Jeffreys's observations may have been pre-empted by the shrewd reader of the twins' diary, and Miss Beckworth's congratulations are perhaps not as huge a surprise for the reader as they are for Charlie. The *actual* reader, at the end of the novels, finds himself or herself interpelated, on different levels, as the *ideal other* which the text addresses. And thus the emphasis shifts from character to reader, subtly raising questions about the reader's relationship to *their own* secret 'doubles', literary or otherwise.

To conclude, I would argue that this complex address to the reader, which gradually develops over the course of the novels, reduces the risk of identification with the main characters of the stories. To paraphrase Maria Nikolajeva, identification is the mark of an unsophisticated reading; to be able to put oneself 'in the shoes' of a fictional character is to put oneself at risk of uncritical acceptance of their actions.[12] These texts, on the contrary, subtly present the heroines' *moving away from* identification with their fantasised and illusory doubles, and towards the complex, unpredictable others which their readership represents. Fiction-writing as presented by the novels is not ultimately an opportunity for self-centred exploration, comfortably balanced over one or several constructed 'doubles': it is a risk, a leap into the unknown.

As the heroines shed their illusions over the stabilities of their own lives and the easy responses of their created 'doubles', the reader is gently enjoined to consider, in turn, the impossibility of finding their own 'doubles' in fictional texts. However enthralling and appealing, Jacqueline Wilson's texts appear here to tug the reader away from narcissistic contemplation of their own woes and difficulties; to wean them gradually from the enthusiastic feeling that they are 'finding themselves' in the text. In so doing, these texts, I argue, accompany their readers on the way to a sophisticated and mature readerly position. They entice them to become readers who will tackle a text to find an *other*, not a *double*; to find complex and new experiences, not just idealised versions of their own existences.

Notes

1 Ruth Berman, 'No Joe Marches'. *Children's Literature in Education*, 29:4 (1998), 237–247, 237.
2 Other books by Jacqueline Wilson which feature writerly heroines and/ or engage in substantial reflection on the writer's professional status include her autobiographical works *Jackie Daydream* (2007), *My Secret Diary* (2009), and *Clean Break* (2005).
3 Lesley Colabucci and Linda T. Parsons, 'To Be a Writer: Representations of Writers in Recent Children's Novels'. *The Reading Teacher* 62:1 (September 2008), 44–52, 48.
4 Jacqueline Wilson, *Double Act* (London: Corgi, 1996), p. 1. All further references in this chapter are to this edition.
5 Jacqueline Wilson, *The Lottie Project* (London: Corgi, 1998), p. 51. All further references in this chapter are to this edition.
6 Jacqueline Wilson, *Four Children and It* (London: Puffin, 2012), pp. 1–3. All further references in this chapter are to this edition.
This conversation is in many ways a rewriting of a very similar, but shorter, argument between Charlie and Jamie in *The Lottie Project*, with Charlie as the disparager of 'boring boring boring' historical fiction (67).
7 All translations mine.
8 Clément Rosset, *Le réel et son double* (Paris: Gallimard, 1984), p. 10.
9 Ibid., p. 41.
10 In *Clean Break*, Wilson creates an explicit 'mimetic double' of herself, successful children's writer Jenna Williams. The association of meta-fiction with doubleness is thus repeated on a biographical level – which I have no space to analyse in this chapter. See Julia Eccleshare, 'Readers' Perceptions of a Writer: Jacqueline Wilson's Persona and Her Relationship with Her Reader' in Evelyn Arizpe and Vivienne Smith (eds.), *Children as Readers in Children's Literature: The Power of Texts and the Importance of Reading* (London: Routledge, 2015).
11 Julia Eccleshare, 'Readers' Perceptions of a Writer.
12 Maria Nikolajeva. *Power, Voice and Subjectivity in Literature for Young Readers* (London: Routledge, 2010).

8

Coming of Age in Jacqueline Wilson's Victorian Fiction

Sheena Wilkinson

Jacqueline Wilson's sequence of Victorian novels – *Hetty Feather* (*HF,* 2009), *Sapphire Battersea* (*SB,* 2011), *Emerald Star* (*ES,* 2012) and *Diamond* (*D,* 2013) – contains much that we associate with the 'typical' Wilson novel – feisty heroine, displaced children, an interest in social stigma and marginalised people – and yet the series differs from the rest of her work in several noteworthy ways, mainly in their historical settings (the 1880s and 90s), and in their sustained exploration of a child maturing into a young adult.

The Victorians have always fascinated Wilson, a passion she explored as early as *This Girl* (1988), and was dismayed to learn modern children might not share. In the introduction to *The Lottie Project* (1992) she expresses hope that 'It would be wonderful if just a few readers … decide that maybe the Victorians aren't so bad after all.'[1] She was inspired to write *Hetty Feather* when she was the inaugural Thomas Coram Fellow at the Foundling Museum, but Hetty's adventures have moved well beyond the short story Wilson initially planned. Apart from the trilogy, a fourth book, *Diamond* (2013), relates the adventures of a young acrobat sold into circus life by a drunken father. Although the narrator is the acrobat, Ellen-Jane (Diamond), her story is being 'written down' by Hetty, her friend and mentor. It seems probable that Wilson intends at least one more sequel. In a recent interview with young readers she reveals, 'I am just finishing a long long Edwardian novel … [*Opal Plumstead,* 2014] but we'll find out what Hetty and Diamond are going to be doing after that'.[2] Clearly, Wilson plans to continue exploring the past.[3]

Catherine Butler and Hallie O'Donovan argue that the term 'historical fiction' is oxymoronic, highlighting as it does 'the uneasiness of the relationship between fact and fiction'.[4] Wilson negotiates this relationship effectively in her Victorian fiction, where inevitable 'lessons' about the past are embedded in exciting narratives described as 'more escapist than her modern fiction'.[5] The books are steeped in Victorian literature, both explicitly – Hetty cherishes a copy of *David Copperfield* and tries to edit her memoirs to resemble the structure of three-decker novels, and Wilson has great fun satirising the 'improving' literature of the time in Buchanan's version of Hetty's story – and implicitly: many of the tropes are familiar Victorian fare – brave waifs, consumptive mothers dying in the arms of said waifs, charlatan mediums, tawdry circuses, perky servant girls walking out with even perkier butcher boys, etc. However, we should remember that these tropes are most unlikely to be familiar to the intended child reader. In a small survey of Jacqueline Wilson readers, 68 per cent said that they chose the Hetty Feather books because they were fans of Wilson rather than of history;[6] and 72 per cent 'never' or 'only occasionally' read historical fiction by other writers. One reader commented, 'They are exciting but you can also learn lots about historical life', a response which would please the 'subtly didactic' Wilson.[7] Lucy Pearson suggests that

> In her own way, Wilson is just as concerned with teaching children appropriate social and moral values as her Victorian predecessors: while the stories she tells are clearly a product of late twentieth-century British society, the messages of tolerance and care for others are not dissimilar from those which appeared in nineteenth-century texts.[8]

Wilson also enjoys educating children about books and reading. Interviewed for Radio Four's *Desert Island Discs* (16 October 2005, while she was Children's Laureate) she described wanting to introduce children to the classics through her stories, whose characters are often bookish: 'If I just have a little reference to [the classics] then children might … read them.' Her books sometimes also teach children *how* to read; in a recent interview for the *Guardian* Wilson tells Rachel Cooke that the voice of Tracy Beaker 'introduces children to the idea of the unreliable narrator', an idea which is explored in more detail in Helen Day's chapter for this volume.[9]

The Hetty Feather books do not merely educate the reader about aspects of Victorian society and literature; they have much to say about the process of writing and editing, and about the place of the imagination in transforming experience. Focusing on the character as artist is not unusual for Wilson, as Clémentine Beauvais discusses in her chapter; what the Hetty Feather series' 15-year timespan allows is the scope for her to explore a writer's development in more depth, linking it to her protagonist's development as a young woman.

Wilson herself says that Hetty, 'a child of enormous creative potential', is now her favourite character, usurping previous favourite Tracy Beaker.[10] While rebellious Hetty may bear a superficial resemblance to Tracy, she is a more complex and developed character. Indeed, I would argue that Hetty's development from birth to 15 represents Wilson's most sustained and ambitious attempt to chart a character's coming of age. Although there are three core books about Tracy, the third, *Starring Tracy Beaker* (2006) is written retrospectively, about a still pre-adolescent Tracy. The four books of the Girls series chart only about a year in the lives of Ellie and her friends in their early teens. Approaching 70, Wilson has said recently that she can no longer 'write for people in their mid teens ... Teenagers are getting up to all sorts that an old lady like me doesn't know about,' which is one reason why she has turned to the past.[11] Even so, it is interesting that Wilson does not allow Hetty to tell her *own* story past the age of 15, shifting the narrative to the younger Diamond, albeit with Hetty's 'help'.

The scope of Wilson's sprawling, somewhat picaresque Victorian odysseys is reminiscent of Dickens or even Sarah Waters, and like them her approach is social realism with a slightly grotesque spin. The action is not set against any war, political uprising or plague. In this, as well as in their three-volume structure, the books have more in common with the Victorian novels they echo than with much modern historical fiction or children.[12] When young soldier Gideon is wounded, Hetty has to ask, 'What was the battle? Are we at *war*?'[13]

Wilson educates young readers about the late nineteenth century partly through vivid evocation of the settings – bucolic village, grim foundling hospital, lively seaside resort (complete with freak show), but also through her typical device of making us empathise with an appealing protagonist. But Hetty must also work as a convincing *Victorian* heroine, without alienating a modern reader. This is always a challenge for the historical writer, perhaps especially when the intended reader is a child. In their introduction to *Historical Fiction for Children: Capturing the Past* (2001) Fiona Collins and Judith Graham identify the balance needed between 'the responsibility owed to historical truth and the need to write a story which in its emotional and narrative truth engages the modern reader'.[14] Thus, Hetty can have 'ideas above her station', but she also takes pride in the domestic skills expected of a Victorian girl: 'She's got a very light hand with her pastry. I doubt I could do better myself,' says Mrs Briskett (*SB*, p. 219). She runs away with the circus, but with full awareness that in doing so she is putting herself beyond the respectable pale. Butler and O'Donovan sum up the dilemma for the writer:

> Historical novels for children must negotiate the fact that many attitudes now generally considered bigoted ... were almost universal at various points in the past ... Writers ... face a difficult choice: that of presenting a sanitised past, with at least the sympathetic characters displaying an ahistorically liberal sensibility; or appearing to normalise and perpetuate these attitudes through fiction.[15]

This 'difficult choice' is played out throughout the Hetty Feather novels. Hetty may not blame her mother for her illegitimacy, but an otherwise sympathetic character, Miss Smith, reinforces more typical contemporary attitudes:

> 'Mama didn't do anything *wrong* – '
> 'She had a child out of wedlock, Hetty', Miss Smith said quietly.[16]

When a stranger (who brings to mind the insouciant mothers in the contemporary-set *The Diamond Girls* or *Lily Alone*) expresses a more 'liberal' opinion – '*My* two kiddies have two fathers and neither father was my husband' – the narrative undermines her view by presenting her as vulgar, drunken and mercenary (*HF,* p. 136).

The Victorians may be, as Philip Pullman suggests, 'more real to us than any age before them', but even so, Hetty's world and world view, and the way she expresses them, must differ from Wilson's modern characters.[17] Pullman suggests, 'If you want readers you have to use present-day English, but that can easily sound incongruous ... The best you can hope for is a sort of dignified neutrality that reads like a good translation.'[18] He reflects that this is a matter not merely of semantics but of rhythm. Wilson's prose style in the Hetty Feather books bears this out. It is more lyrical and expansive than in her contemporary novels. Wilson herself describes the 'challenge' of this: 'she wanted Hetty Feather to be "readable", but still have "some air of Victorian authenticity"' (Womack 2011). We cannot imagine Tracy Beaker expressing herself thus:

> He begged me to carry on, declaring my childish tale a masterpiece. I knew it was nothing of the sort. Still, the story of my life was unusual, to say the least. My former employer, Mr Buchanan, had poured scorn upon my memoir, and yet he had copied it out himself, scarcely changing my words, clearly trying to pass it off as his own work (*ES,* p. 257)

There is no unfamiliar, alienating vocabulary here, even for a child, but the cadences of the sentences give a convincing impression of a

Victorian voice. Like *Jane Eyre*, whose 'passionate and ... arresting' narrative voice invites the reader 'inside and alongside her' and which was, Victor Watson argues, a profound influence on the novels of maturation which came after, Hetty's voice invites identification and empathy.[19] Wilson considers herself 'very much a Victorian girl inside', which is perhaps what helps to make Hetty's voice so engaging.[20]

There is more than voice and attitudes to consider, however, in conveying historical authenticity. John Stephens suggests that 'while historical fiction is essentially a realist genre it also has a pervasive need to make the discourse "strange"'.[21] In Wilson's own memoirs, as a woman in late middle age looking back, it is appropriate to *explain*:

> Shopping was very different in those days.[22]
> Cornwall was considered exotic in 1960, before there were cheap package tours abroad.[23]

The Hetty Feather books, however, are narrated by a child experiencing her own world. It would compromise the relationship between narrator and reader if Hetty were to *explain* what a privy or a hokey-pokey was. The girls I surveyed insisted that 'only occasionally' (32 per cent) or 'never' (68 per cent) did they encounter in the Hetty Feather books any details about Victorian life which they did not understand. Not one girl ticked 'often'. This may have something to do with the fact that all were already at (an academically selective) secondary school, but it may also reflect Wilson's care in presenting the unfamiliar in a clarifying context. She is helped by the fact that Hetty spends nine years in an institution so that the outside world is as unfamiliar to her as it may be to a twenty-first-century reader: 'But now that I was out in this new topsy-turvy world, I realised I had to start learning all over again. I did not know the simplest things ... my own country was a totally foreign land to me' (*SB*, p. 80). As well as their historical settings, I would suggest that the most striking thing about Wilson's Victorian novels is the extent to which they are coming-of-age narratives. Hetty comes of age both as a young woman and as a writer. In the introduction to *Coming of Age in Children's Literature* (2002), Victor Watson identifies the process of 'maturation', describing the maturation of the heroines of nineteenth- and early twentieth-century North American fiction, from *Little Women* onwards: 'Their maturation involves ... suffering, caring for the sick, bereavement, distinguishing and valuing true friendship, and understanding and facing the financial realities that govern their lives.'[24] This exactly describes the stages of Hetty's maturation. Moreover Watson suggests

that 'Maturation has especially attracted writers who have been fascinated by narrative language ... Maturation fiction has been constantly
fascinated by itself, by the practical business of using words to tell stories'.[25] This again has obvious relevance to the Hetty Feather novels.
Wilson's interest in the practical business of using words to tell stories
is discussed elsewhere,[26] but Hetty's is the story which most strikingly
allies emotional and artistic maturity. Tracy Beaker's style, for example,
is raw and immediate, consistent with the device that she is writing
My Book About Me, a tool used by social workers for children in care
to make sense of their lives, and which develops in *The Dare Game*
into a diary. Hetty (like Anne Frank, one of Wilson's heroines) returns
to her memoirs several times, developing them from a spontaneous
outpouring, whose rawness may indeed resemble Tracy's – 'They're
much too bold, too personal, too passionate,' Miss Smith, her mentor,
tells her (*SB*, 38), leading Hetty to reflect, 'Perhaps I would always be
too sharply truthful' (*SB*, p. 210) – into a carefully reworked autobiography: 'I rewrote my memoirs. I kept to the truth but arranged
them like ... three-decker novels ... with lots of conversation and a
proper story structure' (*ES*, p. 305). Hetty loses her childish dream that
her memoirs might make her fortune, but she takes them seriously
as both artefacts and artistic endeavour. The earnestness with which
Hetty approaches her writing sets her apart from Tracy, and even from
more reflective and self-consciously literary characters like Rosalind
(*Four Children and It*). In her seriousness she owes much to the literary-
minded heroines of L. M. Montgomery. Hetty shares with these early
twentieth-century Canadian heroines, Anne Shirley and Emily Starr,
her strong, passionate character, her tendency to befriend the marginalised, her vivid imagination and of course her literary ambitions. She
even physically resembles the skinny, red-headed Anne; and like Emily
the spectre of tuberculosis haunts her: 'The doctor at the hospital
had once said I had a weak chest so Mama still worried terribly' (*SB*,
p. 208). Emily's parents both die of TB and her aunts predict that
Emily will 'probably die of consumption'.[27] Victor Watson says of
Anne Shirley: 'She has had a tough life, and imagination has enabled
her to believe doggedly in alternative possibilities.'[28] This 'dependence
on her imagination' exactly describes Hetty, who shares with other
Wilson heroines like the bed-bound Elsie (*Queenie*) the ability to 'picture' vividly. Wilson uses this imaginative gift, as she uses Hetty's developing craft as a writer, to chart her growing maturity. As an infant she
shares a rich imaginative life with foster-brother Jem, thus endowing
the remembered pastoral idyll of her infancy with magic. As a child,
she uses her gifts to entertain her fellow foundlings: 'I carried on like

Scheherazade' (*HF,* p. 203). As a young teen, she uses invented fairy tales to reassure her friend Freda (a giant in a freak show) of her validity as a large woman: 'I did my best to make up a few fairy stories myself featuring Fearless Freda' (*SB,* p. 373). Later, her developing sensitivity and empathy are shown when she uses her imagination to comfort her disabled, helpless and widowed foster mother, instinctively rejecting stories which might hurt: 'I pictured the past, constructing Mother's days when she was young and tireless' (*ES,* p. 256). In *Diamond,* rather than telling imagined stories to Diamond, 15-year-old Hetty reads from her memoirs and encourages Diamond to write her own, emphasising her new role as mentor. Victor Watson notes the difficulty for writers in handling the imaginative child's development into adulthood: 'The heroically imaginative child must renounce the person she once was in order to accept a diminished adult role.'[29] But Hetty, like Emily Starr, never renounces her imaginative life; instead she learns to accommodate it for her own and others' good.

What sets Hetty apart from Emily and Anne, the fictional predecessors with whom she shares so much, is that Montgomery gives her characters somewhere to belong. Though orphaned and displaced early in life, Emily is brought up in her mother's ancestral home, New Moon, by her aunts. Orphan Anne, though she arrives at Green Gables by mistake, is quickly assimilated: 'The house seems a different place already.'[30] As Mavis Reimer points out in an entry on 'Home' in *Keywords for Children's Literature*: 'houses are often used as both literal and figurative sites for young people to mother or nurture themselves in children's books.'[31] The books' titles highlight this sense of belonging: *Anne of Green Gables*, *Emily of New Moon*. Later books about Anne reprise the device – *Anne of Avonlea*, *Anne's House of Dreams*, etc., whereas Emily's trilogy focuses on her development as writer and young woman – *Emily Climbs*, *Emily's Quest*. All of these titles suggest a character moving on either physically, emotionally or both, but each series *starts* by identifying the orphan child with the house which becomes home. Hetty has no such place, and the picaresque, journeying nature of the narratives reflects her quest to find one.[32] Hetty belongs, emphatically, to herself. Her assertion to Diamond, 'I don't belong to horrid old Beppo. I don't belong to anyone,' is intended to reassure the younger, practically enslaved child: 'When you're my age you won't have to belong to anyone either.'[33] However, it can also be read as expressing regret: 12 pages later Hetty says wistfully, 'I don't even know where my real home is' (*D,* p. 189).

It is significant that every novel is titled with a different version of Hetty's name, none of which is unproblematic. She bears the real surname of neither parent, even though, unusually for a foundling, she finds both of them. 'Hetty Feather' she dismisses in the third sentence of the first novel as 'not my real name' (*HF,* p. 1). She is no more reconciled by the start of the second novel: 'It's just a hateful foundling label' (*SB,* p. 1). It was the real-life Foundling Hospital's policy that each child be baptised with a new name, a practice which continued well into the twentieth century. Abandoned children were, in the main, illegitimate, and for generations they were seen as tainted by their parents' 'sin'. Some orphanages even excluded children born outside marriage on the grounds that 'Children begotten in sin would naturally inherit their parents' weakness and hence they would surely contaminate the minds and morals of the lawfully begotten.'[34] This baptism was thus seen as a symbolic rebirth, not just into Christianity, but out of bastardy. The names were apparently random, but Hetty's name symbolises everything she despises: *Hetty* is a humble name, suitable for a maid, and Hetty dislikes *Feather's* connotations of lightness and insubstantiality, though it could be seen as symbolising the fact that she spends much of the novels in flight in her search for a home. Her delight at discovering that her mother called her 'a fancy pet name, Sapphire, because your eyes were so blue' (*HF,* p. 393) leads her to adopt this and her mother's surname for her second identity, Sapphire Battersea, a name surely even more preposterous in the 1890s than it sounds today. The irony is that *Battersea* was only assumed by her mother, Evie Edenshaw, when *she* in turn needed to reinvent herself to get close to Hetty. With its connotations of lost dogs, Battersea is not the most prepossessing name for a foundling child, but what matters to Hetty is the connection with her 'dear Mama' – who, like everyone else, refuses to call her by it: 'Even she calls me Hetty now' (*SB,* p. 1). Hetty finds it impossible to reinvent herself, perhaps partly because 'Sapphire Battersea' is based on deceit. Her next identity, Emerald Star,[35] though equally fanciful, is more successful. Sapphire Battersea sounds like a prostitute, as Mrs Briskett seems to hint: 'What kind of ungodly, fanciful name is that for a little servant girl?' (*SB,* p. 58), but Emerald Star is at least an obviously made-up stage name. Invented by Hetty for her freak show act as Emerald, the Amazing Pocket-Sized Mermaid, this identity – harking back to childhood memories of being called Little Star by Madame Adeline – serves Hetty well as she discovers her love of performing: 'I guess I'm more of a showgirl than you, Diamond … I miss performing terribly' (*D,* p. 236).

With even her name disputed, Hetty struggles throughout the books to find a place to belong. Such a quest is a common theme in fiction, not least in Wilson's contemporary novels. Tracy Beaker is desperate to be fostered; Andi in *The Suitcase Kid* (1992) yearns for a proper home instead of being a sort of visitor in both her divorced parents' houses. The first chapters of *Hetty Feather* describe an idyllic country childhood. The practice of the Foundling Hospital, in real life as well as in fiction, was to foster infants out until they were five-years old: 'As a system, boarding out had a long history … dating back to Tudor times … Babies from the Foundling Hospital were boarded out in the eighteenth century.'[36] Hetty finds love and security with 'Mother' and 'Father' Cotton. Despite being regularly 'paddled' for naughtiness, and the shadow of imminent return to the Foundling Hospital, she thrives, and finds her own role in the busy family. This gives her an idyll to which she longs to return, like Andi's idealised Mulberry Cottage.

This country infancy in the 'small thatched cottage with whitewashed walls' (*HF,* p. 15), reminiscent of Milly-Molly-Mandy's 'nice white cottage with the thatched roof'[37] functions throughout the novels like Andi's Mulberry Cottage, an Arcadian idyll to which Hetty longs to return: 'the only real home I had ever known' (*HF,* p. 319); 'I thought of the cottage … it shimmered in my mind … I had to sniff to stop myself bursting into tears' (*SB,* p. 151). What makes the idyll more compelling is not simply the fact that it is pastoral – extravagantly so with smocked farmworkers and 'roses and honeysuckle hanging round the front door' (*HF,* p. 15) – but that she belonged, or believed she did, to a family. Not belonging is a frequent Wilson theme. When Andi's parents divorce she longs like Hetty for the happy childhood home with two parents, instead of two houses where she feels like a visitor with no real place: 'I haven't got a home anymore.'[38] Ellie, in the Girls series (1997–2002), feels left out when her widowed father remarries and has another child.

Parents – often inadequate in Wilson's books – are not enough in themselves to make a home. Being a Victorian waif, however, Hetty's position is harsher: no modern Wilson heroine has to put up with a stepmother calling her a 'little harlot' (*ES,* p. 96). Ellie may clash with her stepmother Anna but by the end of the Girls series they are allies. Even though Hetty is taken in willingly by her biological father – 'You are my child and you shall live in my house with me' (*ES,* p. 49) – her stepmother is hostile: 'She's nothing to do with this family' (*ES,* p. 98). When Katherine shows her the family Bible, even the superior thrill she feels at seeing how her despised stepmother stumbles over the reading cannot comfort Hetty for the fact that there is no entry for her.

Nor is it enough simply to be *wanted*. When the free-thinking Greenwoods wish to adopt her, Hetty, though she 'wanted it more than anything' (*SB*, p. 350), is realistic enough to know it would not work: 'I wasn't a real daughter and yet I was too close to them now to be a proper servant ... I didn't really have a place in the Greenwood family though we might all wish I did' (*SB*, p. 350). It is finding a *place* that matters, and a place that she forges on her own terms. This is very different from '*knowing* her place', which is expected of a foundling child: '"I don't want to be anyone's servant," I said, folding my arms obstinately' (*SB*, p. 37). Hetty's inability to be assimilated into Bobbie and Katherine's home is reinforced in the narrative by her failure to take on an age-appropriate role in the hardworking fisher commu-nity. Unable to cope with the work of the flither girls (limpet pick-ers) her own age, she is happy gathering driftwood with the younger children but this is disapproved of: 'I'm not having my daughter set to work with babies and imbeciles' (*ES*, p. 92), so she must gut fish with the older women instead, a distasteful job to which she is never reconciled. This also accentuates her uncertain maturity – at 14 she is neither child nor woman, a theme to which Wilson returns frequently.

'Father' Cotton's sudden death is the catalyst for Hetty to leave her biological father in a quest to rediscover her original place: 'My first family needs me' (*ES*, p. 145). Wilson plays with the reader's expecta-tions here. Even an immature reader must guess that for Hetty to be unproblematically reabsorbed into the pastoral idyll is too simplistic. At first, Arcadia does indeed seem to reject her. The man who gives her a lift is sexually threatening, and the cottage 'wasn't quite as I'd remembered. It was smaller and more tumbledown, the thatch thread-bare' (*ES*, p. 174). 'I seemed a stranger to everyone' (*ES*, p. 177). Of the oft-quoted flowers round the cottage door 'none were flowering now' (*ES*, p. 179). Her foster sisters neither welcome nor even recognise her: 'Oh my Lord, you're one of the foundlings. What are you doing here?' (*ES*, p. 180). For a character who has fought so hard to keep her individuality – 'I had to hang on to myself. I was not going to become just another foundling girl ... inside my head I still had to stay Hetty Feather' (*HF*, p. 167) – to be dismissed as merely 'one of the found-lings' is devastating: 'Oh Lord, this was so terrible. We had all looked on this cottage as our true home ... Yet ... we were dim memories at best, pitiable little foundlings' (*ES*, p. 182). But 14-year-old Hetty is no longer a pitiable little foundling. Newly mature, a trained servant and clever needlewoman, she constructs a place for herself at the very heart of the home, becoming for a time the epitome of the Victorian 'angel in the house'.

Maturity is of course a socially constructed and thus shifting construct, profoundly affected by gender and class. The discrete developmental stage of adolescence was much less recognised in the nineteenth century, particularly for the working classes and for girls. Thus Hetty is ejected from the Foundling Hospital at 14 to step into her new role as a servant. As an under-housemaid she is not exactly an adult – sleeping in a corner of the scullery (once again she has no proper place), and with her manners and morals overseen by the cook-housekeeper – but neither is she any longer a child: "'Playtime!' Mrs Briskett chortled. "Oh, Hetty Feather, you're going to be the death of me! … There won't be any playtime … It will be work work work, seven days a week, with Sunday afternoons off *if* you've been a good girl'" (*SB*, p. 66). This passage clearly shows her anomalous position: adult enough to be expected to 'work work work, seven days a week', she remains child enough to be spoken to like an infant, '*if* you've been a good girl'. Indeed, for the rest of the series, Wilson dramatises this central tension of adolescence – what Watson calls the 'small eddies of progress and clarity' which constitute coming-of-age, and which may not keep pace with external rites of passage.[39] At 14, Hetty puts her hair up, symbolising the end of childhood, but it comes down and flows over her shoulders; she has the domestic skills to allow her to become the mainstay of the Cotton family – 'You're a real little housewife already' (*ES*, p. 249) – but longs to join in with children: 'Oh, how I wanted to join in … I would look a fool if I ran forward with all the little children' (*ES*, p. 365). Hetty continues to switch between child and adult roles, playing out the essential contradictions of adolescence. In *Emerald Star*, 'I'd sunk into the cosy routine of a woman twice my age and it frightened me' (*ES*, p. 286), but later in *Diamond*, by now earning her living as a female ringmaster, she can still regress: 'Hetty forgot she was practically grown up, and gloried in being bold and boisterous, charging round with her skirts tucked up' (*D*, p. 208). As well as the incremental steps towards maturity, Wilson also dramatises several epiphanic moments which chart sudden losses of innocence. At ten Hetty's childish belief that she will marry Jem is shattered, and the renouncing of the dream seems to spell the end of childhood and the painful acceptance of her place in society: 'And my future was plain too. I was Hetty Feather, a foundling, imprisoned in the hospital. When I was fourteen, I'd leave to be a servant. That was all I had to look forward to. I would be a drudge for the rest of my days' (*HF*, p. 285). Hetty's struggle to accept this leads to depression: she becomes temporarily 'listless … dull … slow … sour' (*HF*, p. 293). The reader – and Hetty – must wait for a book and a half before this dream is restored to Hetty, by which time she rejects it. And interestingly, despite the rejections, bereavement and real struggle of her 'bleak upbringing' (*ES,* p. 284), it is only the prospect of married life with Jem which propels the indomitable Hetty back into a similar state of ennui, when she 'couldn't help feeling lonely and disappointed' (*ES,* p. 286). The process of maturing is thus shown as difficult and slow. Wilson has said that she feels out of sympathy with modern teenage girls: 'I struggle to get into that mindset', which is one reason why she has devoted so much energy recently to historical fiction.[40] Hetty shares some of the preoccupations of a modern teen: she is, for example, interested in her appearance and frustrated with her lack of physical development, but she is too busy surviving to be over-preoccupied by this.

Hetty herself knows that maturity is profoundly influenced by social class. The first time she meets the Greenwood family she reflects that 'That little baby ... would be able to stay a child well into her teens' (*SB,* p. 279). Next day, 'I wished ... I could be a blessed child like Maisie, when the worst thing that could happen to her was getting lost on a beach' (*SB,* p. 319). Wilson suggests the difference in the girls when they are running, Hetty's physical encumbrance symbolising the baggage of her foundling background: 'The girls both surged forward, skirts flying. I ran along beside them, my case bumping awkwardly against my legs' (*SB,* p. 282–3). But if Hetty lacks the freedom to be a child, she doggedly retains the freedom to be *herself.* Wilson reinforces this point most strikingly when she meets Polly again in *Diamond.* Polly, 'so grown up and ladylike' (*D,* p. 223), may be still at school, but her adoptive parents will not support her desire for higher education: 'I would dearly love to ... study further at a ladies' college, but Papa does not want me to become a bluestocking' (*D,* p. 223). Although Polly's lack of freedom to be herself is given the extreme form of her adoptive parents naming her after their dead child, Wilson is also dramatising pressing contemporary arguments about young women's education.[41] This scene is short but significant: it reinforces Hetty's status as outside respectable Victorian norms, her pride in herself, but also her pain: '"We should be pleased and proud. It is a very fine, rare thing to be a circus girl", she said, but she was crying properly now' (*D,* p. 225). She has rejected premature maturity as Jem's wife in favour of circus life, and the expression of her own talents, but she must accept the consequences.

And then, of course, there are boys. The place of romance in the Hetty Feather books is fascinating, and Wilson uses it rather as she does Hetty's development as a writer: as a device to show the complexities of her maturation. The consequences of unguarded sexual relations haunt the novels – Hetty may not condemn her unmarried mother, but almost everyone else does, and Wilson allows Ida only brief happiness with her daughter before her horrible death from consumption. This is mainly a device to force Hetty into independence and adventure, but it accurately echoes the fate of other wronged Victorian young women, in fact and fiction. Hetty's peripatetic life renders her vulnerable to predatory men – 'There's gentlemen and gentlemen', warns the more streetwise Sissy (*HF,* p. 352).

Hetty's uncertain maturity is reflected in her changing relations with the opposite sex. At five, she believes she will marry Jem; at ten she realises this was a fantasy. At 14, Wilson presents it as a real possibility, but by now Hetty is able to see Jem dispassionately, as a good man and brother, but not as a mate. Like Anne and Emily, the heroines she so resembles, she must reject the *apparently* perfect lover in favour of the true one. However, Wilson reverses Montgomery's model: Emily and Anne return to their childhood loves/friends, Gilbert and Teddy, and there is no real doubt that they will. Wilson's model is closer to that of Louisa M. Alcott, where Jo must break the heart of Laurie, her childhood friend, and make her way alone (until she meets Professor Bhaer). Like Alcott, Wilson sweetens the pill by placing the jilted lover's true sweetheart (in this case the loyal Janet) in the wings. When Hetty returns to Jem, he is no longer a romantic figure, like the enchanted Squirrel House of Hetty's memory, which is now revealed as merely 'quite small and spindly' (*ES,* p. 328). He may be her foster brother, but there is nothing of the Heathcliff about him: handsome, kind and gentle, his attractiveness is undercut when Hetty describes him in bovine terms: 'I couldn't help thinking of Farmer Woodrow's docile cows' (*SB,* p. 285). It is Hetty who is the wild outsider, and her 'angel in the house' role gradually becomes untenable: 'My days are so … restricted. I cook the same meals, wash the same sheets, see the same folk, even talk the same talk, over and over again. I can't stay because I'm starting to make Jem unhappy – and I'm unhappy too' (*ES,* p. 384). Although Bertie, the indomitable butcher's boy, may appear to be a temporary distraction from Jem, it is significant that when Hetty fantasises about writing a novel – an idealised version of her own life – she leaves out the Jem character entirely and imagines her heroine meeting '…her true sweetheart, a former workhouse inmate, now cheerily earning his living as … a baker's boy? I blushed in the darkness of the scullery, ashamed to have let myself get so carried away' (*SB,* p. 210). This is an early clue that Bertie is the suitor designed for Hetty: *Emerald Star* ends with the Bertie story unresolved, but *Diamond* ends with a strong hint of a reunion. Bertie is presented as potentially Hetty's 'true sweetheart' because they are equals. The model offered by Jem – where a disparity of age and outlook may be compensated for by security and one-sided love – is a more conventional Victorian model, and one which doomed many a nineteenth-century heroine before Hetty.[42] The possibilities offered by Bertie are more 'modern': Jem idealises Hetty; Bertie treats her as an equal. While this may seem anachronistic, relations between men and women were beginning, albeit in more advanced and bohemian circles, to alter in the late nineteenth century. Besides, Wilson depicts their walking out as essentially two *children* experiencing the outside world together, but always with the promise of something more: 'It would be grand to do a double act with you' (*SB*, p. 231). They share more than their institutional origins; they share a sense of adventure whereas 'Jem won't ever be anything but a farmer, I'm sure of it' (*SB*, p. 232). In *Opal Plumstead*, Wilson goes rather further in depicting 'advanced' relationships between the sexes, when Opal's sister becomes the mistress of an older artist, bearing his illegitimate child.

Nicholas Tucker suggests that '[The] enormous success of Jacqueline Wilson is a reminder that children also relish stories set in far from glamorous surroundings and where the emphasis is firmly on everyday reality'.[43] In her Victorian novels, Wilson moves far beyond this. The surroundings may remain far from glamorous, but Hetty's everyday reality has what Hilary Mantel calls 'the shock of the old' for the modern reader.[44] Moreover, we see, in more depth and detail than her contemporary novels give scope for, the development and coming of age of the heroine as writer and young woman.

Notes

1 Jacqueline Wilson, foreword to *The Lottie Project* (London: Corgi, 2012).
2 Rachel Cooke, 'The Story of Jacqueline Wilson', *The Observer* 23 March 2014, http://www.theguardian.com/books/2014/mar/23/the-story-of-jacqueline-wilson [accessed 8 August 2014].
3 Since this chapter was written, Wilson has announced the next chapter of Hetty Feather's adventures: *Little Stars* (2015) follows Hetty's adventures as a music hall star.
4 Catherine Butler and Hallie O'Donovan, *Reading History in Children's Books* (London: Palgrave Macmillan, 2012), p. 3.
5 Philip Womack, 'Interview with Jacqueline Wilson', *Telegraph* 9 December 2011, http://www.telegraph.co.uk/culture/books/bookreviews/8943303/Interview-with-Jacqueline-Wilson.html [accessed 7 August 2014].
6 I surveyed 26 Jacqueline Wilson readers aged 11/12 in Methodist College Belfast, in February 2014, using a questionnaire.

7 Philip Womack, 'Interview with Jacqueline Wilson'.

8 Lucy Pearson, *Children's Literature* (with Peter Hunt) (London: Longman, 2011), p. 82.

9 Rachel Cooke, 'The Story of Jacqueline Wilson'.

10 Jacqueline Wilson, *Hetty Feather* (London: Corgi, 2010), p. 387. All further references in this chapter are from this edition and are given in parentheses in the text.

11 Claire Donnelley, 'Tracy Beaker Author Jacqueline Wilson Reveals Her Suffering Over Kidney Failure', *The Daily Mirror* 16 December 2013, http://www.mirror.co.uk/news/real-life-stories/tracy-beaker-author-jacqueline-wilson-2931891 [accessed 7 August 2014].

12 For example, books such as *The Boy in the Striped Pyjamas* (John Boyne, 2006), *Fire, Bed and Bone* (Henrietta Branford, 2002) or *All Fall Down* (Sally Nicholls, 2012).

13 Jacqueline Wilson, *Emerald Star* (London: Corgi, 2013), p. 311. Emphasis in the original.
All further references in this chapter are from this edition and are given in parentheses in the text.

14 'Introduction' to Fiona Collins & Judith Graham (eds.), *Historical Fiction for Children* (London: David Fulton Publishers, 2001), pp. v–vi, p. v.

15 Catherine Butler & Hallie O'Donovan, *Reading History in Children's Books*, p. 4.

16 Jacqueline Wilson, *Sapphire Battersea* (London: Corgi, 2012), p. 16. Emphasis in the original. All further references in this chapter are from this edition and are given in parentheses in the text.

17 Philip Pullman, 'Daddy, or serendipity', in Fiona Collins & Judith Graham (eds.), *Historical Fiction for Children*, pp. 102–107, p. 104.

18 Ibid., p. 105.

19 Margaret Meek & Victor Watson, *Coming of Age in Children's Literature* (London and New York: Continuum, 2001), p. 8.

20 Philip Womack, 'Interview with Jacqueline Wilson'.

21 John Stephens, *Language and Ideology in Children's Fiction* (London: Longman, 1992), p. 202.

22 Jacqueline Wilson, *Jacky Daydream* (London: Doubleday, 2007), p. 62.

23 Jacqueline Wilson, *My Secret Diary* (London: Corgi, 2010), p. 201.

24 Margaret Meek & Victor Watson, *Coming of Age in Children's Literature*, p.21.

25 Ibid., p. 43.

26 This is discussed in depth in Clementine Beauvais's chapter for this volume.

27 L. M. Montgomery, *Emily of New Moon* (London: Virago, 2013), p. 45.

28 Margaret Meek & Victor Watson, *Coming of Age in Children's Literature*, p. 18.

29 Ibid.

30 L. M. Montgomery, *Anne of Green Gables* (London: Harrap, 1961).

31 Mavis Reimer, 'Home' in Philip Nel & Lissa Paul (eds.), *Keywords for Children's Literature* (New York and London: New York University Press, 2011), p. 106.

32 I do not see the Hetty Feather books as archetypal 'Home – Away – Home' narratives, as Hetty returns 'home' to the cottage only to leave again.

33 Jacqueline Wilson, *Diamond* (London: Doubleday, 2013), p. 177.

34 Ivy Pinchbeck & Margaret Hewitt, *Children in English Society* (London: Routledge & Kegan Paul, 1973), p. 584.

35 Incidentally, in light of her resemblance to Montgomery's heroine, it is interesting to note how closely Emerald Star echoes the latter's full name of Emily Byrd Starr.

36 Ivy Pinchbeck & Margaret Hewitt, *Children in English Society*, p. 519.

37 Joyce Lankester Brisley, *Milly-Molly-Mandy Stories* (London: Harrap, 1955), p. 9.

38 Jacqueline Wilson, *The Suitcase Kid* (London: Corgi, 2006), p. 18.

39 Margaret Meek & Victor Watson, *Coming of Age in Children's Literature*, p. 40.

40 Rachel Cooke, 'The Story of Jacqueline Wilson'.

41 Wilson seems to be interested in the history of girls' education. *Opal Plumstead*, its title clearly echoing the Hetty Feather titles, is about an Edwardian girl with academic aspirations, who must leave school to work in a factory.

42 Catherine Earnshaw, Emma Bovary, Eustacia Vye, to name a few. The intended child reader will be unaware of these heroines, but may, when encountering them later, feel a spark of recognition from their remembered reading of Hetty Feather.

43 Nicholas Tucker, 'Jacqueline Wilson', in Nicholas Tucker and Nikki Gamble (eds.), *Family Fictions* (London and New York: Continuum, 2001), pp. 68–84, p. 69.

44 Celia Brayfield & Duncan Sprott, *Writing Historical Fiction* (London: Bloomsbury, 2014).

9

Jacqueline Wilson and the Problem Novel in Comparative Context

Rebecca Morris

Jacqueline Wilson's problem novels have earned critical and popular acclaim for their realistic, reader-centred approach to the difficult psychological, social and familial issues that children and teens face. In her article '"So Good It's Exhilarating": The Jacqueline Wilson Phenomenon', Kay Waddilove observes that it is 'the "situations" in her books that have made Wilson one of the most controversial, as well as popular, authors of the twenty-first century'.[1] Waddilove offers examples such as eating disorders, abandonment, mental and physical illness, paedophilia and emotional abuse, and there are several others that could be added to this list, including divorce, death, sex, financial worries and bullying. While controversial, such issues are hardly unique to Wilson's work and have appeared frequently as the subject matter of problem novels in the Anglophone world since the mid-twentieth century, when books such as Judy Blume's became enormously influential. The focus of this chapter is to locate Wilson's contributions within the broader context of the problem novel genre in Anglophone literature for children and teens during the late twentieth and early twenty-first centuries by examining her work in relation to that of her US predecessor, Blume, to whom Wilson is often compared in American popular and social media.

Some book professionals such as Roger Sutton, editor in chief of *Horn Book*, have observed that Jacqueline Wilson's novels are not as well-known in the United States as they should be. However, when Wilson's work does receive mention in US pop culture outlets, it is frequently likened to that of Blume. For instance, a photograph caption headlining Moira Redmond's article 'Who is Jacqueline Wilson? And Should Americans Read Her?' for *Slate* dubs Wilson 'the United Kingdom's Judy Blume'.[2] Parents and teens posting to message boards such as Goodreads looking for recommendations for readers who have enjoyed Blume or Wilson are frequently pointed to Wilson or Blume respectively. Such comparisons crop up on UK sites as well. On the popular lifestyle website xoJane's UK site, for example, a posting celebrating YA fiction identifies Wilson as Blume's 'British equivalent'.[3]

Indeed there are several similarities that would prompt such a comparison. Blume (b. 12 February 1938) is just shy of eight years Wilson's (b. 17 December 1945) senior, and they published their first children's books within four years of each other (Blume's *The One in the Middle is the Green Kangaroo* was published in 1969, and Wilson's *Ricky's Birthday* appeared in 1973). Both authors have been celebrated for their profoundly child-centred approaches to their books, with each woman frequently identifying in interviews and speeches tendencies to write based on the books she enjoyed (or wishes she could have enjoyed) and the feelings she experienced when she was young. Both have received top national literary awards in their respective countries for their efforts. Neither has shied away from controversial subjects in her writing, and each has made it a point to deal honestly with the issues that preoccupy children and adolescents. As a result of this candid treatment of controversial issues, Blume and Wilson have also both come to be seen as writers of bibliotherapeutic novels, amongst the pages of which confused, worried or hurt children might find validation and consolation.

Based on the observation of such similarities, there is a clear impulse, at least amongst those audiences more familiar with Blume, to link Blume and Wilson and either to view the two as literary sisters or to consider Wilson something of a literary descendant of Blume, the heir who has ushered the problem novel of the 1970s and early 80s into the late twentieth and early twenty-first centuries. To consider this relationship and highlight Wilson's position in the broader context of the problem novel, this chapter will focus on texts by Blume and Wilson with similar target audiences and subject matter. In particular, this chapter examines texts for young adult readers, including *Amber* (1986), *Girls in Tears* (2002) and *Love Lessons* (2005) by Wilson, and *Deenie* (1973) and *Forever* (1975) by Blume, all of which focus heavily on topics of adolescent sexuality, a central preoccupation in YA literature. Roberta Seelinger Trites notes, 'Teenage characters in YA novels agonize about almost every aspect of human sexuality', largely because the experience of sexuality serves as an important 'rite of passage', as well as a 'common metaphor for empowerment'.[4] Trites also points out the historical tendency to moralise on the topic, writing 'sexuality in YA novels often includes a lesson for the reader to learn'.[5] While Trites's analysis focuses on American adolescent literature, Lucy Pearson, who also indicates the influence of American adolescent literature in the British market, emphasises that similar moralising pervaded British adolescent literature, with trends towards 'strong warnings' against unsavoury behaviour and didactic messages that would offer teens 'required guidance in an increasingly perilous world'.[6]

In the Blume and Wilson novels identified above, however, both authors validate the complexity of adolescent sexuality, with each focusing on its pleasures as well as its confusions. *Forever's* Katherine ends up splitting from her first sexual partner, and *Deenie's* titular character uses masturbation as an escape from dealing with her scoliosis diagnosis. Wilson's novels move these complexities to more dangerous extremes such as encounters with paedophiles (*Girls in Tears*) and worst-case scenarios such as unplanned teenage pregnancy (*Amber*). Wilson, thus, positions sexuality as more problematic and potentially more threatening than Blume does, and while this tendency may seem to recall the admonitory flavour of mid-century problem novels before the tone of books like Blume's took over, critic Michael Cart has argued that the presentation of threatening sexuality in problem novels after the popularisation of the Blume formula is not necessarily a regression back to the harsh style of mid-century adolescent books. Instead, such texts are a natural progression. Because Blume's novels introduced a candid discussion of sexuality into the literature 'other writers have had the liberty of beginning the important work of investigating other, less savoury aspects of sex – notably its perversion by the interjection of violence in the form of rape and sexual abuse'.[7] This observation highlights just how pervasive Blume's work has been in crafting standards for the genre and leading possibilities for its continued evolution in Anglophone children's literature.

With novels that readily include sexuality as assumed central content, Wilson draws on the type of problem novel forged by Blume, but her work is among that which extends the content into the dangers that Blume leaves on the periphery. Moreover, Wilson's novels also chip away at the typical features and formulas present in and popularised by Blume's problem novels. For instance, Wilson's protagonists shift from the intentionally ordinary narrators of Blume's books to narrators who are crafted as outsiders. Furthermore, Blume's linear narrative and cheerful, pat endings give way to nonlinear chronology and, as Ika Willis has observed in her chapter of this volume, 'murky' resolutions. When compared to Blume's *Deenie* and *Forever*, then, Wilson's young adult books evolve the comfort of the problem novel formula and the normalising effect that formula has on sexual experience, to reveal instead narrative trajectories and treatments of sexuality that are more unsettled.

Titled the 'confidante' to teens and children,[8] Blume has often been celebrated for her devotion to writing about the 'real problems' of 'real' young people, assuring them that they are normal in their feelings, in their bodies and in their worries. Readers frequently speak of an intimate connection to her stories, characters and the issues they relay. One 13-year-old boy, for example, whose letter is included in Blume's collection *Letters to Judy: What Your Kids Wish They Could Tell You*, writes, 'I think the main point of kids' books is to show that things that happen to you also happen to other kids. It makes kids feel like they are normal. I thought I was weird for doing and thinking some things but your books make me feel okay.'[9] Indeed, Blume's books are remembered fondly by audiences for mainstreaming literary treatment of such issues as divorce, disability, body image, the emotional confusion of adolescence, and sex, the issue most closely under consideration in this chapter.

Blume achieves the normalisation of previously controversial and clandestine issues largely through the tactic of employing 'normal', first-person narrators. Many of Blume's narrators are ordinary by mid-century US standards. They are members of white, middle-class, nuclear families (or at the very least, they hail from the wreckage of former nuclear families). Comparing Blume to something of an 'Ann Landers for the younger set', Stephen Garber observes that Blume's characters tend to be 'types' who are 'derived from averaging' the typical population of children or teens.[10] Of course, Blume's characters boast unique particularities such as their own favourite foods (eggplant parmesan for Deenie) or a penchant for a certain sport (tennis for *Forever*'s Katherine), but Blume's 'ability to juggle the specific incident and the generally applicable truth' is what assures children that they are 'normal' and part of a 'cultural pattern' rather than exceptions and outsiders.[11] Following the observations of Sheila Egoff, many critics such as Brian Sturm and Karin Michel argue that one of the primary reasons adolescents turn to problem novels is to know that they are not alone in their angst, and so the assurance of normalcy has become a hallmark of the genre.[12] Writers too who helped establish standards for reader-centred, realistic young adult fiction, as opposed to cautionary and moralising tales, have identified as an express aim of their fiction the desire to portray their protagonists, and their protagonists' problems, as typical. Blume's friend and contemporary Phyllis Reynolds Naylor, for instance, whose titular character in her Alice series shares many similarities with Ellie in Wilson's Girls series, has, like Blume, remarked, 'I always wanted to write about an ordinary girl.'[13]

For the most part, however, Wilson's protagonists veer from this ordinary quality, and her novels push their markedly different protagonists to more uncomfortable and less common places than Blume's novels. While Blume works to establish her first-person narrators as ordinary and normalise the problems and concerns they face, Wilson devotes her efforts to making her narrators unusual, and she places them in extreme and difficult situations. Blume's protagonists are encouraged to be smart, confident and strong individuals, but their stories often ask for social validation. Wilson's novels, however, are far wearier of this concept of 'normalcy' and social validation. In *Amber* and *Love Lessons*, for instance, the protagonists are both isolated and praised because they are 'different', something each text makes a point of elaborating.

Amber's titular character is the daughter of a 1960s groupie, whom she calls 'Jay' instead of mother or mum, and a roadie, who kills both himself and the pop star he was escorting in a car accident. Amber spends her childhood living on communes and in shacks with Jay and Jay's various boyfriends before mother and daughter take up an attic room when Amber is 15 in a home with a family they know from a commune. Amber is deeply ashamed of her mother, whose clothes, attitude and actions seem to be stuck in her 1960s groupie and 1970s commune lifestyles, and Amber spends her days dreaming that she is a girl from a tidy home near the park who attends a school for rich and clever children and whose mother prepares normal food, not the damaged and outdated products Jay brings home from the health food store where she works. Before Amber and Jay move into the attic room, Amber had never attended school, and when she does begin, she works dispassionately to fit in. She buys very plain new clothes in navy and grey because the clothes she had been making herself for years 'made me look conspicuous'.[14] At school she 'tried hard to act ordinary … I kept quiet and copied the other girls' (p. 45), and for the most part, the other girls ignore her. She is neither friend nor enemy. However, one boy, Justin, an odd character himself who uses his sleeve as a puppet, takes interest in her, precisely because she is 'not a bit like the other girls at school' (p. 48). Amber resents the comment, but Justin explains, 'I'm *glad* you're not' (p. 48). The tension between the desire to be normal and the reality of being different appears commonly in Wilson's books, with most protagonists eventually settling into their difference.

Love Lessons also makes a point of positioning its narrator and protagonist, Prudence, as an outsider rather than a 'normal' teen girl.

From the beginning, it is obvious that Prue is different from her peers when she tells readers on the first page, 'I don't really know any other teenage girls' because her overbearing father has kept Prue and her sister, Grace, isolated from their peers and much of the social world.[15] Prue hasn't been allowed to shop, go to the movies, or even attend school. She longs to be allowed to do the things other teens her age do, and she often remarks on her self-described weirdness. She is also feisty, hot-headed and defiant.

Prue starts attending school after her father has a stroke and can no longer homeschool her, and while the girls at school make fun of her for her difference, male characters admire and are attracted to her for it. Toby, the most popular and good-looking boy at school, appreciates that Prue 'really [doesn't] care' about social norms or rules. He also observes, 'You're so different from all the other girls, Prue', and though Prue quips back, 'I wish I wasn't', she is also often quick to defend her difference (p. 132). Toby repeats these sentiments again at the mall when he offers to go shopping with Prue after she gives him a reading lesson. Prue assumes it's because of her outfit:

> I was wearing last year's dreadful blue cord dress, which was way too short for me, and a shapeless hand-knitted purple sweater that had stretched in the wash. I'd threaded blue and purple glass beads into a strand of my hair and painted a blue cornflower on one of my old black shoes and a purple daisy on the other. I was worried that these home-spun embellishments made me look weirder than ever. (p. 161)

But Toby insists, 'I love the way you look. You're not boring like all the other girls, you've got your *own* style' (p. 165). Mr Raxberry, the art teacher who takes a special interest in Prue and whose romantic relationship with her will be discussed later in this chapter, also notices that Prue is a 'funny kid' (p. 182), and he quips, 'There'll be no forgetting you' (p. 209). Like Toby, Mr Raxberry is attracted to Prue because of her difference. This praise, however, masks the fact that Prue, and Amber as well, often attract the wrong kind of attention – troublesome sexual attention – for their difference. In Wilson's novels, this attention results in confusing sexual feelings and the introduction of troublesome extremes and dangerous scenarios. At the same time, though, Wilson always stops short of allowing these extremes and dangers to reach fruition, and so her characters are left neither rewarded nor punished. Instead they and their sexual experiences occupy more ambiguous ground than that found in novels like Blume's.

Conversely, those presentations of sexuality told through the experiences of normal protagonists, who occupy the safe, sanctioned and ordinary confines of typical middle-class life, appear more normal as well. Joyce Maynard, an American novelist also known for writing about the 'real world', observes in her essay 'Coming of Age with Judy Blume' that 'By dealing with sexuality in the very comfortable, familiar context of suburban towns, among middle-class families, in the lives of ordinary kids, they [Blume's novels] make sexuality a less strange and shameful thing.'[16] In fact, Blume's novels not only show normal young people experiencing and experimenting with sexual feelings, but her books also commonly feature normal adult characters who explicitly validate those feelings. Roberta Trites observes that the 'practice of employing a wise adult to guide a confused adolescent is so commonplace in adolescent literature that it is practically invisible even to the trained eye', though whether the 'transactions between adolescents and adults in YA literature are heinous, enabling, or inevitable' is up for debate.[17] In regard to the problem novel genre specifically, Sheila Egoff has noted that adolescents are typically 'alienated and hostile toward adults', but that 'some relief from unhappiness comes from a relationship with an adult outside the family'.[18] While adult figures in Blume's novels certainly operate as sources of contention at times, there are also many examples of adults, within the family and without, who offer information that allows adolescents to explore sexual experience. Blume's work thus borrows familiar features of adolescent fiction, but it also pushes bounds for the problem novel genre by offering adults who acknowledge expressions of adolescent sexuality as a normal and acceptable part of young adult life. This kind of normalisation and validation is clearly at work in *Deenie*, a novel that treats two 'issues': masturbation and disability.

Deenie follows a 13-year-old protagonist who faces common teen problems such as a pushy mother – one of those adults who causes contention – alongside more unusual struggles, namely her scoliosis diagnosis. Deenie finds that masturbation provides a way to forget the pressures of her life, relax and feel good. Before readers ever learn of her sexual exploration and her scoliosis, though, Blume introduces them to a main character who is in no way strange, special or extraordinary. Deenie goes shopping with friends, tries out for cheerleading and is disappointed when she doesn't make the cut, has a boy who is interested in her, she cares about her looks, gets her period, and holds hands at the movies. Deenie lives with her father, who loyally heads off to work every day, her mother and her smart older sister. There is no indication in the text that Deenie stands out from her peers in any way. The protagonist's utter ordinariness comes first in the narrative, and then her 'problems' of scoliosis and masturbation come second.

By the time readers reach Deenie's descriptions of masturbation, they already have an impression of her as an average American girl.

The text goes even further to normalise sexual expression by including a conversation, led by the well-meaning gym teacher, Mrs Rappoport, which introduces sexual vocabulary into the students', and readers', lives, assuring them that their questions, curiosities and feelings are normal. The conversation comes as part of a new programme at the school in which students submit questions anonymously, and then the teacher selects a few for discussion each week. Deenie's question asks, 'Do normal people touch their bodies before they go to sleep and is it all right to do that?'[19] As the wording of the question makes clear, Deenie wants to know if she is normal. The conversation that emerges amongst the class after hearing the question reveals a great deal of misinformation. For example, several of the students have heard that masturbation can cause blindness, pimples and deformity. In the straightforward internal dialogue that Blume's fans have come to appreciate, Deenie immediately worries,

> Could it possibly be true? ... Maybe that's why my spine started growing crooked! Please God ... don't let it be true, I prayed. I felt my face get hot and I had to go to the bathroom in the worst way but I didn't move a muscle. I hoped nobody could tell what I was thinking. (p. 83)

Deenie's fears, however, quickly subside when the conversation takes on an air of community and curiosity. Students volunteer information they have heard, and Mrs Rappoport assures the students that 'it's normal and harmless to masturbate' both for boys and girls and that masturbation is 'not a word you should be afraid of' (p. 84). She even has the students repeat the word, which they do 'together' (p. 84), creating a sense of collectivity and breaking through the taboo of the subject, while still recognising the intimacy of the issue.

Blume employs many of the same tactics to normalise sexuality in *Forever*, which was published just two years after *Deenie* and is often considered to be Blume's most sexually forward book because the plot focuses on the protagonist's choice to have sex with her boyfriend. Like *Deenie*'s narrator, *Forever*'s main character, Katherine, is also as the *Kirkus* review of the novel puts it 'deliberately ordinary'.[20] She has a mother, father and a younger sister, who is irritating at times but loved nonetheless. Katherine is preoccupied with things most high school seniors would be preoccupied with: getting into college, finding a summer job and hanging out with her boyfriend, Michael, whom she meets at a New Year's Eve party at the start of the novel. The *Kirkus* review of the book also notes that aside from these details, Katherine is 'pretty much a blank', an observation which, though tinged with some disdain in the review, admits that the character will act as a sort of 'magnet' for readers who have enjoyed other Blume books, hinting that her protagonists are transferrable types. Importantly, though, what such critics read as 'blankness' is the space that allows for familiarity between character and reader. Because we know only enough about Katherine to know that she is an ordinary teenager, it is fairly easy for readers to access her and concentrate on her 'issue', her sexual relationship with Michael.

Katherine's relationship with Michael is immediately physical. The two exchange a kiss the first time they hang out, and an intense relationship quickly develops. From there, Blume shares graphic details of Michael and Katherine's intimate moments, speaking to readers' curiosity and demonstrating, as Mrs Rappoport does, that there should be no shame in considering sexuality and that teens should have access to honest information. Blume's act of putting detailed language and vivid descriptions on the page for readers to witness has something of the same effect as the class's speaking the word 'masturbation' in *Deenie*; it removes the stigma, secrecy and otherness of it. Kim Reynolds identifies the straightforward detail and plain language as the unique contributions that parlayed the novel to its status as a classic and that continue to set the novel apart. Even as sex has become an increasingly visible component of adolescent literature, Reynolds observes, other books have not matched Blume's in its descriptions of the mechanics of sex.[21] Giving Katherine and readers this language casts sex in a normal and everyday light, while it also significantly transfers a sense of power, and indeed, Blume affords Katherine, and implicitly her readers, considerable power and control over sexuality.

Readers learn early on in the book that Katherine is not willing to be pressured into sex. Before Katherine meets Michael, she dates a boy named Tommy Aronson and she explains to readers, 'Sex was all he was interested in, which is why we broke up – because he threatened that if I wouldn't sleep with him he'd find somebody who would. I told him if that was all he cared about he should go right ahead. So he did.'[22] Michael, readers are told, is immediately 'different from Tommy' because he is interested in talking to Katherine and finding out about her as a person. Though Michael wants to have sex earlier than Katherine does, he respects her decision to wait. When they do have sex, Katherine proves to be well informed, and she is the one who insists that Michael wear a condom. Michael on the other hand is misinformed and thinks that women get pregnant only when they have their periods. Katherine is the one who explains to him, 'Every woman has a different cycle' (p. 113). Katherine also takes the initiative, after receiving a letter and informational pamphlets from her grandmother in another show of adult validation, to visit Planned Parenthood to get a prescription for the birth control pill. The episode acts as an introduction to and demystification of the resources available for adolescents. In a very matter-of-fact manner, the chapter walks readers through a group session with general information about methods of birth control, Katherine's personal counselling session with a social worker and a physical exam with a doctor, after which Katherine promptly receives her birth control prescription. Blume also affords Katherine the power to insist on enjoying sex, to take control over the act of sexual intercourse, and to experience both physical pleasure and emotional closeness with her boyfriend from it. Blume has recalled on her website and in several interviews that she wrote *Forever* at the request of her daughter, Randy, who 'asked for a story about two nice kids who have sex without either of them having to die'.[23] Growing up in the 1970s, Randy 'had read several novels about teenagers in love', but 'If they had sex the girl was always punished – an unplanned pregnancy, a hasty trip to a relative in another state, a grisly abortion … sometimes even death. Lies. Secrets. At least one life ruined.'[24] In Katherine's ability to make independent decisions, enjoy sex and show both power and responsibility, all while being a normal teen, Blume counters those negative depictions of adolescent sexual experience, which Wilson interestingly reintroduces.

At the same time, Blume does not leave the dangers of sex out entirely even alongside her efforts to normalise it. The novel includes conversations about sexually transmitted diseases, and it is revealed that Michael contracted chlamydia from the one sexual partner he had had before Katherine, a girl whom Michael met only briefly on the beach. Thus readers encounter the potential repercussions of casual, unprotected sex. The difficulty of navigating sexual identity receives brief attention when Archie, who is dating Katherine's best friend, attempts suicide, in part because of his inability to mould to heteronormative sexuality. The novel also includes mention of teen pregnancy, when one girl, Sybil Davison, who is described in the first line of the novel as a girl who 'has a genius I.Q. and has been laid by at least six different guys' falls pregnant (p. 9). Readers also find out that Sybil is sexually active for the wrong reasons: her 'fat problem and her need to feel loved' (p. 9). The pregnancy does not have catastrophic consequences – Sybil quietly decides to give the baby up for adoption, picks a good college of her many choices and opts to have an IUD inserted to avoid another pregnancy before she is ready – but rather the episode seems thrown in as a token warning. More importantly, neither pregnancy nor STD ever affects Katherine, the character on whose side the readers are. Wilson's protagonists, we will see, suffer complications like these first-hand. Katherine does experience some of the emotional toll involved in having sex during adolescence. Though Michael and Katherine believe they will be together forever, Katherine begins to have feelings for someone else while she is away teaching tennis at a summer camp. Katherine struggles with confusion and guilt and ultimately breaks up with Michael in a painful fight. At the end of the novel, though, Katherine is able to have an amicable, albeit bittersweet, exchange with Michael, and there is the suggestion that she is smoothly transferring into a new relationship.

Though not without its complications and dangers, sex, overall, is presented as a positive and normal component of adolescent life and relationships largely because the story comes from the perspective of an innocuous, everyday protagonist who suffers no punishment for having sex. Rather than telling the story from the perspective of a character who contracts an STD or becomes pregnant, Katherine, much like Deenie, is never damaged or broken because she experiences and acts on her sexuality. Neither young woman represents an extreme nor, many reviewers and critics suggest, is either even particularly unique, and that is precisely the point. By featuring regular protagonists, Blume engages and validates the issues that preoccupy 'ordinary' children and teens, making those issues ordinary as well. Though the struggles of many Blume protagonists pale in comparison to the harsh problems of poverty, violence, racism or abuse that have come in problem novels since,[25] Blume positioned the comparatively mundane struggle of coming to terms with sexual feelings as an important subject of fiction, one worthy of attention.

In addition to the ordinary and, as Sheila Egoff has noted with distaste, flat first-person narrators, Blume's novels display, and in some cases have worked to forge, other formulaic qualities of the problem novel that add to the audience's delight in reading from this class of fiction.[26] Describing the problem novel in contemporary adolescent literature, Amy Pattee observes that these books follow a predictable pattern: they introduce a problem or controversial issue, develop a specific scenario around the issue and then offer 'narrative resolution', a pattern that has roots in Blume's novels.[27] Through observation of the characters and the narrative resolution, readers leave the stories knowing how they should feel about an issue that might otherwise be confusing or overwhelming. This quality accounts for part of the comfort readers find in the novels. In both *Deenie* and *Forever*, readers can conclude that acknowledging their sexuality is normal and acceptable because the characters, the narrative and the conclusions condone it. Both novels discussed above end pleasantly. Deenie attends a party, wearing her brace, and the boy she likes finally kisses her. Katherine, as noted previously, is able to have a nostalgic moment with Michael and then return home to a phone call from another nice guy. While scholars such as Egoff and Cart have noted that the stock characters and predictable narrative trajectories of problem novels can quickly devolve into 'recycled formula, making subject … and theme the tail that wags the dog of the novel',[28] Pattee asserts that there is pleasure in the familiar. In Blume's novels – which are innovators of the formula rather than straight 'recyclers' of it – where the aim is comfort and reassurance, indulging such formulas seems an apt tool for the task.

For all the comparisons that have been drawn between Blume and Wilson, the treatment of sexual experience diverges markedly in Wilson's novels because they showcase precisely those dangers and extremes that Blume leaves on the periphery. For instance, both *Love Lessons* and *Amber* include romantic infatuations with older men, taboo fantasies, which the characters move from the realm of fantasy to 'reality' by acting on their infatuations. The tryst is relatively short-lived in *Amber*. Amber, devastated by the loss of her best friend because she has had sex with his brother and fearing that the episode has left her pregnant, seeks comfort in Davie, an older man she has known since she was a little girl. She recalls his 'knack of making me feel special' with his songs and stories (p. 61), and since the days at the commune, the two have kept in touch, with Davie sending her small gifts that she tucks away in a secret casket. He even visited Jay and Amber once and took Amber to a bookstore, usually much too expensive for her, so that he could contribute a book to her beloved collection. As the story develops, it is clear that Amber has feelings for Davie both as a father figure and as an idealised romantic partner.

When Amber withdraws emotionally and physically from the external world because of her suspected pregnancy (another dramatic result of sexuality that will be discussed later), her mother assumes she is ill and, in a rare act of understanding, writes to Davie who then comes to visit. Davie arrives, looking old and sickly, with holes in his socks and dirty feet. Nevertheless, he takes Amber out for a day in London. They visit a bookstore, indulge in sweets and fantasise about sharing a quaint house in the park. They exchange 'I love yous', and then 'He kisses me. It's a little soft kiss with closed lips. It only lasts a second but I can still feel his mouth long after it's over' (p. 147). When Davie protests that Amber is too young to continue with such behaviour, Amber shares her news about the pregnancy, and the two envision a domestic life together, raising the baby as a couple. The suggestion of romantically pairing an older man, and a father figure no less, with a teenage girl certainly troubles the normality found in the lives of Blume's characters, but the show of support Amber receives also counters the admonition of older problem novels, indicating that Wilson is interested in engaging another approach to the genre: one that permits first-hand experience of even perverse expressions of sex without necessarily condemning the teen.

Furthermore, Wilson snuffs out the romantic infatuation between Davie and Amber quickly, again demonstrating that Wilson's protagonists can delve into taboo expressions of sexuality without having their lives permanently destroyed. After revealing her news to Davie, Amber gets her period, and though she still craves Davie's attention, he begins to return to a fathering role. He takes her home and listens to the problems she has been having with Justin. He sits with her as she takes a nap, kisses her head gently in a re-enactment of the Sleeping Beauty fairy tale, and gives her advice about going on to art college to make a career for herself. This is not to say that positioning Davie in the fathering role wipes all sexual complexity with pat closure. Bookending Amber's relationship with Davie with these scenes reminiscent of father and daughter also serves to highlight how unconventional and uncomfortable the middle bit is. Adding to the sexual complexity of the scene is Amber's observation that Jay is 'jealous of me' when Jay sees Amber and Davie hugging during Davie's visit (p. 161). Though Davie is largely a benevolent character, a melancholy reminder of both ideal father and husband figures unrealised, his scenes also carry undercurrents of paedophilia, sexual competition, and the unrealistic expectations of fairy-tale notions of relationships. Nevertheless, the return to Davie as a pseudo – albeit incompetent – father figure is significant. The interaction with Davie allows Amber to wander into taboo and even perverse territory, areas that have potential for catastrophe and that would likely result in catastrophe in the pre-Blume tradition of the problem novel. With Davie's return to a more proper adult role akin to that of father rather than lover, there is, for Amber, a return from the darker threats of sexual experience rather than punishment for dalliances in those experiences.

In *Amber's* story, there is additional positioning of sexuality as problematic beyond the issues with Davie. In one brief scene, there is an assertive and unsettling suggestion of paedophilia when Amber remembers an episode from her life at the commune when she would go off by herself into town. In the scene, a man spots her 'hanging around hungrily at the fish and chip shop' (p. 62). The man buys her a bag of food, and the smell tempts her,

> but I was scared there was a catch. He looked silly but harmless enough in his shorts and stout walking boots, the top of his balding head burned strawberry by the sun, but there was something about the way he was looking at me that reminded me of Tim, of Zap, of all the other men who messed Jay about. I became painfully conscious of my tight T-shirt and shorts. (p. 62)

While she runs back to the compound – and to Davie – unharmed, the threat is nevertheless introduced.

The even more pervasive problem linked to sexuality is that of unexpected teenage pregnancy. Amber is the child of teen pregnancy, and the scare of Amber herself being pregnant is one of the driving conflicts of the novel. Amber has sex only once in the book, following an argument with Justin at his house. After the argument, Amber runs into Jonathon, Justin's older and much more suave brother, in the hallway, and he brings her back to his room. Amber's feelings about sex with Jonathon are mixed: 'Up in my head I still hated him but my body was acting with a compliance that astounded me. I'd thought it would be so awkward and uncomfortable. I'd had no idea it would be overwhelming' (p. 126). She begins to enjoy the act, though she also feels sore. But any physical enjoyment is quickly replaced with terrible consequences. Justin walks in on them, and then her period is late. Sex, here, is linked with worst-case scenarios and confusion. While Blume's Katherine has her first sexual experience in a committed relationship with an attentive boyfriend and the extremes of STDs and pregnancy are left on the periphery, Wilson's main character experiences those extremes first-hand. Though sex is not without its complexities in *Forever*, it is for the most part safe, normal and enjoyable. In *Amber*, however, sex becomes much darker, and even the narrative style of the book, which reveals Amber's fear of pregnancy not immediately but in small, non-chronological clues throughout the story, a style which seems to anticipate Laurie Halse Anderson's adolescent novel on rape *Speak* (1999), provides a formal reflection of the feelings of confusion Amber experiences.[29] This style connotes fear, uncertainty and worry, while the more straightforward and predictable style of *Deenie* and *Forever* provide information and comfort.

The treatment of sexuality and romantic relationships in *Love Lessons*, published a full 30 years after Blume's *Forever*, also comes in dramatic form. The plot is set in motion when Prue's father suffers a stroke. The stroke has clearly been a long time coming from the stress of debt, managing a failing business and struggling to write his 'magnum opus', but the final straw comes over breakfast when amidst the bills, Prue's father finds a letter from her maths tutor saying that Prue has not been attending her lessons. The father demands to know what Prue has been doing with the money if she has not been going to tutoring. After a tense shouting volley, Prue goes to her room to retrieve the underwear she has purchased with the money, and she '[throws] them down on the table in front of [her] father' (p. 30). The black and pink lace-trimmed set are much different than the family's usual homemade 'grey-white, baggy, slackly elasticised' underwear, each pair nearly indistinguishable from another so that all the pairs are 'almost interchangeable', revealing the atmosphere of sexual and identity repression, which Wilson clearly critiques, in the home. When Prue lays out her purchase, her father 'recoiled as if they were hissing vipers', accuses Prue of being a 'sleazy disgusting little trollop' and then collapses on the kitchen table. This moment recalls the seriousness of the typical pre-1970s form of the problem novel in which expressions of adolescent sexuality brought catastrophe. However, the scene is rife with melodrama, indicating a jab at the older tradition, which is personified vigorously in Prue's father. Expressions of sexuality do result in trouble for Prue throughout the novel, as they do for Amber, but Wilson offers a rebuke of the older punishments and a reshaping of the formula popularised by Blume by allowing protagonists' problems to have dramatic turns without dire and lasting effect.

Prue's father does not die from the stroke but has to remain in the hospital for several weeks, leaving Prue, Grace and their mother to adjust their lives at home. One of these adjustments means sending the girls to school for the first time because their mother fears that she and her husband will face legal trouble for not properly educating their children. While Grace settles into school life well, Prue struggles to relate to her peers, teachers and the structured environment. The only class she looks forward to is art, and this is where Wilson develops the most involved and most extreme relationship between a teen girl and an older man to appear in her novels. Prue is immediately drawn to her art teacher, Keith Raxberry, whom the students affectionately call Rax, and when she begins to babysit for his children, her infatuation grows. Alone in their house, she 'imagined being Mrs Raxberry. This was my house, these were my children, he was my husband' (p. 145). Here Prue, again like Amber, appears to be reaching for ideals of father and husband (in the same man, as was the case with Amber), and she also will come to find those ideals as frustrated. When Rax first drives Prue home, she lingers on details. She does not know how to fasten her seatbelt, so when Rax leans over to help her with it, 'For one mad magical moment I thought he was going to kiss me' (pp. 152–153). He puts his hand on hers in a show of sympathy when she describes her father's condition: 'The car took off like a rocket, soaring into space, whirling up and over the moon, his hand on mine, his hand on mine, his hand on mine' (pp. 154–155). Wilson grows the tension in the car after that moment. Neither of the two characters speaks. Prue hears Rax swallow. Finally, Rax is able to diffuse the tension by making a joke.

A later scene in the car intensifies the attraction, primarily on Prue's initiative. The two discuss art and books and memories, and Prue longs for Rax to see her as an equal. Furthermore, Prue has no qualms about expressing her feelings towards Rax. For instance, she tells him, 'I'm simply trying to impress you', and Rax responds, 'You don't have to try, Prue. You do that already' (p. 182). When Rax finally observes, 'We're starting to act as if … as if there's something between us', Prue insists, 'There is' (p. 183). Rax tries to resolve the situation by emphasising the bounds of the student/teacher relationship: 'I know we get on really well, and it's a privilege for me to help you with your art, but that's all it can be, Prue. You do know that don't you?' But Prue presses him to embrace and reveal what he is really feeling inside. Rax insists it doesn't matter, again establishing the bounds of the relationship: 'Don't, Prue. Look this is all my fault. I should have kept my distance. You're going through a difficult time, you're feeling very vulnerable, your dad's not well. It's not surprising you've got overly attached to me' (p. 184). Rax's observation that Prue is upset about her father's illness has little support in the text, which makes Prue's continued urging, as well as her admission of love for him, appear all the more aggressive. Rax refuses to confess he feels the same way, though she sees him whisper his affirmation when she finally exits the car.

After this episode, Rax attempts to maintain boundaries. He avoids Prue at school and insists that she stop babysitting, but she resists, insisting that she must see him and thwarting his efforts to keep her away from his home. Their interaction culminates with a passionate exchange, again in Rax's car. Prue initiates a kiss, and though Rax tries to pull away, he eventually gives in: 'I kissed him again, sliding my arms round his neck and holding him tight so that he couldn't pull away from me. After a few seconds he stopped trying. He kissed me back, deeply and passionately' (p. 206). The moment develops into an elaborate fantasy indulgence. They drive to a secluded location, they kiss more and exchange 'I love yous' and they imagine a life in the future. Prue suggests that they

> start driving and keep on driving all through the night, until we get somewhere we've never been before, where no one knows us, and we'll start our new life together, Prue and Rax. We'll find some old cottage or beach shack, we'll live very frugally on bread and cheese – maybe chips! – and you won't go to work and I won't go to school. We'll paint all day. You'll teach me lots of things. We'll go for long walks hand in hand and in the evenings we'll curl up together and then we'll read. Maybe you'll read to me – would you like that? (p. 211)

Prue even wraps a makeshift promise ring – a strand of her unruly hair, which Rax 'love[s]' – around the ring finger of his left hand.

Like Amber, then, Prue acts on her feelings towards an older man, but with even more initiative and sexual undertones. Though crushes on older men and teachers in particular are common enough in adolescent problem novels (Blume's Margaret and her friends in *Are You There, God? It's Me, Margaret*, for example, gossip about their handsome young male teacher), permitting both student and teacher to act on the crush offers a more extreme indulgence of the fantasy, as well as a dramatic departure from the sexual exploration with peers and with one's own body presented in Blume's adolescent novels. In an article for the *Guardian*, Stephanie Merritt argues that the relationship in this book is so different from the realism of other problem novels that it acts more like a 'piece of escapism' than a reflection of 'real life'.[30] Prue shuns what would be considered more normal expressions of teen sexuality by refusing Toby's advances, and instead, she explores taboo expressions of sexuality that cause her problems over the course of the book.

Even amongst the tamest of Wilson's young adult novels, such as *Girls in Tears*, there are extreme presentations of sexuality and its dangers. Throughout *Girls in Tears*, the most Blume-like of the Wilson novels discussed here, the protagonist Ellie's gothic and sophisticated friend Nadine engages in an online flirtation with whom she believes to be a 19-year-old named Ellis.[31] Nadine brags that Ellis is 'so *cool*', with a penchant for sending romantically poetic messages and a shared interest in *Xanadu*.[32] As soon as Ellie hears about Ellis, however, she is leery of the relationship, asserting that he could be some 'pervy creep' (p. 65) who is playing Nadine. Sure enough, Ellis proves to be 'an old guy with a beard' who is shown 'having a good peer at the topless girls' on a movie poster in his first physical appearance in the book (p. 153). The poster is stationed in front of an X-rated movie theatre where the man has arranged to meet Nadine, telling her that they are going to see a special showing of *Xanadu*. In the scene, Ellie, Nadine and a third friend Magda are able to stand up to the would-be paedophile and all ends well. The message, important as it is, again positions sexuality as dangerous and offers another extreme example of the threat male sexuality poses to girls. In fact, all male sexuality is treated with some mistrust in the book. Though the girls discuss sex and enjoy kissing, both Ellie and Magda struggle with boyfriends who incessantly encourage them to go further than they want to. Furthermore, both Ellie and her stepmother, Anna, assume that Ellie's father is having an affair when he stays out late night after night without offering an explanation. It turns out that he is merely working on a self-portrait in hopes of stimulating his languishing art career, but that idea never occurs to Ellie nor Anna. In many ways, the story has the effect of warning girls of dangerous male sexuality and leaving them with the impression that it is better to trust in a sort of sisterhood instead.

In the case of *Love Lessons*, the relationship with the older man drags on longer than it does in *Amber* and more intimately than the episode in *Girls in Tears*; nevertheless, it ends with relatively little scandal. After Prue and Rax are caught in the art room hugging, Rax downplays the relationship, explaining that Prue has a schoolgirl crush on him and that nothing has happened. He is allowed to keep his job, and Prue is transferred to another school, one with a head teacher who proves to be more understanding of Prue than her previous head teacher. The novel seems set for a tidy ending with this action, but there is never any real resolution for Prue, other than that life will go on. In the book's final pages, Prue laments, 'I knew I'd never be really happy again. I missed Rax so much. I couldn't bear to be without him. Sometimes it was so overwhelming that I had to shut myself away and cry and cry' (p. 263). The novel closes with Prue imaging herself walking along the seashore with Rax. In a formal indication of the unsettled narrative resolution, the last sentence of *Love Lessons* ends with an ellipsis. This conclusion disrupts the reassuring end typical of Blume's problem novels and, instead, leaves readers not entirely certain of what will happen to Prue or how they are supposed to evaluate the novel's central issue, her infatuation with her teacher. But while this ending is foggy, it is not damning. As Wilson has done in her other problem novels discussed here, she permits her protagonists and readers to wade through taboo and dangerous sexual encounters, but she punishes neither for the experience.

Wilson has often stated in interviews that she aims for happy, or at least hopeful, conclusions. At the same time, though, many reviewers have also noted her tendency towards 'open-ended' conclusions, which indicates a shift away from the formulaic structure of problem novels like Blume's.[33] In Blume's novels, elements such as the typical narrators, predictable narrative structures and clear resolutions all work to reinforce the normalisation of sexuality in the stories and protagonists. Wilson's trajectories for her protagonists and their narratives are more unsettled. With such elements as the slow revelation of information (*Amber*) and open-ended conclusions (*Love Lessons*), Wilson's narratives move the plots from the comfortable and the stereotypically familiar to less stable ground. Along with the plots, the positioning of sexuality also becomes less comfortable and less safe with all three of the young adult problem novels covered here presenting, to some degree, extreme, dramatic and problematic treatments of sexual experience and sexual feelings. Significantly, none of Wilson's protagonists meet the kind of grisly consequences typical in the fallout of sexual expression in pre-Blume young adult novels, but neither is it the safe and sanctioned experience presented in the normal lives of Blume's protagonists. And Wilson sees this emphasis on troublesome scenarios as part of her role as an author. Wilson's approach to the problem novel, then, and her contributions to the field might best be summed up in her own words: 'My job', Wilson explains,

> is not just to write about what I think will interest children, but to touch on tricky subjects they may have to confront in their lives. Over the years people have implied that I'm not responsible in the way I write, that I'm deliberately going round upsetting children, but my responsibility is to help to gently open their minds.[34]

Blume on the other hand has commented that her writing is 'saying to kids, this is OK and it is normal'.[35] Both quotations indicate profound concern for the reader, but the nuance in each mirrors the different approaches these authors have taken in shaping the problem novel genre. While both authors maintain some hint of the didactic, which has always been a feature of the problem novel genre, Blume's philosophy seems to be more reflective and reassuring, while Wilson's seems to be more proactive and preparatory, and these differences in philosophy are reflected both in the treatment of subject matter and in the treatment of form. Returning to the impulse to label the two as literary sisters or to mark Wilson as Blume's literary descendant, the identification is perhaps not as neat as some readers and reviewers would like it to be. Nevertheless, both women have notably worked to evolve the genre in a way that keeps the reader at heart.

Notes

1 Kay Waddilove, 'So Good, It's Exhilarating'. *Bookbird: A Journal of International Children's Literature* 50:3 (July 2012), 75–78, 76.

2 Moira Redmond, 'Who is Jacqueline Wilson? And Should Americans Read Her?', *Slate.com* 11 October 2005, http://www.slate.com/articles/arts/culturebox/2005/10/who_is_jacqueline_wilson.html [accessed 4 December 2013].

3 Jane Bradley, '"I Must, I Must, I Must Increase My Bust!" Oh How We Love YA Fiction…', *xoJane* 6 June 2012, http://www.xojane.com/fun/bring-me-books-my-youth-jane-b-brilliance-ya-fiction [accessed 8 October 2013].

4 Roberta Seelinger Trites, *Disturbing the Universe: Power and Repression in Adolescent Literature* (Iowa City: University of Iowa Press, 2000), p. 84.

5 Ibid., p. 85.

6 Lucy Pearson, *The Making of Modern Children's Literature in Britain: Publishing and Criticism in the 1960s and 1970s* (Farnham: Ashgate, 2013), p. 60, p. 61.

7 Michael Cart, *From Romance to Realism: 50 Years of Growth and Change in Young Adult Literature* (New York: HarperCollins, 1996), p. 145.

8 Articles in such papers as the *New York Times* and the *Chicago Tribune* have featured this label in their titles. These articles can be located at the following links respectively: http://www.nytimes.com/2004/09/15/books/15AWAR.html?_r=0 and http://articles.chicagotribune.com/2013-05-31/features/ct-prj-0602-judy-blume-tiger-eyes-20130531_1_judy-blume-margaret-simon-printers-row-journal.

9 Judy Blume, *Letters to Judy: What Your Kids Wish They Could Tell You* (New York: Putnam, 1986).

10 Stephen M. Garber, 'Judy Blume: New Classicism for Kids'. *The English Journal* 73:4 (April 1984), 56–59, 59.

11 Ibid., 56, 59.

12 Brian W. Strum and Karin Michel, 'The Structure of Power in Young Adult Problem Novels'. *Young Adult Library Services* 7.2 (Winter 2009), 39–47.

13 Monica Hesse, 'Phyllis Reynolds Naylor, Oracle for Teenagehood, Says Goodbye to "Alice"', *The Washington Post* 13 October 2013, http://www.washingtonpost.com/lifestyle/style/phyllis-reynolds-naylor-oracle-for-teenagehood-says-goodbye-to-alice/2013/10/13/457f465e-2528-11e3-b75d-5b7f66349852_story.html [accessed 1 January 2013].

14 Jacqueline Wilson, *Amber* (Oxford: Oxford University Press, 1986), p.45. All further references in this chapter are from this edition and are given in parentheses in the text.

15 Jacqueline Wilson, *Love Lessons*, ill. Nick Sharratt (London: Doubleday, 2005), p. 1. All further references in this chapter are from this edition and are given in parentheses in the text.

16 Joyce Maynard, 'Coming of Age with Judy Blume', *New York Times* 3 December 1978, https://www.nytimes.com/books/98/09/13/specials/maynard-blume.html [accessed 17 December 2013].

17 Roberta Seelinger Trites, *Disturbing the Universe*, p. 80.

18 Sheila Egoff, 'The Problem Novel' in Sheila Egoff, G.T. Stubbs and L.F Ashley (eds.), *Only Connect: Readings in Children's Literature* 2nd edn. (New York: Oxford University Press, 1980), pp. 356–365, p. 357.

19 Judy Blume, *Deenie* (New York: Laurel Leaf, 1973), p. 83. All further references in this chapter are from this edition and are given in parentheses in the text.

20 Kirkus Review, '*Forever* …, by Judy Blume', *Kirkus Reviews* 1 October 1975, https://www.kirkusreviews.com/book-reviews/judy-blume/forever-4/ [accessed 9 October 2013].

21 Kimberley Reynolds, *Radical Children's Literature: Future Visions and Aesthetic Transformations in Juvenile Fiction* (New York: Palgrave, 2007), p. 117.

22 Judy Blume, *Forever* (New York: Pocket Books, 1975), p. 21. All further references in this chapter are from this edition and are given in parentheses in the text.

23 Judy Blume, 'Forever'. *Judy Blume on the Web*, n.d., http://www.judyblume.com/books/ya/forever.php [accessed 8 October 2013].

24 Ibid.

25 Blume does take on some of these issues in other novels. *Iggie's House* (1970), for example, deals with racism, and *Tiger Eyes* (1981) revolves around a father's murder.

26 Sheila Egoff, *Thursday's Child: Trends and Patterns in Contemporary Children's Literature* (Chicago: American Library Association, 1981).

27 Amy Pattee, 'YA or STFU: Got a Problem with Problem Novels?', *Kirkus Reviews* 30 May 2011, https://www.kirkusreviews.com/features/ya-or-stfu-got-problem-problem-novels/ [accessed 10 November 2013].

28 Michael Cart, *From Romance to Realism*, p. 32.

29 Laurie Halse Anderson, *Speak* (New York: Farrar, Strauss and Giroux, 1999).

30 Stephanie Merritt, 'Love at School Rings No Bells', *Guardian* 10 December 2005, http://www.theguardian.com/books/2005/dec/11/booksforchildrenandteenagers.bestbooksoftheyear2 [accessed 10 November 2013].

31 *Girls in Tears* is one of the four titles in Wilson's Girls series. Unlike the protagonists of *Amber* and *Love Lessons*, Ellie is a relatively normal and ordinary teen. She is entrenched in social institutions, attends school, makes frequent references to popular culture and is comfortable navigating typical teenage hangouts. She has a particular talent for art, taking after her father, but that exceptional quality is tempered by the fact that

she is the frumpiest in her trio of friends (similar to Stephanie in Blume's *Just As Long As We're Together*), making her seem evenly average. Her mother died when she was a little girl and there is mention that Ellie at one time struggled to accept her stepmother, but for the most part, Ellie's family fits the middle-class, nuclear mould.

32 Jacqueline Wilson, *Girls in Tears* (New York: Delacorte, 2002). All further references in this chapter are from this edition and are given in parentheses in the text.

33 Roger Sutton, 'Parent Trap', *New York Times* 13 January 2008, http://www.nytimes.com/2008/01/13/books/review/Sutton-t.html?_r=0 [accessed 4 December 2014].

34 Eleanor Morgan, 'This Much I Know: Jacqueline Wilson', *Guardian* 25 February 2012, http://www.theguardian.com/books/2012/feb/26/jacqueline-wilson-author-this-much [accessed 10 November 2013].

35 Jamia Wilson, 'So Many Kinds of Longing: An Interview with Judy Blume', *Rookie* 8 July 2013, http://www.rookiemag.com/2013/07/an-interview-with-judy-blume/ [accessed 30 March 2014].

Blume makes this point specifically in reference to *Deenie*, though the claim holds true for her other novels on adolescent sexuality as well.

10

A Writing Life: Interview with Jacqueline Wilson

Lucy Pearson and Jacqueline Wilson

LP You started – as is well known – writing with D. C. Thompson. How connected were you with their efforts for teenagers?

JW It all started by chance. I was just 17 and had just finished a secretarial course at a technical college and was looking for a job as a junior typist. I was looking at the Situation Vacant pages of the London evening newspapers, feeling depressed – when I came across an advert at the bottom of the page saying *Wanted, Teenage Writers.* I was a teenager and I desperately wanted to be a writer so I had a go at writing an article for them. To my enormous surprise D. C. Thompson wrote back almost by return of post, saying they wanted to buy my article – for the bizarrely archaic sum of three guineas. I sent them more articles, and various short stories, and after several months they offered me a job working in their offices up in Dundee. I'd never been to Scotland, I didn't know anyone there – but I felt this was my big chance to earn my living as a writer. I thought I'd be working on a new teenage magazine (to be called *Jackie*) but I worked on several other women's magazines instead, though I still continued to contribute to *Jackie* too.

LP *Jackie* was such a ground-breaking magazine and was – I think – ground-breaking in the world of writing for children more broadly. Do you see the seeds of your later work in the writing that you did then?

JW Well, not really, because I became very conscious that I was writing for a magazine which had its own ideas and house style. It wasn't reflecting what *I* thought. I had several articles and stories turned down by *Jackie* because I couldn't always adopt the right attitude. I've never been a romantic soul and though I had various boyfriends I'm afraid I never felt in awe of them. I tended to have too much of a sense of humour to take them desperately seriously. The editor, Gordon Small, wrote me a lovely letter when I started writing for *Jackie* saying that he liked the piece I'd sent him, but it just wasn't suitable for a teenage magazine. I'd suggested that pop stars were really just ordinary human beings and probably would be a bit boring if you ever got to know them properly. He said, 'No, no, no, we *need* the girls to hero-worship pop stars. We want to nurture their romantic dreams.' I understood, of course. This was what teenage magazines were all about. I still retained a colloquial jokey style, so that some of my early articles and stories are quite recognisably by me, but I wasn't projecting *my* ideas and beliefs and values. I went on writing endless short stories for magazines not only in my teens, but in my 20s and 30s too. I needed to make money! But I was also writing a lot of books at the same time, and I took satisfaction in expressing myself properly in all those early novels and children's books. I could develop my own style and write exactly how I wanted – whereas I had to monitor myself doing the magazine work. I knew it was no use putting in long passages of description or trying to use metaphors or similes, or striving to give my writing a little bit of sparkle or originality or humour. My job was to tell a romantic story in plain prose and involve the readers. The sub-editors were ready with their red pens to tidy your manuscript into a neat package that did the job. There was the occasional crossover in subject matter. I might be writing about teenage life in a magazine short story in the morning and in my own novel in the afternoon, but I'd tackle the material very differently. I'm not knocking the magazines because they were very important to young girls, especially *Jackie*. The magazine was a success right from the start, but I think it only came into its own in the 70s, when I wasn't so much involved with it. Whenever I give family talks, I tell the audience about writing for D. C. Thompson's, mentioning *Jackie* in particular. The moment I say the name *Jackie* all the mums and teachers and librarians nudge each other and whisper, 'Do you remember the Cathy and Claire problem page?' So I'm very much aware that it did have a big influence and I think what was so extraordinary was that the magazine went right across the board. It didn't matter what kind of girl you were, or even what class. You read *Jackie*. I feel touched to be a little part of this, but I don't feel that it had anything to do with what I consider my real writing.

LP So you were writing for yourself at the same time. At that point did you have a sense of audience?

JW Yes, for the magazines. But this was very much secondary work. I always wanted to write books – for myself, although obviously I've always been aware that I have to make things interesting and accessible for my readers. I wrote my first full-length novel when I was about 15 and had the common sense to know that it wasn't really publishable. It was about a teenage girl and her sister on a journey abroad. There was no real plot whatsoever. Then all the time I was a journalist in Dundee, from 17 to 19, I wrote at least two novels. I sent the *next* novel to a publisher and it got turned down. They were very kind and wrote quite a long letter. I was so stupid – I thought they were just being kind to me. I didn't realise it was quite unusual to get a long letter, and you usually just got a brief rejection slip. I didn't have the sense to try it anywhere else or to try to rewrite it. Eventually, by the time I was 23 or so, I did get my first, very short, children's book published – and I was off!

LP And that was *Ricky's Birthday* in Macmillan's Nippers series? How did it come about that you wrote for that series?

JW I was married by this time (at 19, much too young!) and I had my daughter. We practically lived in Kingston Library because we didn't have much money to buy many books then. Luckily Emma loved being read to. So when she was about two we were sitting on the floor in the library, working our way through the picture books. I saw a nearby shelf of smaller books with big print for beginning readers and noticed one very distinctive series, slim paperbacks with white covers and bright child-friendly illustrations. You could see right away from the titles like *Fish and Chips for Supper* and *Who's Coming in the Van with Me?* that these stories were about urban children from poor families. They weren't anything like the Ladybird Peter and Jane in their smart little coats and Start-Rite sandals. I loved these new books. So I wondered if I could possibly write one. They just seemed my sort of territory. I had no idea that Leila Berg, the editor, had commissioned well-known children's authors to contribute to her series. I simply tried to work out how to write something that would fit the format. I saw each had 32 pages and I counted the number of words on each page too. I made up my own story – not a particularly great story actually – about a little boy desperate for a special birthday present and divided it up into 30 pages, because I didn't count the end papers. Then I sent it off, crossing my fingers. Leila Berg said she was surprised but tickled that I'd sent her this story on spec and said she'd like to publish it. I was absolutely thrilled. Although it was only a little paperback and it certainly wasn't widely distributed, it meant so much because I'd actually got a book in print at last. This had been my ambition right from when I was six or so.

LP   Did you have much contact with Leila Berg?

JW   No, sadly I never met her, though I read about her. I'd heard her interviewed on Woman's Hour and read her own Little Pete children's stories. It sounds as if she was an amazing woman. She just wrote me a few letters.

LP   That's surprising, because it's striking how closely the ethos of Nippers can be applied to your books. Leila Berg was one of a number of people at that time who were really interested in creating different kinds of books for children. How aware were you of those conversations?

JW   I had absolutely no idea. I didn't know any people in publishing or education at that time. But I'd always been slightly dissatisfied with children's books, even though I loved reading. I rushed through a lot of Enid Blyton when I was six and then by the time I was seven or so I loved Noel Streatfeild, and then all those girly classics, *Little Women, What Katy Did, The Secret Garden, A Little Princess...*
I read my way round all the shelves in the children's room in Kingston library. I loved them but I felt there was something missing. They didn't seem *real* to me. The parents never quarrelled, there were rarely any money concerns in the family, the children didn't worry or have nightmares. They didn't reflect my kind of life at all. So I started reading adult novels about children. I knew nothing about the literary cannon – at the age of 13 I raced through Catherine Cookson's books about a tough little Tyneside child and then secretly read *Lolita* and enjoyed both because they were 'real'. I was a huge fan of the child star Mandy Miller, and the subject matter of her films totally appealed to me: a lonely deaf child at boarding school, a child with divorcing parents, a child whose father was a criminal, a dying child in hospital. You didn't find this sort of subject matter in children's books in the 50s and 60s. The only book I could find about so-called working-class children was *The Family from One End Street*, which I loved, especially the illustrations, but it was very light-hearted, and I wanted drama and

tragedy. I had no idea that there was a continuing conversation about the need for more realism in children's books.

By the time I started writing teenage novels for OUP I'd discovered various American teenage titles and saw that they were nearly all written in the first person. I've always loved first-person narratives. I love *The Bell Jar*, I love *Catcher in the Rye* and my favourite classics are *Jane Eyre* and *Great Expectations* – so writing in the first person came naturally to me. So I wrote *Nobody's Perfect* – which clearly wasn't perfect because a handful of publishers rejected it. OUP hung on to it for an endless nine months, but at last they said they wanted it. It was my first young person's hardback, a story about a girl trying to find her real father.

I'd had novels published before – adult crime novels. I didn't set out to write a crime novel at all. I'd written an adult novel about two little girls getting kidnapped. I thought it was a straight novel, but Macmillan put it on their crime list. So then I was stuck because I wanted them to carry on publishing me, but I really didn't much *like* crime novels, either reading or writing them. I was actually married to a policeman at that time, which made Macmillan very excited because they thought he could help me and I could do police procedural writing. I didn't want to do that at all! I had enough of the police in my ordinary life and I didn't want to have it in my fictional life too. I did struggle through about five more crime novels. They were very dark and certainly not at all suitable to be read by children – but they were all *about* children. I seem to have concentrated nonstop on children throughout my writing career.

LP   And then you eventually did get that first book published by Oxford University Press. Who was your editor at OUP?

JW   Ron Heapy was the chief editor. I think *Nobody's Perfect* appealed to him because he'd experienced something similar himself. I was delighted to be published by OUP and went on to write about five more teenage books for them. I wrote books for other publishers too and started to do school and library visits. One school got in touch with me, and then it escalated rapidly. I found giving talks rather an ordeal at first. As many of my books were for teenagers I was often invited to talk to Year 9. Individually they can be delightful but en masse they can be a bit of a nightmare. I realised that my books in those days appealed to the more literary child or teenager, who already loved reading. I deliberately aimed at the odd ones out, the quirky and imaginative and awkward, the person who would not be captain of the school team or the first person to be asked for a dance. At first I wanted to concentrate on this sort of readership. I knew my books wouldn't necessarily be popular but I didn't mind. I certainly didn't want to write a bestseller. However, after a while I started to think it might be good to try to interest the sort of kids who said they thought reading boring. I thought the dense pages of text in my books might be part of the problem. When I was young I loved all the black-and-white illustrations and colour plates in books and pored over them for hours. My OUP books had no illustrations and rather old-fashioned covers.

So I changed tack slightly. I moved to Transworld (which became Random House and is now Penguin Random House). One of the editors, David Fickling, was very approachable, so I told him that I wanted to write a different sort of book. I wanted to write the story of a child in a children's home desperate to be fostered. I thought it would work best if I could have lots of black-and-white illustrations all over each page, as if the child herself were drawing them. This way I thought the text would look interesting and easy to read, a fun experience. David was very affable and agreed at once and introduced me to the illustrator Nick Sharratt. It just seemed to be the most perfect match ever. That was how we came to work on *The Story of Tracy Beaker* together. Nick came up with a busy, lively, contemporary cover that was totally eye-catching. He did countless perfect illustrations throughout the text, often elaborating on my bossy instructions in the margin. (Now I always leave everything to Nick because I know he'll always come up with wonderful ideas.) I decided to write *Tracy* in a different kind of way. When I'd been researching foster care I'd been sent the booklet all children in care were given at that time. There were all sorts of questions and suggestions. This was a gift. I imagined Tracy herself filling in the booklet, being deliberately subversive, scribbling in the margin and telling fibs. It was her way of coping with institutional life, battling against her social worker and the whole care system. I loved writing this way – rather like a diary – and felt it was especially easy to read. I trusted children to understand Tracy and know why she often behaves badly. To my delight, this idea worked. So many children have happily told me that they hated reading, but when they picked up *The Story of Tracy Beaker* they liked the humorous pictures, relaxed when they saw the big print and frequent paragraphs and immediately got sucked into the story.

The Story of Tracy Beaker didn't instantly become a huge hit, but I suppose it established me as a writer, even though I'd already written about 40 books for children. It was shortlisted for the Carnegie and started to do well. I loved writing in this style. I wanted to write about a child's experience of divorce, but I didn't want to revert to a plain chapter book, so I divided *The Suitcase Kid* into sections, one for every letter of the alphabet: *A is for Andy, B is for Bathroom, C is for Cottage*, etc. I hadn't dreamt that I'd be translated into many different languages, so this book has been a nightmare for translators! *The Mum-Minder* was in seven sections, one for each day of the week. There were different food-themed passages in *The Bed and Breakfast Star* because Elsa is living in a hotel for homeless people and food treats are very important to her. When I wrote a book about those dreaded Year Nines I had nine chapters and nine lists of heroes, dilemmas, resolutions, etc. I knew lists are very popular with young teenage girls. I went on trying to present each book in a novel way, but there's a limit to the number of tricks you can play. Now I'm back to writing Chapter One.

LP   Because you are so popular and the books are so accessible, I think people are often not as conscious of them as literary artefacts. In fact, they are very sophisticated. One of the things that is striking about Tracy is the fact that she is such an unreliable narrator.

JW   It's very pleasant for someone to be thinking about the way I write my books, rather than the content! For a long time people dismissed me as an 'issue' writer, which made my books sound pretty dreary. Also some middle-class parents have been very wary of my books, thinking they contain a lot of sex and drugs, though perhaps not rock and roll. There's no sex, there's no drugs, and I think they're subtly moral books. I'm pleased that most children, even very young unsophisticated readers, get the whole concept of an unreliable narrator. They understand that Tracy is badly behaved because she's unhappy and missing her mother and has been let down so many times. I don't point this out in my text and avoid any overt instruction. I used to hate it in 1950s stories when the author would write 'Oh, wasn't she a naughty girl?' or 'You wouldn't do that, would you, children?' I think children nowadays would find this even more irritating. I find it interesting that older teenagers often write to tell me that they've reread their favourite childhood books when they're ill or depressed and find there's another depth to them.

   I'm writing the stories I want to write now, and luckily I haven't needed to churn out those magazine stories for money for a long time now. I feel my books are quite complex and I often play around with language, but I still want them to be easy to read. I try hard to start with an arresting beginning and make the book easy to get into. I avoid long pages of description and get on with the action straight away. Most children nowadays aren't prepared to struggle through several introductory chapters before the story actually gets started. I know most readers rush through a whole book in a couple of days, just to see what happens. But then they nearly always reread the story and ponder passages and generally understand less obvious points.

LP *The Story of Tracy Beaker* is often identified as the turning point, but looking back at the early teenage novels, there are lots of themes you come back to later on. David Fickling told me that *Tracy Beaker* was also a book that required very little editing. Were you conscious of having found the right voice and then being able to go back and mine that earlier material, or was it more of an unconscious process?

JW No, I don't think I mined the earlier books. I can't find most of them (I've got about twenty thousand books crammed into my house) and I've forgotten what they were about. I think it's just the type of book I'll always write, because of the person that I am. If you pick up an Anne Tyler or an Anita Brookner book, that world is distinctive and easily recognisable as theirs. *My* world is always going to be about misunderstood girls: shy ones, bookish ones, lonely ones, naughty ones, fierce ones. Girls who are generally going through a hard time. It's a safe bet that there is probably not going to be a full complement of parents who are comforting and lovely and mature. This is the type of book I always write – well, up till now!

I do find it a little bit disconcerting if I give a talk in a library or a school where there are books of mine on the shelves that have been there 20 or 30 years. A child might have read one of these books only last week and will ask me a detailed question about the characters or plot. It's quite a struggle for me to come up with a coherent answer because they've simply faded from my mind (not surprising when I've now written 103 books). I suppose I could go back and reread some of those earlier titles but I'd find that torture. I hate rereading my work because I always itch to alter things – and times change too. I *have* reread *Ricky's Birthday*, my Nippers title, which is hardly a trial because it probably took all of ten minutes. I'd write it so differently now. Those early 1970s characters seem so stereotyped now. Ricky's big sister is very girly and only interested in her appearance, and her brother is the one who gets to ride the powerful motorbike. If I wince at one tiny early reader then goodness knows what I'd think of some of the others.

I did have to reread a long-ago OUP book *Falling Apart* because it was reissued in Australia recently. I wouldn't write this book now, though I think it's quite powerful and works well – perhaps too well. It's about a girl contemplating suicide. She makes a serious attempt in the first chapter, then you get the whole backstory before her eventual recovery at the end. I wouldn't write that story now, because initially it's quite persuasive. I didn't have much of a readership when my OUP titles were published, but now lots of impressionable young girls read my books. I couldn't live with myself if just one unbalanced girl didn't read right to the end of the book and thought suicide the only possible response to the sad end of a love affair. I try to be extremely careful now: I might write about children going through hard times and coping with all kinds of difficulties but I never suggest that destructive behaviour is a solution.

I didn't realise then just how books can influence children and that they can identify with the strangest characters. I once took a friend and her granddaughter to a stage adaption of my book *Bad Girls*, about bullying. There's a character in this book called Kim who's really cruel and spiteful. She's a horrible character who makes the main girl Mandy's life a misery. My friend's grandchild watched absolutely absorbed. We were very pleased, because she was only just six and we wondered if she'd get bored and fidget. At the end of the play she clapped enthusiastically and said she loved it, her eyes shining. I asked her which part you liked the most. 'I loved Kim! All the bits about Kim. I want to *be* Kim!' she declared. This was funny but very alarming! (Luckily that little girl has grown up to be kind and sunny-natured and very caring.) I know some of my fellow writers think you should only write for yourself. I like to do that too, but I do think you have to be responsible and steer away from anything that might be a malign influence on a child.

LP   One of the contexts in which your books often come up in is a kind of therapeutic context. I know Judy Blume, a writer with whom I think you share some commonalities, has very much embraced that kind of agony aunt position. How do you see yourself in relation to that sort of role?

JW   I never set out to be an agony aunt but I seem somehow to have become one. I get hundreds of letters and emails from children telling me about their problems Thank goodness there's never been any situation where I feel I've got to inform someone because a child is in actual danger. Mostly the problems are prosaic, though horrible for the child: they worry that no one likes them at school; they're scared their parents will split up; they're anxious about school tests. I can't possibly write back to everyone, it would take 24 hours each day. I try to reply to children going through a really difficult time. I have to be very careful. They've written to me, probably without their parents knowing, so if I write back and say, 'Yes, your stepdad does sound a bit of a bully', the stepdad himself might be insisting on reading it, which would make the situation worse for that child. My answers have to be comforting and positive, but I can't give specific advice, just hints and suggestions: 'I'm so sorry you're going through a bad time and feel so fed up. Does your mum know how you feel? I'm glad you've got a really good friend at school though. If you both like reading my books perhaps you could start up a library club together.' Thousands of children want to be writers and send me their stories and ask me how to get published. That's a difficult one for me, because obviously most children aren't ever going to see their stories in print, except maybe on one of the many Internet sites. I'll reply, 'It's great that you enjoy writing and I can see you've tried really hard with your fantastic story. You'll probably have to wait till you're grown up before you can think of getting published, and then you might want to do something else anyway.' I always try to be kind, and it's a privilege to get so many letters – some are a total joy. However, I worry about the piles of letters always waiting on my desk, or on the sofa, or scattered over the carpet. I sometimes think of all those children waiting hopefully each day for a reply. I feel so bad when a child says to me that they wrote but I never replied, and they were so disappointed. But realistically how can anyone reply to every single letter? I don't want to employ anyone to respond for me, and I don't want to send out a specially printed token reply, because children compare their letters. They want personal replies, in my own handwriting. It's a perennial problem – but if the time comes when I *don't* get lots of fan letters I shall probably worry about that too!

LP   What about books? You've talked about really wanting, as a child reader, to see books that were more realistic, and one idea that's often discussed is that children need more realistic books in order to make sense of their own lives. Has that influenced your approach to social realism?

JW   I think it's something that *I've* always wanted, but there are lots of children (and their parents) who want to read about safe, cosy idealised worlds in children's books. Luckily there's such a choice of children's literature now to cater for all needs – and of course the main purpose of a book is to delight and entertain, not necessarily to enlighten and inform, though it's wonderful if one book can do all these things. Life is strange for twenty-first-century children. Most parents try hard to protect their children. They're taken to school, to sport and leisure activities, they're supervised on play dates, they're looked after in every way, so that they're much less independent than the young people of my generation. Yet children nowadays have access to all sorts of information on the Internet, and even the soaps on television deal with very adult content. They know so much more than I did – and they're much more aware of all sorts of adult things. I'm writing for these children. I don't pretend that life is a fairy tale, but I try not to be too graphic or depressing. I might show a child going through a very bad time, but I want the message to be that life can be dreadful sometimes, but somehow or other you get through a bad patch and learn how to cope and be happy again. I want my books to have a satisfying ending, not necessarily a hundred percent happy, but I want things to be positive. I don't want children to close one of my books and think that life is bleak and depressing and unfair. I want them to close a book and smile.

LP   Do you think that that commitment to an optimistic ending, if not a happy one, is something that has become stronger as you've moved into writing for younger children?

JW   Probably. I think older teenagers can deal with bleak situations. In fact, they often enjoy wallowing in them when they're in a really dark mood. It's weirdly comforting then to read a really tragic book. But I don't think young children can manage this. I don't want to write anything too sad or ultra melancholy. My books aimed at six to eight year olds are all quite light in tone: *Sleepovers*, *The Cat Mummy*, *The Butterfly Club*. I still try to be very careful when I'm writing for 9–13-year-olds. *Lola Rose* is probably one of my bleakest books. It deals with two very frightening things. There's a violent dad, even though he can be loving at times. Mum makes a break for freedom with her two children, but later she develops cancer. Obviously these are very controversial subjects for a children's book. The saddest letters I get from children are the ones that say 'My mum's got breast cancer. Will you promise me she is going to be all right?' If only I *could* promise that. All I can do is write truthfully that I've had friends with breast cancer who have made a full recovery and that I very much hope that their mum will get better too. When I decided to write *Lola Rose* I wanted to deal truthfully with violence and cancer, but I didn't want any graphic scenes and I didn't want to be too morbid either. I actually wrote the book because a mother with cancer got in touch with me and said her children were going through such a difficult time and asked if I could write a story about children in this situation. So I tried my best. I didn't have the mother in the story making a full recovery because some mums don't make it, and I didn't want to anger those child readers – and yet I needed to reassure the children still desperately hoping their mum would get better. So I end the book with the mother seeming to get much better for a while, but not necessarily recovering totally. Mum and the children are now living with their lovely capable Aunt Barbara, so there's a feeling of safety and security, no matter what else happens. At the moment there's a fashion for teenage books about death – what it's like to be a young person dying of leukaemia, for instance. Some of these are beautifully written sensitive stories, but I don't think I'll ever write one myself. I've *known* so many kids with leukaemia and other potentially fatal illnesses through private charity work. Some of these children make it – but some don't. If I wrote a book about a child dying then all those kids in hospital battling through treatment would find it frightening and depressing. And if I wrote about a child getting better and everything being fine, then it would be very upsetting for the children getting weaker and going downhill. So it seems better not do it at all.

LP One of the things that I find very striking, actually, when I teach your books, is how effectively you walk that line. Because students will read *The Illustrated Mum* and they are often very excited – they read it as children and they remember it – and then they come and say, 'I can't believe how upsetting this is.' As child readers they were able to take the optimistic note of that book, whereas as adults, they are bringing something different.

JW I think this is very true and it's strange. Obviously I don't see the reactions of people when they are reading my books – well, it's very rare if I actually *see* someone reading one – but I've been to a lot of play adaptations. When the lights go up at the end it's always the adults who are tear-stained. I think children do believe that things will somehow turn out all right for the family in *The Illustrated Mum*, whereas adults aren't at all sure and find some of the scenes harrowing. It *is* a terribly sad book, yet I felt compelled to write it, and I didn't want to fudge it at the end. I have the mother in hospital, her two girls visiting her, and they seem fine and if you're an optimistic child you can think 'Mum's going to get completely better and then they'll all live together and be happy', whereas an older or adult reader won't see it like that but will know that there's a foster mother who'll be able to look after them if Mum can't stay stable. It's difficult trying to work things out so that I feel I'm writing a truthful ending, one that satisfies me, and yet at the same time I want it to be a comforting ending for child readers.

LP   In recent years you have turned towards historical fiction. What motivated you to do that? Do you see a fundamental difference between those novels and the contemporary novels?

JW   I didn't set out to write historical novels. I was made a Coram Fellow at the Foundling Museum in London and met up with the then director, Rhiann Harris, to see how we could work together. She said that what they'd *really* like would be for me to write a children's novel about a foundling. I liked this idea. I knew Jamila Gavin had written *Coram Boy* about an eighteenth-century boy foundling, so I decided to write a late nineteenth-century book about a foundling girl. I love that period in history. However, I knew I was taking a big risk with this book. Children have always said they like my work because it's very contemporary and modern and reflects their own lives and experiences. I wasn't at all sure they'd like an historical book. I tried to find a voice for my main character that was engaging and immediate but would have a reasonably authentic Victorian tone, but even so I thought it would only appeal to a minority of my readers. I was so relieved and excited when almost immediately Hetty became one of my most beloved characters. Hundreds of children wrote to ask me what was going to happen next. They all wondered whether she would be a servant when she left the Foundling Hospital so I decided that we'd all find out. I've now written four books about Hetty and I'm halfway through the fifth. I've also written about an Edwardian girl, Opal Plumstead, a bright girl who has to leave school and work in a factory and becomes involved with the Suffragette movement. But I still write contemporary books too. My latest book *The Butterfly Club* is about little girls in Year Three, when they've just gone up into the junior school, and how they cope. I'm happy writing about modern younger children, but I'm not sure about writing for older modern teenagers now. Social media has changed things so much, and if this is the preferred form of communication it's pretty hard to get an emotional plot going! I feel happier writing about a 14-year-old in Victorian or Edwardian times because I can have a reasonable stab at guessing what they're thinking about and what they like to do. I'm not sure I'd get it right about modern teenagers. I'm not into modern technology in any way. My publishers have me on Facebook and Twitter but it's certainly not my favourite way of being in touch with people. I feel comfortable with younger children and we get on well at signings and I feel I know what I'm doing. Once girls go off into their own teenage world where the most important thing is to get your eyebrows threaded then I'm lost.

LP   I was never that girl.

JW   No, me neither. Of course there are many girls now who feel they don't fit and they don't belong. I'm very glad I'm not 14 or 15 now.

LP   Well, the historical fiction certainly does seem to have been a rich, new vein for you.

JW   I love writing it. It's a treat to try something different and to find it works. Maybe I'll try something else entirely in the future!

Further Reading

Jacqueline Wilson has been widely discussed in the media, but has received very little scholarly attention. I have therefore arranged this selection of further reading into three main sections:

1. A bibliography of Jacqueline Wilson's published works, comprising her published books, a limited selection of journalism and a list of adaptations of her work.
2. A list of material about Jacqueline Wilson, including a selection of journalism which covers some biographical material and a range of responses to Wilson's work.
3. A brief selection of material not pertaining to Wilson specifically, but dealing more generally with issues raised by the chapters in this volume. Some of this material briefly addresses Wilson's work as part of a broader discussion.

Works by Jacqueline Wilson

In order of publication.

Fiction

Illustrators' names are provided where known. In several cases Wilson's picture books have been reissued with new illustrations; only the first edition is given. Titles marked with an asterisk are adult novels.

Hide and Seek (London: Macmillan, 1972)★.
Ricky's Birthday, ill. Margaret Belsky (London: Macmillan, 1973).
Truth or Dare (London: Macmillan, 1973)★.
Snap (London: Macmillan, 1974)★.
Let's Pretend (London: Macmillan, 1976)★.
Making Hate (London: Macmillan, 1977)★.
Nobody's Perfect (Oxford: Oxford University Press, 1982).
Waiting for the Sky to Fall (Oxford: Oxford University Press, 1983).
School Trip, ill. Sally Holmes (London: Hamish Hamilton, 1984).
The Killer Tadpole, ill. Rebecca Campbell-Grey (London: Hamish Hamilton, 1984).
The Other Side (Oxford: Oxford University Press, 1984).
How to Survive Summer Camp (Oxford: Oxford University Press, 1985).
Amber (Oxford. Oxford University Press, 1986)
The Monster in the Cupboard, ill. Kate Rogers (London: Hamish Hamilton, 1986).

The Power of the Shade (Oxford: Oxford University Press, 1987).
Glubbslyme, ill. Jane Cope (Oxford: Oxford University Press, 1987).
Stevie Day: Lonely Hearts (London: Armada, 1987).
Stevie Day: Supersleuth (London: Armada, 1987).
Stevie Day: Vampire (London: Armada, 1988).
Stevie Day: Rat Race (London: Armada, 1988).
This Girl (Oxford: Oxford University Press, 1988).
The Party in the Lift, ill. Thelma Lambert (London: Blackie, 1989).
Is There Anybody There? Volume 1 – Spirit Raising (London: Armada, 1989).
The Left-Outs, ill. Ian Newsham (London: Blackie, 1989).
Is There Anybody There? Volume 2 – Crystal Gazing (London: Armada, 1989).
Take a Good Look, ill. Jo Worth (London: Blackie, 1990).
The Dream Palace (Oxford: Oxford University Press, 1991).
The Werepuppy, ill. Janet Robertson (London: Blackie, 1991).
The Story of Tracy Beaker, ill. Nick Sharratt (London: Doubleday, 1991).
Mark Spark, ill. Bethan Matthews (London: Hamish Hamilton, 1992).
Video Rose, ill. Janet Robertson (London: Blackie, 1992).
The Suitcase Kid, ill. Nick Sharratt (London: Doubleday, 1992).
Mark Spark in the Dark, ill. Bethan Matthews (London: Hamish Hamilton, 1993).
Deep Blue (Oxford: Oxford University Press, 1993).
The Mum-Minder, ill. Nick Sharratt (London: Doubleday, 1993).
The Wooden Horse, ill. Jan Nesbitt (Aylesbury: Ginn, 1994).
Come Back, Teddy!, ill. Stephen Holmes (Harlow: Longman, 1994).
Freddy's Teddy, ill. Stephen Holmes (Harlow: Longman, 1994).
Teddy Goes Swimming, ill. Stephen Holmes (Harlow: Longman, 1994).
Teddy at the Fair, ill. Stephen Holmes (Harlow: Longman, 1994).
Twin Trouble, ill. Philippe Dupasquier (London: Methuen, 1994).
Love From Katy, ill. Conny Jude (Aylesbury: Ginn, 1995).
Cliffhanger, ill. Nick Sharratt (London: Yearling, 1995).
Jimmy Jelly, ill. Lucy Keijser (London: Piccadilly, 1995).
My Brother Bernadette, ill. Stephen Lewis (London: Heinemann, 1995).
Sophie's Secret Diary, ill. Natacha Ledwidge (Aylesbury: Ginn, 1995).
The Dinosaur's Packed Lunch, ill. Nick Sharratt (London: Doubleday, 1995).
Double Act, ill. Nick Sharratt and Sue Heap (London: Doubleday, 1995).
Bad Girls, ill. Nick Sharratt (London: Doubleday, 1996).
Beauty and the Beast, ill. Peter Kavanagh (London: A&C Black, 1996).
Connie and the Water Babies, ill. Georgien Overwater (London: Methuen, 1996).
Mr Cool, ill. Stephen Lewis (London: Kingfisher, 1996).
Girls in Love, ill. Nick Sharratt (London: Doubleday, 1997).
The Lottie Project, ill. Nick Sharratt (London: Doubleday, 1997).
The Monster Story-Teller, ill. Nick Sharratt (London: Doubleday, 1997).
Buried Alive!, ill. Nick Sharratt and Sue Heap (London: Doubleday, 1998).
Rapunzel, ill. Nick Sharratt (London: Scholastic, 1998).

Girls under Pressure, ill. Nick Sharratt (London: Doubleday, 1998).
Monster Eyeballs, ill. Stephen Lewis (London: Egmont, 1999).
Girls out Late, ill. Nick Sharratt (London: Doubleday, 1999).
The Illustrated Mum, ill. Nick Sharratt (London: Doubleday, 1999).
Lizzie Zipmouth, ill. Nick Sharratt (London: Corgi, 2000).
The Dare Game, ill. Nick Sharratt (London: Doubleday, 2000).
Vicky Angel, ill. Nick Sharratt (London: Doubleday, 2000).
Dustbin Baby, ill. Nick Sharratt (London: Doubleday, 2001).
Sleepovers, ill. Nick Sharratt (London: Doubleday, 2001).
The Cat Mummy, ill. Nick Sharratt (London: Doubleday, 2001).
Girls in Tears, ill. Nick Sharratt (London: Doubleday, 2002).
Secrets, ill. Nick Sharratt (London: Doubleday, 2002).
The Worry Website, ill. Nick Sharratt (London: Doubleday, 2002).
Lola Rose, ill. Nick Sharratt (London: Doubleday, 2003).
Midnight, ill. Nick Sharratt (London: Doubleday, 2003).
Best Friends, ill. Nick Sharratt (London: Doubleday, 2004).
The Diamond Girls, ill. Nick Sharratt (London: Doubleday, 2004).
Clean Break, ill. Nick Sharratt (London: Doubleday, 2005).
Love Lessons, ill. Nick Sharratt (London: Doubleday, 2005).
Candyfloss, ill. Nick Sharratt (London: Doubleday, 2006).
Starring Tracy Beaker, ill. Nick Sharratt (London: Doubleday, 2006).
Kiss, ill. Nick Sharratt (London: Doubleday, 2007).
Cookie, ill. Nick Sharratt (London: Doubleday, 2008).
My Sister Jodie, ill. Nick Sharratt (London: Doubleday, 2008).
Hetty Feather, ill. Nick Sharratt (London: Doubleday, 2009).
Ask Tracy Beaker, ill. Nick Sharratt (London: Doubleday, 2010).
Little Darlings, ill. Nick Sharratt (London: Doubleday, 2010).
The Longest Whale Song, ill. Nick Sharratt (London: Doubleday, 2010).
Lily Alone, ill. Nick Sharratt (London: Doubleday, 2011).
Sapphire Battersea, ill. Nick Sharratt (London: Doubleday, 2011).
Big Day Out, ill. Nick Sharratt (London: Yearling, 2012).
Emerald Star, ill. Nick Sharratt (London: Doubleday, 2012).
Four Children and It, ill. Nick Sharratt (London: Puffin, 2012).
The Worst Thing About My Sister, ill. Nick Sharratt (London: Doubleday, 2012).
Diamond, ill. Nick Sharratt (London: Doubleday, 2013).
Queenie, ill. Nick Sharratt (London: Doubleday, 2013).
Opal Plumstead, ill. Nick Sharratt (London: Doubleday, 2014).
The Butterfly Club, ill. Nick Sharratt (London: Doubleday, 2015).
Katy, ill. Nick Sharratt (London: Puffin, 2015).
Little Stars, ill. Nick Sharratt (London: Doubleday, 2015).

Autobiography

Jacky Daydream, ill. Nick Sharratt (London: Doubleday, 2007).
My Secret Diary: Dating, Dancing, Dreams and Dilemmas (London: Doubleday, 2009).

Anthologies

Wilson has edited or provided forewords for several anthologies of others' work, and as Children's Laureate produced a list of recommended books for reading aloud.

Agnew, Kate, *Love and Longing: A Collection of Classic Poetry and Prose* (Cambridge: Wizard, 2004) (foreword by Jacqueline Wilson).

Eating Words for Breakfast (London: Penguin, 2004) (foreword by Jacqueline Wilson).

Wilson, Jacqueline, *Great Books to Read Aloud* (London: Corgi, 2006).

Wilson, Jacqueline (ed.), *Green Glass Beads: A Collection of Poems for Girls* (London: Macmillan, 2011).

Wilson, Jacqueline (ed.), *Paws and Whiskers*, ill. Nick Sharratt (London: Doubleday, 2014) (includes a short story by Jacqueline Wilson).

Quizzes and trivia books

The Jacqueline Wilson Quiz Book, ill. Nick Sharratt (London: Doubleday, 2002).

The World of Jacqueline Wilson, ill. Nick Sharratt (London: Doubleday, 2005).

Totally Jacqueline Wilson, ill. Nick Sharratt (London: Doubleday, 2007).

The Tracy Beaker Quiz Book, ill. Nick Sharratt (London: Doubleday, 2009).

Articles

Wilson, Jacqueline, 'Not in Front of the Children'. *Signal* 94 (January 2001), 17–28.

Wilson, Jacqueline, 'On Being the Children's Laureate'. *Books for Keeps* 162 (January 2007) http://booksforkeeps.co.uk/issue/162/childrens-books/articles/other-articles/on-being-the-children%E2%80%99s-laureate

Wilson, Jacqueline, 'Hopelessly Addicted to the Written Word', *TES* 11 May 2008 https://www.tes.co.uk/article.aspx?storycode=353749

Television adaptations

Directors and screenwriters are given where available.

Cliffhanger, Channel 4 Schools Television (1995).

Ware, Cilla (director), *Double Act*, Channel 4 Schools Television (2002).

The Story of Tracy Beaker, CBBC Television (2002–2005).

Islitt, Debbie (screenplay) and Cilla Ware (director), *The Illustrated Mum*, Channel 4 Schools Television (2003).

Morris, Mary (screenplay) and Joss Agnew (director), *Tracy Beaker's 'The Movie of Me'*, BBC Television (2004).

Best Friends, ITV (2004).

Girls in Love, ITV (2005–2005).

Blakeman, Helen (screenplay) and Juliet May (director), *Dustbin Baby*, BBC (2008).
Tracy Beaker Returns, CBBC Television (2010–2012).
The Dumping Ground, CBBC Television (2013–).
Blakeman, Helen (writer) and Paul Blakeman (director), *Hetty Feather*, CBBC Television (2015).

Stage adaptations

Listed according to the year and location of first performance. Details of published scripts are given alongside where relevant.

Ireland, Vicky, *The Lottie Project* (Polka Theatre, London, 1999). Published playscript: Ireland, Vicky, and Jacqueline Wilson, *The Lottie Project (play edition)* (London: Nick Hern, 2006).
Ireland, Vicky, *Double Act* (Polka Theatre, London, 2003). Published playscript: Ireland, Vicky, and Jacqueline Wilson, *Double Act (play edition)* (London: Collins Educational, 2003).
Ireland, Vicky, *Bad Girls* (Polka Theatre, London, 2004). Published playscript: Ireland, Vicky, and Jacqueline Wilson, *Bad Girls* (London: Nick Hern, 2006).
Ireland, Vicky, *Midnight* (Haymarket Theatre, Basingstoke & Peacock Theatre, West End, 2005). Published playscript: Ireland, Vicky, and Jacqueline Wilson, *Midnight (play edition)* (London: Nick Hern, 2006).
Ireland, Vicky, *The Suitcase Kid* (Orange Tree Theatre, London, 2007). Published playscript: Ireland, Vicky, and Jacqueline Wilson, *The Suitcase Kid (play edition)* (London: Nick Hern, 2009).
Ireland, Vicky, *Secrets* (Polka Theatre, London, 2008). Published playscript: Ireland, Vicky, and Jacqueline Wilson, *Secrets (play edition)* (London: Nick Hern 2009).
Novel Theatre Company, Emma Reeves (adaptor) and Sally Cookson (director), *Hetty Feather* (Rose Theatre, London, 2014). Published playscript: Reeves, Emma and Jacqueline Wilson, Jacqueline Wilson's Hetty Feather (London: Oberon Books, 2014).

Works about Jacqueline Wilson

For children

Carey, Joanna, *An Interview with Jacqueline Wilson* (London: Egmont, 2000).
Parker, Vic, *All About: Jacqueline Wilson* (Oxford: Heinemann Library, 2003).
Bankston, John, *Jacqueline Wilson* (New York: Chelsea Press, 2013).

Scholarly articles

Sources given here focus principally or exclusively on Wilson's work.

Butler, Rebecca, 'Different Lives: Disability in Contemporary Children's Literature'. *Journal of Children's Literature Studies* 2:1 (March 2005), 15–26.

Carter, James, 'Jacqueline Wilson' in *Talking Books: Children's Writers Talk About the Craft, Creativity and Process of Writing* (London: Routledge, 1999), pp. 232–255.

Leeson, Robert, 'Jacqueline Wilson' in Tracy Chevalier (ed.), *Twentieth-Century Children's Writers* (Chicago and London: St James Press, 1989), pp. 1057–1058.

Eccleshare, Julia, 'Readers' perceptions of a writer: Jacqueline Wilson's persona and her relationship with her reader' in Evelyn Arizpe and Vivienne Smith (eds.), *Children as Readers in Children's Literature: The Power of Texts and the Importance of Reading* (London: Routledge, 2015).

Pearson, Lucy, 'Real Lives: Alcott, Ashley, and Wilson' in *Children's Literature* (with Peter Hunt) (London: Longman, 2011), pp. 61–89.

Tucker, Nicholas, 'Jacqueline Wilson' in Nicholas Tucker and Nikki Gamble (eds.), *Family Fictions* (Continuum, London and New York, 2001), pp. 68–84.

Waddilove, Kay, '"So Good, It's Exhilarating": The Jacqueline Wilson Phenomenon'. *Bookbird: A Journal of International Children's Literature* 50:3 (July 2012), 75–78.

Journalism

Armitstead, Claire, 'Profile: Jacqueline Wilson: The Pied Piper of Kingston', *Guardian Saturday Review* 14 February 2004, http://www.theguardian.com/books/2004/feb/14/booksforchildrenandteenagers.jacquelinewilson

Benn, Melissa, 'Bad Girl for Laureate', *Guardian* 11 February 2005, http://www.theguardian.com/books/2005/feb/11/booksforchildrenandteenagers.jacquelinewilson

Cooke, Rachel, 'The Story of Jacqueline Wilson', *The Observer* 23 March 2014, http://www.theguardian.com/books/2014/mar/23/the-story-of-jacqueline-wilson

Eccleshare, Julia, 'Authorgraph No. 115: Jacqueline Wilson'. *Books for Keeps* 115, March 1995, http://booksforkeeps.co.uk/issue/115/childrens-books/articles/authorgraph/authorgraph-no115-jacqueline-wilson

Eccleshare, Julia, 'In Dol's House', *Guardian* 25 March 2000, http://www.theguardian.com/books/2000/mar/25/booksforchildrenandteenagers.guardianchildrensfictionprize2000

Eccleshare, Julia, 'Jacqueline Wilson: Happy 100th Book'. *Books for Keeps* 209, November 2014, http://booksforkeeps.co.uk/issue/209/childrens-books/articles/jacqueline-wilson-happy-100th-book

Healey, R. M., 'Jacqueline Wilson'. *Book and Magazine Collector* 191 (2000), 18–26.

Pearson, Lucy, 'The Stories That Made Tracy Beaker Real'. *V&A Magazine* 34 (Summer 2014), 66-71.

Robinson, Winifred, 'The Hypocritical Ms Wilson: Why Children's Authors are to Blame for Loss of Innocence', *Daily Mail Online* 4 March 2008 http://www.dailymail.co.uk/news/article-526369/The-hypocritical-Ms-Wilson-Why-childrens-writers-hugely-blame-loss-innocence.html

Williamson, Charlotte, 'Jacqueline Wilson: I'm Afraid of Replying to Children's Letters', *Telegraph* 27 September 2009, http://www.telegraph.co.uk/culture/books/authorinterviews/6235183/Jacqueline-Wilson-Im-afraid-of-replying-to-childrens-letters.html

Womack, Philip, 'Interview with Jacqueline Wilson', *Telegraph* 9 December 2011, http://www.telegraph.co.uk/culture/books/bookreviews/8943303/Interview-with-Jacqueline-Wilson.html

Other relevant scholarly works

Family stories

One of the hallmarks of Wilson's work is her representation of 'alternative' families. These works are a good starting point for thinking about these issues. Alston and Pearson discuss Wilson briefly within the broader context of family stories.

Alston, Ann, *The Family in English Children's Literature* (Oxford: Routledge, 2008).

Pearson, Lucy, 'Family, Identity and Nationhood: Family Stories in Anglo-American Children's Literature, 1930–2000' in Catherine Butler and Kimberly Reynolds (eds.), *Modern Children's Literature: An Introduction* 2nd edn. (London: Palgrave Macmillan, 2014), pp. 89–104.

Reynolds, Kimberly, 'Changing Families in Children's Fiction' in M. O. Grenby and Andrea Immel (eds.), *The Cambridge Companion to Children's Literature* (Cambridge: Cambridge University Press, 2009), pp. 195–208.

Thiel, Elizabeth, *The Fantasy of Family: Nineteenth Century Children's Literature and the Myth of the Domestic Ideal* (Oxford: Routledge, 2007).

Tucker, Nicholas and Nikki Gamble (eds.) *Family Fictions* (Continuum, London and New York, 2001).

Fairytale, narrative, metafiction

As this volume shows, the question of narrative is a recurring theme throughout Wilson's books. She has repeatedly returned to issues relating to fantasy, storytelling and metafiction. How do we tell stories, what stories do we tell and why? These titles offer a useful introduction to some of these themes. Though old, a range of the essays in the section on 'The reader' in *The Cool Web* are relevant to this topic and give a good picture of ideas circulating at the time Wilson started her career.

Bettelheim, Bruno, *The Uses of Enchantment: The Meaning and Importance of Fairy Tales* (London: Penguin, 1991).

Booth, Wayne C., *The Rhetorics of Fiction* 2nd edn. (Chicago: The University of Chicago Press, 1983).

Colabucci, Lesley and Linda T. Parsons, 'To Be a Writer: Representations of Writers in Recent Children's Novels'. *The Reading Teacher* 62:1 (September 2008), 44–52.

Crago, Hugh, 'Healing Texts: Bibliotherapy and Psychology' in Peter Hunt (ed.), *Understanding Children's Literature* 2nd edn. (London: Routledge, 2005), pp. 86–102.

D'hoker, Elke and Gunther Martens (eds.), *Narrative Unreliability in the Twentieth-Century First-Person Novel* (Berlin: Walter de Gruyter, 2008).

Meek, Margaret, Aidan Warlow and Griselda Barlow (eds.), *The Cool Web: The Pattern of Children's Reading* (London: The Bodley Head, 1977).

Wilkie-Stibbs, 'Intertextuality and the Child Reader', in Peter Hunt (ed.) *Understanding Children's Literature* 2nd edn. (London: Routledge, 2005), pp. 168–179.

Ideology and ethics

As Kay Waddilove's chapter for this volume shows, Wilson's books engage directly with ideological debates about gender. More broadly, social realism has an important role to play in constructing ideas about the world. Children's literature scholarship has dealt extensively with questions of ideology and didacticism: here follows a small selection of relevant works which take various approaches to exploring what and how children's books teach. Daniels and Sainsbury discuss Wilson specifically.

Daniels, Carolyn, *Voracious Children: Who Eats Whom in Children's Literature* (London: Routledge, 2006).

Mallan, Kerry, *Gender Dilemmas in Children's Fiction* (Basingstoke: Palgrave, 2009).

Paul, Lissa, *Reading Otherways* (Stroud: Thimble Press, 1998).

Sainsbury, Lisa, *Ethics in British Children's Literature* (London: Bloomsbury, 2013).

Stephens, John, *Language and Ideology in Children's Fiction* (London: Longman, 1992).

Historical fiction

Wilson's recent turn to historical fiction situates her in a new tradition of writing for children with its own concerns and conventions.

Butler, Catherine and Hallie O'Donovan, *Reading History in Children's Books* (London: Palgrave Macmillan, 2012).

Collins, Fiona and Judith Graham (eds.), *Historical Fiction for Children* (London: David Fulton Publishers, 2001).

De Groot, Jerome, *The Historical Novel* (London and New York: Routledge, 2010).

Social realism and young adult fiction

Jacqueline Wilson's work is rooted in a tradition of social realism which has been particularly strong in books for teenage readers. Her early writing was aimed directly at teenagers; later work has continued to explore themes of maturation even when written for slightly younger audiences. Much of the scholarship on this topic deals with the American scene; however, it offers some useful perspectives. Day's concept of 'narrative intimacy', for example, is very relevant to Wilson's books, while Cart's work and the early essays from Egoff and Eccleshare give a good sense of the tradition in which Wilson's early work can be situated. Pearson and Reynolds offer an overview of the development of social realism in children's books more broadly.

Cart, Michael, *From Romance to Realism: 50 Years of Growth and Change in Young Adult Literature* (New York: HarperCollins, 1996).

Day, Sara K., *Reading Like a Girl: Narrative Intimacy in Contemporary American Young Adult Literature* (Jackson: University Press of Mississippi, 2013).

Eccleshare, Julia, 'Teenage Fiction: Realism, Romances, Contemporary Problem Novels' in Peter Hunt (ed.), *International Companion Encyclopedia of Children's Literature* (London: Routledge, 1996), pp. 387–396.

Egoff, Sheila, 'The Problem Novel' in Sheila Egoff, G. T. Stubbs and L. F. Ashley (eds.), *Only Connect: Readings in Children's Literature* 2nd edn. (New York: Oxford University Press, 1980), pp. 356–369.

Egoff, Sheila, *Thursday's Child: Trends and Patterns in Contemporary Children's Literature* (Chicago: American Library Association, 1981).

Meek, Margaret and Victor Watson, *Coming of Age in Children's Literature* (London and New York: Continuum, 2001).

Pearson, Lucy and Kimberley Reynolds, 'Realism' in David Rudd (eds.), *The Routledge Companion to Children's Literature* (London: Routledge, 2010), pp. 63–74.

Trites, Roberta Seelinger, *Disturbing the Universe: Power and Repression in Adolescent Literature* (Iowa City: University of Iowa Press, 2000).

Index

abandonment, parental   24, 61, 67,
    87, 106–115, 176
adolescence
    Hetty Feather   170–71
    and gender   94
    and parenting   112
    historical recognition of   186–9
    see also maturation, teenage novels
adult novels, Wilson's   3–4, 18–19,
    34, 202
Alcott, Louisa M.,
    Little Women   164, 172, 201
Amber   4, 19, 20, 34, 37, 38, 42–3,
    45, 49, 58, 59, 177, 178, 180,
    187–9, 194
anorexia   47, 58,
audience, Wilson's understanding
    of   97, 200
Austen, Jane
    Mansfield Park   62–3
autofiction   141, 155
awards and honours   1–2, 7, 27–30,
    60, 177

Bad Girls   8, 25, 36, 45, 46, 48, 104,
    111
    stage adaptation of   206
BBC adaptations, *see* television
    adaptions
Beckman, Gunnel   19
Belsky, Margaret   57
bereavement   8, 38–9, 41, 55, 58
Berg, Leila   56–57
Best Friends   45
Bettelheim, Bruno   58–9, 60, 61,
    67, 69, 106, 112
bibliotherapy   10, 55–74
    and realistic fiction   55–8
    and fantasy   58–9
    through shared reading   73–4

through writing   141–59
Blume, Judy   13, 18–19, 57, 176–182
    as agony aunt   58
    Are You There, God? It's Me,
        Margaret   62
    comparisons with Wilson   177
    Deenie   182–3
    Forever   183–6
    normalisation of controversial
        issues   179, 181–2
    representation of
        sexuality   182–7
Bok, Sissela   126, 138
Booth, Wayne C.   120
boys
    fearful   80–1, 92–3
    impact of conventional
        masculinity on   92–3
branding   25–32
    in the USA   9
    importance of Nick Sharratt to
        26, 34
    as a series   25–26
Bronte, Charlotte,
    Jane Eyre   63–5, 70, 76(n), 164,
        202
Butler, Judith   82–4
Butterfly Club, The   208

Candyfloss   35, 82–3, 89, 90,
    93, 94
Carnegie Medal   2, 7, 20, 29,
    see also awards and honours
Cat Mummy, The   208
children
    changing tastes as readers   23–4
childhood
    as a distinct phase   115–6
    in the twenty-first
        century   208

Children's Laureate   1, 30–31, 74,
    161, 215
  see also awards and honours
Chodorow, Nancy   104–5, 114,
    116
class, 137, 46, see also working class
  cross-class romance   36, 38–40
  impact on constructions of
    maturity   169–71
  Wilson's changing representation
    of   45–6
  in work of Judy Blume   179,
    181–2
classics
  Wilson's books as introduction to
    the   161
  Wlson's reading of   201–2
Clean Break   31, 48, 79, 88–9,
    90–1, 92–3, 157
clothes   83, 135, 147
  and relationships with
    parents   42, 83, 180, 190
  as symbol of (un)
    conventionality   70, 180, 181
coming of age, see also
    maturity   12, 143
  in children's literature   164–165
  in Hetty Feather   160–73
Cookie   35, 36, 47, 79, 83–5, 89, 90,
    93, 94
Coram Fellow   9, 31, 160, 210
  see also Foundling Museum
Cormier, Robert   18, 57
crime novels, see adult novels

Dahl, Roald   1, 26–7,
Dame Commander of the Order of
    the British Empire   1, 30
Dare Game, The   165
Daydreams and Diaries: the Story
    of Jacqueline Wilson   2, 6–7,
    31, 99(n)
D.C. Thompson   2 3, 4, 198–9, see
    also Jackie magazine
Dickens, Charles   162
  David Copperfield   161

Deep Blue   34, 36, 38, 40–1, 47, 50,
    58
Diamond   160, 166, 167, 170, 171,
    172–3
Diamond Girls, The   8, 35, 45,
    100(n), 104, 105, 111, 163
diary / diaries, as literary
    device   141–159, 165,
didacticism
  in children's and teenage
    fiction   82–3, 178, 194–5
  in Wilson's work   95–6, 152,
    158, 161, 208–10
  in The Story of Tracy Beaker (BBC
    adaptation)   137
Dinosaur's Packed Lunch, The   7
divorce   24, 25, 65–6, 89, 148, 168,
    176, 179, 204,
Double Act   25, 27, 34, 141, 144–146,
    150–3
double   12, 141–59
  antagonistic   148
  aspirational   149–50
  complementary   145–6
  mimetic   148–9
  parallel   146–7
  reader as   155–8
Dream Palace, The   1, 4, 34, 35,
    39–40, 42, 44, 47, 49
drugs   1, 40, 42, 44, 58, 204
Dumping Ground, The   1, 132
Dustbin Baby   8, 40, 45, 103, 104,
    105–110

Edwardian   46, 147–8, 153–4, 160,
    210, see also Four Children and
    It, Opal Plumstead
Egoff, Sheila   95–6, 179, 182, 186,
    187, 220
Emerald Star   9, 160, 167, 170, 172
endings
  open-ended   64–5
  happy   59, 67–8
escapism   5, 10, 38, 39, 59–60,
    61–64, 66, 71–2, 146–7, 161,
    192 see also fairy tales, fantasy,

fairy tales   38, 55–74, 91, 94, 105,
    112, 115, 122, 129–30, 148,
    166, 188, 208, 218-19
  bibliotherapeutic qualities
    of   58–9
  see also fantasy
family   7–8, 10–11, 16, 20, 24–5,
    31, 36, 57, 68–9, 78–101, 102–
    118, 128–9, 148, 167–9
  changing cultural dynamics of
    86–9
  see also fathers and fathering,
    mothers and mothering;
    parents
fantasy   1, 10, 12, 44–5, 50, 55–74,
    133–4, 147, 149, 154, 172,
    191–2, 218–19
  bibliotherapeutic qualities of
    58–9
  see also escapism, fairy stories, lies
    and lying
fathers and fathering   35, 36,
    39–40, 68, 78, 82–5, 88–96,
    116–17, 168–9, 181, 190, 202
father-romance   40–43, 187–8
femininity   79–80, 84–5, 90, 94
  see also gender
feminism   5, 10–11, 88–9, 96–7,
    104–5,
Fickling, David   6, 22–3, 25, 203,
    205
Fine, Anne   20, 23, 24, 73
food   94, 204
  as symbol of family   71, 104,
    111–12, 114, 180,
  affective qualities of   48–9
Foundling Hospital   11, 31, 162,
    167, 168, 170
Foundling Museum   9, 160, 210
  see also Coram Fellow
Four Children and It   1, 12, 50, 59,
    141–2, 143, 144, 147–150,
    153–4, 156, 157,165

gay and lesbian content   38, 39
gender   78–97, 117, 219

binaries   78
characteristics, schemata for
    79–80
and family life   85–94
and ideology   79–82
impact on construction of
    maturation   169
performativity and
    socialisation   82–85
Gerhardt, Sue   103–4
girls
  as audience for Wilson's
    books   28
  'feisty'   78–101
  friendships   44–5, 94
  as a focus for Wilson's work   10,
    11, 19
  impact of constructions of
    femininity on   94–5
  as writers   141–2
Girls in Love   36, 59,
Girls in Tears   177, 178, 192–3,
    196–7(n)
Girls under Pressure   40, 47,
Glubbslyme   1, 21,
Great Books to Read Aloud   30
Guardian Children's Book Award
    29

Heap, Sue   143–4
Hetty Feather series   12–13, 147,
    160–173
  versions of Hetty's name in   166–7
  influence of Victorian literature
    on   162
  as historical fiction   161–164
  as coming-of-age
    narrative   164–173
  reader responses to   164
  romance in   170–173
  prose style of   163–5
Hetty Feather   1, 9, 11, 31, 50, see
    also Hetty Feather series
  stage adaptation of   1
  BBC adaptation of   1
Hide and Seek   3–4, 14(n)

historical fiction   1, 9, 12–13, 31,
        147, 159(n), 160–175, 210
    tension between historical and
        contemporary attitudes in
        162–3
Hollindale, Peter   81–2, 89
How to Survive Summer Camp   21
humour   4, 5, 7, 20, 57 199

ideology   79–82, 219
illness   154, 176, 191, 209–210,
    see also mental illness
Illustrated Mum, The   7, 8, 10, 29, 35,
        36, 37, 39, 42–4, 45, 47, 48, 49,
        50, 56, 59, 100(n), 103, 209–10
    bibliotherapy in   65–74
    mothering in   110–17
intertextuality   60–65, 143, 147–50
Jackie magazine   2–3, 17–18,
        198–9
    see also D.C. Thompson
Jacky Daydream   50, 86

Katy   9–10
Killer Tadpole, The   21
Kingtown   40, 41, 47,
    see also worldbuilding
Kiss   35

lesbian and gay content   38, 39
libraries, Wilson as most-borrowed
        author from   1, 2, 30
    bravado   123–5
    developmental model of, see also
        Piaget
    fantasy   129
    prosocial   122–3
    antisocial   122–3
    self-protective   123–5
Lily Alone   48, 104, 163
Little Darlings   45
Lizzie Zipmouth   1
Lola Rose   79, 89, 92, 95, 208–9
Lottie Project, The   12, 35, 36, 38,
        45–6, 49, 59, 141, 143, 144,
        146–7, 151, 154–6, 160

Love Lessons   177, 180–1, 187,
        189–92, 193, 194

Macmillan (publishing house)   3–4,
        200, 202
magazines, Wilson's career in   2–3,
        26, 59–60, 198–9
    see also D.C. Thompson, Jackie
        magazine
marketing   21, 22–3, 25–9, 34,
        101(n)
masculinity   79–81, 83–4, 90, 92–3,
        93
    see also gender; boys; fathers and
        fathering
maturation, see coming of age
mental illness   8, 37, 43–4, 56, 58,
        60, 63–5, 66–7, 70–2, 108,
        110–13, 115
    see also illness, suicide
metafiction   141–158, 218–19
Midnight   35, 37, 38, 39, 41, 59, 89
Monster Story-Teller, The   7
Montgomery, L. M., 165–6   172
    Anne of Green Gables   165
    Emily of New Moon   165
morality, see didacticism
Moss, Elaine   62
mothers and mothering   7, 11, 37–38,
        50, 60–72, 84–5, 87–9, 102–17
    distributed   103, 116–7
    good-enough   103–4, 107–110
    pressures on women   104–5
Mum-Minder, The, 204

narratee   119–20
narrative
    first-person   5, 6–7, 21, 22, 25,
        120, 125–6, 179–80, 186, 202
    unreliable, see unreliable narration
narrator
    lying   119–20
    first-person, see narrative, first-
        person
Nesbit, E.   157
    Five Children and It   143, 148, 154

Nestlé Smarties Book Prize   2, 7,
Nobody's Perfect   4, 5, 10, 11, 19, 34,
        35–6, 37, 40, 41, 42–3, 48, 49,
        50, 58, 59 202
Nünning, Ansgar   120–1

Opal Plumstead   7, 78, 160, 173, 210
Order of the British Empire
        (OBE)   1, 30
Other Side, The   10, 19, 34, 35, 36–7,
        38, 43–5, 48, 56, 60–6, 71–4
OUP novels   10–11, 34–54
        see also, teenage novels
Oxford University Press
        (OUP)   4–5, 6, 22, 202–3

parents, *see* family; mothers and
        mothering; fathers and
        fathering
Paul, Lissa   96
Piaget, Jean   121–2, 136,
Power of The Shade, The   19, 34, 37–8,
        39, 40, 41, 45, 47, 48, 49, 59
primary carers, *see* family; fathers
        and fathering; mothers and
        mothering
problem novel   13, 34–41, 50–1,
        57–8, 176–195
publishing, *see also* Fickling, David;
        Macmillan; Transworld
    changes over Wilson's career   2,
        5–6
    children's, 1990s   19–20, 27–29
    emergence of teenage   3, 18–19
    magazine   3, 17–18

Queenie   1, 9, 50, 165

Random House   203, *see also*
        Transworld
reader
    child (as inexperienced)   121–2
    critical   121–2
    as double   155–8
reading,
    collaborative approach to   72–4

realism   1, 4, 7–9, 10, 34–5, 94–7,
        201–2
    as contrasted with fantasy and
        romance   35, 50–1
    emphasis on during 1960s and
        1970s   56–8, 61–74
    see also problem novel
reception of Wilson's work
    by children   1–2, 21, 28–9
    by media   8–9, 29, 30, 55–6
    by reviewers and librarians   4–5,
        7–8, 20–1, 29–30, 194
    international   9–10
    by parents   8–9, 27–8
    scholarly   1
Red House Children's Book
        Award   1, 2, 7
Ricky's Birthday   1, 4, 14(n), 18,
        57–8, 177, 201–2, 205
romance
    as a literary mode   34–51, *see
        also* escapism, fantasy
    and relationships   36–40, 41–3,
        47, 171–3, 180–193
    cross-class   36, 38–40
    teacher-student   38, 41, 47–8,
        181, 190–2
    see also father-romance
Rosset, Clément   151–3

Sapphire Battersea   9, 160, 167,
        see also Hetty Feather series
Secrets   7–8, 35, 36, 41, 45, 46
self, writing the, *see* doubles
Seven Stories, the National Centre
        for Children's Books   2, 31
    see also Daydreams and Diaries:
        the Story of Jacqueline Wilson
sexuality   13, 58, 84, 177–79, 181,
        183–194
Sharratt, Nick   6–7, 15(n), 22–3,
        26, 31–2, 34–5, 41, 132–5,
        143–4, 203–4
    see also branding, marketing, *Double
        Act, The Story of Tracy Beaker*
Sharratt books   34–5

Sleepovers   208
Small, Gordon   199,
  see also D.C.Thompson,*Jackie*
  magazine
social realism, *see* realism
Spare Rib   5, 10
stage adaptations   1, 206
Steedman, Carolyn   155
Stephens, John   79–80, 164,
Stevie Day series   5, 6
Story of Tracy Beaker, The   1, 5, 28,
  55, 78, 89, 96, 141, 157, 162,
  165, 167–8, 203–4
  gender roles in   80–1
  unreliable narration in   11–12,
    119–39, 161
  television adaptation of   1, 132–8,
  as a 'breakthrough book'   2, 6–7,
    21–5, 34
  Nick Sharratt's illustrations
    for   6–7, 132–3, 135, 203
suicide   4, 37, 38–9, 44, 58, 59–60,
  106, 108, 206
Suitcase Kid, The   25, 27, 34, 35, 36,
  168, 204

teenage fiction   2, 18–19, 57–8,
  177–8
  Wilson's   4, 6, 9, 19–21, 34–51,
    56, 59, 65, 176–195, *see also*
    OUP novels
teenage pregnancy   4, 37, 58, 178,
  187–9
This Girl   19, 34, 38, 44–6, 160
*Tracy Beaker, see Story of Tracy Beaker,
  The*
Tracy Beaker Returns   1
translations of Wilson's work   9, 204
Transworld (publishing imprint)
  3, 21–2, 203
Trites, Roberta Seelinger   96,
  177–8, 182

unicity   12, 151–3
unreliable narration   11–12, 81,
  119–140, 161, 205
  cognitive approach to   1215

rhetorical approach   125–9
stylistics approach   130–2

Vicky Angel   8, 45
Victorian
  literature, influence of on
    Wilson's novels   9–10, 11–12,
    160–173, 210–11
  period in Wilson's work   38,
    44–6, 142, 143, 155–6

Waiting for the Sky to Fall   19, 34,
  35, 36, 45, 50
Welldon, Estella   105, 116
Westall, Robert   20, 24
Wilson, Jacqueline
  advocacy of reading
    aloud   30–31
  as agony aunt   8–9, 206–7
  awards and honours   1–2, 7,
    28–30
  childhood and family life   17
  early career   2–5, 17–21, 34
  public events   1, 28–30
  views on her role as children's
    writer   82, 194, 204–5,
    206–7
Winnicott, Donald   103–4, 114,
  116,
world-building   10, 48–9, 51
  setting   41
  vocabulary and idiolect   49–50
Worst Thing About My Sister, The
  87–8, 101(n)
working class
  in children's literature   56–7,
    201–2
  representations in Wilson's work
    4, 7–8, 104

young adult fiction, *see* teenage fiction
young carers   114–5
Young Observer / Rank
  Organisation Fiction Prize   4

Zindel, Paul   18, 57–8
Zipes, Jack   59